GHOSTS *of* PASSION

GHOSTS
of
PASSION

*Martyrdom, Gender, and the Origins
of the Spanish Civil War*

BRIAN D. BUNK

Duke University Press   Durham and London   2007

© 2007 Duke University Press
Printed in the United States of America on acid-free paper ∞
Designed by Heather Hensley
Typeset in Bembo by Keystone Typesetting, Inc.
Library of Congress Cataloging-in-Publication Data appear
on the last printed page of this book.

An earlier version of chapter 3 was published in *History and Memory* 14, nos. 1–2 (fall 2002): 65–92; and portions of chapter 5 appeared in *Journal of Women's History* 15, no. 2 (summer 2003): 99–122. Both of these journals are published by Indiana University Press.

A Laura, por supuesto

CONTENTS

ACKNOWLEDGMENTS

I begin here by thanking Laura Sizer and Zoe Bunk Sizer, whose love and support made possible the completion of this project. I would also like to thank my family, especially my mother Patricia, but also Amy, Joe, and Bridget, who helped me over the many years I spent working and writing. I owe an enormous debt to Jordi Getman Eraso who helped me in ways too numerous to count. I could never thank him enough for all he has done, except to say that he is a true friend. Jordi's family also deserves special mention, his *yaya*, Laura Aquilué Grasa, generously allowed me to live in her Barcelona flat where she fed me tortilla and rabbit. Pilar Eraso, John Getman, and Laura and Joan Poqui, along with Xavi Poqui, Enric Caujapé, and Susanna Getman, gave me friendship, great food, and a visit to Camp Nou. Other friends and colleagues who were of great assistance include Benita Blessing, Patrick Michelson, Simon Hall, Luca De Caprariis, Sean Perrone, Sasha Pack, Dan Kowalsky, Javier Morillo Alicea, Diana Correa, and Daniella Sarnoff.

The research for this project could not have been completed without major financial assistance from the J. William Fulbright Foreign Fellowship; the Program for Cultural Cooperation between Spain's Ministry of Education and Culture and United States Universities; and a Bernadotte E. Schmitt Research Grant from the American Historical Association. My work was made immeasurably easier thanks to the staffs of the Biblioteca Nacional, Fundación Pablo Iglesias, Archivo General de la Guerra Civil Española, Pavellón de la República, Biblioteca de Asturias, and the U.S. Library of Congress. In addition, Paloma Aguilar Fernández and David Ruiz provided guidance and advice while I worked my way through the archives, and Laura Estévez Fernández helped me obtain recent materials on Aida Lafuente. Finally, the libraries and interlibrary loan departments at Central Connecticut State University and the University of Massachusetts, Amherst, allowed me to access a wealth of valuable material.

Many other historians have helped me over the years. Stanley Payne, through his encyclopedic, seemingly limitless knowledge of Spanish history and his intellectual rigor, taught me how to be a historian. Pamela Radcliff read the manuscript, offered suggestions for revisions, and helped in numerous other ways. Carla Rahn Philips, Adrian Shubert, and Christopher Schmidt-Nowara all willingly shared their opinions and expertise. I'd also like to thank my colleagues in the history departments at Xavier University, Central Connecticut State University, and the University of Massachusetts, Amherst, along with the members of the Five College History Seminar, all of whom provided me with an intellectual community and an opportunity to continue working on this project. I'd especially like to acknowledge Heather Munro Prescott, David Glassberg, Laura Lovett, Audrey Altstadt, Andrew Donson, and Heather Cox Richardson, whose admonition "you've got to get it off your desk" provided the final push to complete the manuscript. I must also thank the folks at Duke University Press: Valerie Millholland, Miriam Angress, Justin Faerber, and the anonymous readers who all worked hard to make this book better. A tip of the hat also to Boot Liquor Radio (www.bootliquor.com), which provided an appropriate soundtrack for my final few months of writing. Finally, let me again thank Laura Sizer, whom I love beyond words.

INTRODUCTION

The history of the insurrection, like descriptions of the great battles, should be made when the ghost of passion has disappeared.

—Segundo Serrano Poncela,
El Partido Socialista y la conquista del poder

The military revolt of July 1936 marked the collapse of the Spanish Second Republic and the beginning of a bitter three-year civil war. Although the insurgency proved to be the ultimate rebellion against the short-lived Republic, it was by no means the first. Periodic revolts by anarchist groups and a previous military uprising had been unable to seriously disrupt the parliamentary system.[1] The revolution of October 1934, however, emerged as the first legitimate threat to democracy in Spain, when a coalition of leftist groups launched an armed insurrection against the conservative administration then in power. Although it was planned as a nationwide uprising, sustained fighting occurred only in the northwestern province of Asturias, where a long history of worker mobilization and the recent worldwide depression had exacerbated an already difficult economic situation. The revolutionaries enjoyed some success during the first days of the uprising by capturing Oviedo, the provincial capital, along with several other important towns. In response the government mobilized army units, including sections of the Foreign Legion and the Moroccan Regulares. After nearly two weeks of bitter fighting, the armed forces defeated the rebels and placed the province under martial law. Both during and after the events public discussion of the rebellion consumed the country, as politicians, writers, and artists disputed both its causes and its effects.

Debate over the motives and consequences of the insurrection has continued among the historians who have studied the revolt.[2] Stanley Payne concludes that the October revolt exacerbated the long-standing structural defects of the Republican system and revealed the unwillingness of the major political organizations—left, right or center—to fully commit to parliamentary democracy.[3] In contrast, Helen Graham has argued that the radical parties on the political left posed no serious threat to the Republican system and that the events of October 1934 confirmed the rebels' weakness by revealing the lack of support for the insurrection and the relative ease with which it could be defeated. Instead, it was the ability of conservative forces to mobilize a strong movement against even moderate Republican reforms that made a successful military uprising possible.[4] Others have asserted that it was the rebellion of October 1934 and not the military coup of July 1936 that represented the true beginnings of the Civil War. This interpretation was a common theme of Francoist propaganda and scholarship following the war, and it has recently seen a revival in Spain. In a series of popular books, Pío Moa assigned virtually all blame for the Civil War to the Partido Socialista Obrero Español (Spanish Socialist Workers Party, PSOE) and to a lesser extent, to the other revolutionary groups, including anarchists and communists.[5] Furthermore, he stated categorically that the October revolt "constitutes, literally and rigorously, the start of the Spanish Civil War, and is not a distinct episode or a simple precedent for it."[6]

Despite the claims of Moa and others, the larger conflict that erupted less than two years following the conclusion of hostilities in 1934 was not assured. Instead the commemorative imagery and interpretations of the rebellion that appeared in 1935 and 1936 created the atmosphere of polarization that ultimately exploded into civil war. In the period between the two events, the October revolt suffused all aspects of society and culture from artistic creation to parliamentary debate.[7] The idea of the revolt emerged as a potent symbol for both pro- and anti-revolutionary sympathizers.[8] Even as the smoke cleared in the streets of Oviedo and other cities, groups and individuals began to employ descriptions and commemorations of the revolt in political discourse. The conservative organizations portrayed the events as a struggle for the future of the nation with only the army able to definitively save Spain. The leftists, on the other hand, depicted a scenario in which only political unity could prevent the victory of fascism and help inaugurate a revolutionary society. These representations encouraged political extremism and helped to render untenable the moderate positions within both sides. Furthermore, both groups used gendered imagery as a way of promoting violent action in defense of one side or the other. These contested representations combined with other factors to eventually plunge Spain into civil war. My analysis of this imagery and how it helped create an atmosphere ripe for conflict forms the subject of this book.

The October revolution took place in a context of increasing polarization both within Spain and throughout Europe. World War I had shattered the social, cultural, and political status quo that had emerged over the long nineteenth century.[9] Not only had the conflict ushered in a terrifying vision of industrialized war, but out of it also came potent new symbols that would be used to generate political radicalism. The Russian revolution, if not exclusively a result of the war, sent shock waves throughout Europe and the world. Just as in many nations, Spanish opinion on the Bolshevik seizure of power ran the gambit from enthusiastic acceptance to hysterical condemnation.[10] The revolt in Russia emerged as one result of the Great War, but the conflict was also crucial to the development of counter-revolutionary ideologies that strengthened extreme nationalism and ultimately led to fascism. Developments in communications technology combined with improved techniques of mass propaganda meant that the messages of political extremism permeated society in previously unmatched ways. Politics and society across Europe during the interwar years seemed to be more polarizing and more violent than in previous decades.

If the era proved to be fertile ground for radical politics, it has also inspired an enormous variety of historical interpretations. In particular, the vast cultural remains of World War I and the impact that the conflict had on subsequent political developments led to an explosion of studies examining cultural memory and commemorations.[11] Both the pioneering research by Maurice Halbwachs and the current scholarship stress that collective memory is not simply an amalgamation of individual memories but instead constitutes a process of remembering.[12] In order to reflect this focus on the active nature of cultural memory, Jay Winter and Emmanuel Sivan have proposed using the term "collective remembrance" rather than the more common "collective memory." In so doing they hope not only to eliminate the imprecision of the traditional terminology but also to highlight the fact that the public act of recalling is what bridges the gap between individual and group memory.[13] Daniel Sherman employs similar reasoning to define commemoration as "the *practice* of representation that enacts and gives social substance to the discourse of collective memory."[14] James Wertsch, in his *Voices of Collective Remembering*, emphasizes that recalling past events is an interaction between the events of the past and communities of individuals as mediated through cultural representations.[15] He stresses the key role played by texts in framing the response by individuals to historical events since they provide a lens through which such events are remembered. The definition of texts is not limited to printed matter (even though this type of material is often the most important); instead, the phrase "cultural resources" better captures the diversity of representational formats.[16]

Identifying and analyzing representations of the past allows historians to better understand the relationship between historical events and subsequent developments. Since collective memories are formed through the public discussion and analysis of past events, they can best be studied through an investigation of the imagery used to convey meaning.[17] Ultimately societies rely on culturally meaningful images in order to create "textual communities" whose shared understanding of past events is based on a common set of cultural resources depicting that history. The formation of such communities creates and reaffirms collective identities by both encouraging a sense of cohesion within the group and at the same time emphasizing differences with those outside of it.[18] Although recalling collective memories is based on past events, the act of remembering itself takes place (instantiated in cultural resources) in a particular historical context. The content and meaning of past events can and does change based on current political, social, and cultural needs.[19] The nature of collective remembering suggests that meaning can only be found in the shared understandings between members of these textual communities and not in the beliefs of single individuals. In this study I focus precisely at the point when cultural resources were being created to provide individuals with the means for interpreting the events of the October insurrection. I explain how the act of remembering the past played a key role in triggering the much larger conflict that followed. The creators of representations of the rebellion were necessarily both influenced and constrained by the sociocultural context in which they lived. The re-membering of the events took place within the long-term framework of cultural tradition as well as in the current political and social situation both nationally and internationally. Spanish cultural heritage limited the types of available narratives with which to tell the story of, and give meaning to, the revolt. These "schematic narrative templates" are generally specific to a particular culture and form the basic building blocks out of which meaning is constructed.[20] Representations of the October revolt were quickly framed using the templates of "martyrdom" and "preserving gender stability."

Commemorations of World War I employed similar scripts to remember and give meaning to the enormous tragedy of the conflict.[21] The emotional excitement, known as the "spirit of 1914," that greeted the outbreak of war provided many combatant nations, especially Germany, with a powerful symbol of social cooperation and political unity. The evocation of this spirit continued even after the realities of the conflict had dimmed the enthusi-asm.[22] According to George Mosse, the cult of the fallen soldier that emerged following the Great War helped create what he terms the "Myth of the War Experience." The myth celebrated the conflict as a meaningful and sacred experience, and through the glorification of the dead it transformed the terrible sufferings of war into potent symbols of renewed nationalism.[23] Spain, however, had remained neutral in the Great War, and thus the ceme-teries and monuments so central to the creation of the myth never mate-rialized.[24] Nevertheless, similar concepts of redemption through suffering and the political use of this imagery had long played an important role in Spanish history. Chroniclers well into the twentieth century, for example, remembered and celebrated the suicidal defense of Numancia by native Iberians against the Roman legions.[25] The memories of past heroes could be used to support current political positions, as when patriotic writers in the nineteenth century christened the ninth-century Martyrs of Cordoba as the first Spanish nationalists.[26] Francisco Goya's painting of the fighting in Madrid during the failed revolt of 2 May 1808 is less celebrated than is the famous scene depicting the executions of prisoners by the French on the

following day. Eventually the uprising and combat against Napoleon became legendary components of what the Spanish call the War of Independence.[27] The use of martyrs and heroes to support a political position
continued into the twentieth century as imagery of suffering and death
emerged following the revolution of 1934. In effect, Spaniards created their
own version of the "Myth of the War Experience" based on the sacrifices of
individuals during the revolt and in the repression that followed. Conservatives and revolutionaries both employed similar images of martyrdom to
promote their political agendas. Each group used graphic descriptions of the
cruelties perpetrated by their opponents in order to make explicit the nature
of the enemy and the consequences should they prevail. Because pro- and
anti-revolutionary forces presented the choice as one between good and
evil, they motivated people to support one side or the other and thus helped
to spark the Civil War.

War has traditionally been viewed as an exclusively masculine domain
where women are relegated to the roles of either victims or spectators;
likewise, commemorations of war serve to reinforce established gender
roles. Sometimes the social instability resulting from conflict provides a brief
opportunity for women to escape conventional norms, but often the post-
conflict period witnesses a powerful reversal as traditional views return and
are even intensified.[28] The interplay between the events of the October revolution and the social roles of men and women became a fundamental aspect of the interpretations of the revolt for both pro- and anti-
revolutionary commentators. In an effort to halt the social and political
disorder that at the time seemed to be overtaking the nation, commentators
on the events of October exploited gender stereotypes to show their side as
the defenders of social order against chaos. They accused their enemies of
promoting such changes and portrayed themselves as the only true men
willing and able to properly defend women and the home. Such notions
served to escalate tensions by turning political struggles into a conflict that
challenged men's self-image and threatened women and the home with
violence and destruction.[29] The imagery of martyrdom and masculinity
helped bridge the gap between rhetoric and action as, in the words of
Eduardo González Calleja, "an ever-growing proportion of the population
felt afraid and so, at least morally, supported the defense of their interests and
ideals by means of illegal armed action."[30]

My focus here on the act of remembering through an examination of cultural representations of the past clearly defines my area of study but does not address the problem of reception. Since detailed records of public opinion or extensive oral histories often are not available, it can be problematic to determine the extent to which the imagery actually had an effect on political and social developments.[31] This study deals with reception by examining the use of the past in a very constrained period of time, since the Civil War began less than two years after the October revolution. This compressed interval allows for a more concentrated examination of the ways that images of the past affected social communities and makes the identification of such imagery clearer and its effects easier to trace. Representations of the insurrection had a short but intense and ultimately decisive effect on the political and social process. The brevity of the period allowed little chance for diffusion or for reflection on the events, and instead favored reliance on oversimplified and easily communicated frameworks in order to generate widespread approval for particular memories.[32] Unlike the Weimar Republic, for instance, the construction of memory did not develop through years of armed conflict, dramatic political development, and generational change.[33] The simplified visions of October coalesced into two main "textual communities," either pro- or anti-revolutionary, that directly competed with each other to provide compelling memories of the events. Despite some governmental censorship, no repressive apparatus existed to enforce a monolithic version of past events as happened in many totalitarian regimes during this period. The explicit struggle between competing interpretations of the revolt allowed people greater freedom to choose the message they felt to be more meaningful given their political and social identity. Memories that are freely chosen by individuals, and not forced by state coercion, stand a much better chance of being accepted.[34]

The volume of material produced in the aftermath of the insurrection and the widespread distribution of the imagery meant that it permeated all aspects of public discourse. All the major newspapers published extensively on the revolt right up to the outbreak of the Civil War.[35] The political and legal aftermath of the October revolt meant that newspapers throughout 1935 included coverage of the trials of those accused of criminal actions, especially famous leftist politicians such as Manuel Azaña and Francisco Largo Caballero.[36] In his study of the February 1936 elections, Javier Tusell carefully examined papers from across the nation. His detailed breakdown by province revealed that although regional differences existed, the insurrection of 1934 occupied a central place in election propaganda throughout virtually all parts of the country.[37] The success of the full-length books that were written to describe the events demonstrated the enormous public interest in the rebellion and its aftermath. Precise figures on the circulation of the texts can be difficult to determine; nevertheless, certain factors indicate that many of the titles had the potential for widespread distribution. Some of the publications, such as those by Manuel Benavides and Fernando Solano Palacio went through multiple editions in a relatively short time, including at least ten for Benavides and at least three for Palacio.[38] Those who participated in the revolt, including several revolutionary leaders as well as General Eduardo López Ochoa, the field commander of the armed forces that put down the insurrection, also penned histories.[39] Other works were written by famous and influential figures, including Manuel Villar, the director of the anarchist newspaper *Solidaridad Obrera*, along with the popular conservative author El Caballero Audaz (the Bold Knight) who produced an entire series of tracts.[40] Still more books included introductions or postscripts by leading political personalities such as the anarchist leader Federica Montseny and the Jesuit priest Emilio Herrera Oria.[41] Many of the pamphlets had close connections to political organizations ranging from conservative Catholics to revolutionary communists.[42] Despite censorship and the closure of party offices, revolutionary groups managed to print and distribute thousands of pamphlets and other materials.[43]

On both sides in early 1936 the imagery of the October revolt dominated the electoral propaganda, where it appeared in booklets, posters, and speeches. The Catholic Confederación Española de Derechas Autónomas (Spanish Confederation of Autonomous Rightist Groups, CEDA) alone produced millions of pieces of electoral propaganda, most of which referred to the revolution in some way.[44] The walls of many Spanish cities were covered with posters, and the streets literally became a sea of paper.[45] All parties held rallies and meetings throughout the country, so it is likely that many people were exposed to such imagery at some point. In Catalonia, for example, conservative groups put on an average of 30 meetings per day throughout February 1936, and in Seville on one day alone the political right held at least 93 meetings while the leftist groups managed 128.[46] While many of the assemblies were undoubtedly fairly small, others attracted tens of thousands of people. On 30 June 1935 the CEDA held meetings in two different cities that attracted at least 120,000 people.[47] In addition, the imagery produced by conservatives continued into the Civil War and helped form the ideological foundations of the Franco dictatorship.[48]

Finally, there is the testimony of contemporaries who, without taking strong ideological positions, described the effects of the imagery on politics and society. Some of these were foreigners who were in Spain during the period and published accounts of the general atmosphere following October 1934. Claude Bowers, the ambassador from the United States, declared that rumors and innuendo dominated political discourse in the aftermath of the revolt. He described the stories of atrocities that emerged after the conclusion of the uprising, and he reported, "Hate was in the saddle, and Hate had become the order of the day."[49] The British ambassador, meanwhile, characterized the atmosphere in the country as one of "sullen disaffection."[50]

Spanish authors of moderate views also commented on the polarizing effects of the competing interpretations of the events of October. One book titled *Asedio y defensa de la cárcel de Oviedo* (Siege and defense of Oviedo jail) by the director of prisons, Eraclio Iglesias Somoza, recognized the risk that commemoration could be abused. His work was a firsthand account of his experiences while under siege during the October revolt. Iglesias Somoza claimed not to be political and expressed sympathy for the economic plight of the workers, yet he believed that socialist utopias were unrealistic and not a proper solution. Although his work contained some descriptions of revolutionary crimes, Iglesias Somoza ultimately judged the events to be terrible for people of all social classes. In one section he described the symbolic value of martyrs but stated that no political position could justify destruction and murder. Perhaps alluding to the government's actions during the aftermath of the revolt, he wrote that unjustified killings created martyrs "in the name of which are raised revolutionary flags."[51] Consuelo Bergés, in her 1935 *Explicación de octubre: Historia comprimida de cuatro años de República en España* (Explanation of October: A condensed history of four years of the Republic in Spain), attempted to sort out the causes of the current political crisis. She agreed that, contrary to the propaganda of both sides that dehumanized and distorted their political rivals, the country was not a nation of deranged people: "Spain is neither an immense camp of crazies nor an endless wilderness of bandits."[52] In a chapter titled "Why the Revolution Failed," Bergés judged that ultimately the revolt failed because it did not attract the sympathy of the vast majority of the people.[53] One of the great successes of the public campaign against the repression, however, was its ability to attract support from sectors outside the proletariat, most notably the educated elites. The author prophetically stated that the events of the revolution would undoubtedly have important political and social consequences. She termed the revolt itself a brutality that transcended patriotism and legality, but she also believed that existing laws could justly punish those responsible for the insurrection and that abusive actions of repression were unnecessary. Bergés described how the actions and propaganda of both sides exacerbated the developing political polarization, and she predicted that the ultimate result would be the end of the Republic: "It will remain standing for some time; some weeks; some months—I won't dare to say years."[54] Bergés's statement proved to be all too correct as the Civil War broke out in July 1936.

In this volume I begin in chapter 1 with a brief background on the events leading up to the revolt, and I offer a general narrative of the insurrection itself. In chapter 2, "Sacred Blood: The Martyrs of Turón and Conservative Politics," I analyze the case of nine ecclesiastics who were killed during the uprising. In so doing I explore how conservative writers hoping that the textual and visual imagery of martyrdom could mobilize support for their political programs used the martyrs' stories to support a violent reaction. The commemorations of the martyrs performed two important functions. First, the commemorations served to divide Spaniards into groups of good and evil beings, with the former presented as individuals who embodied the traits most prized by conservative society, while the latter appeared as dehumanized creatures bent on destruction. Second, the martyrs served as a vehicle for eroding the boundaries between religion and politics. In the conservative literature, the protection of religion became fused with the defense of the nation, and being a good Christian was equated with patriotism. Violent response was justified through historical associations with a martial, crusading form of Catholicism and with modern notions of nationalism that promoted the military as the saviors of an independent and unified Spain. The extremist vision of a life-and-death struggle between good and evil encouraged violent action by eliminating the possibility of political change through legal means.

Leftist imagery also stressed the suffering and sacrifice of fallen revolutionaries in order to support a radical political position. In chapter 3, " 'Your Comrades Will Not Forget!' Revolutionary Martyrs and Political Unity," I demonstrate how commentators shifted perceptions of the revolt as a violent uprising so as to highlight it instead as a cruel repression. As a result, the commemorations of the October revolution largely became memories of distress and horror. Pro-revolutionary memory proved successful at mobilizing support and unifying the political left, and the effort contributed to their electoral victory in February 1936. Commemorations of the uprising helped tie moderate leftists to more revolutionary organizations, thus eliminating the political center. Once in power the coalition continued to use the treatment of fallen revolutionaries as a means to defend a radical political agenda.

In chapter 4, "Grandsons of the Cid: Masculinity, Sexual Violence, and the Destruction of the Family," I argue that the commemorations of October 1934 sought to restore traditional values by carefully defining proper male conduct. Changing gender roles produced anxiety in many Spaniards who viewed the patriarchal family as the foundation of social stability. Writers, poets, and artists accused their opponents of upsetting social order by encouraging shifts in traditional gender roles. Each side depicted itself as better embodying masculine virtues while implicitly or explicitly criticizing the manliness of their opponents. Commentators also used threatening images of sexual violence and the destruction of the family to mobilize political support, and special focus was placed on the actions of the Foreign Legion and the Moroccan troops. Apprehension over changing gender roles merged with the political tensions provoked by the revolt, and together they created the heightened social and cultural anxieties that contributed to the outbreak of the broader conflict in 1936.

In chapter 5, "Hyenas, Harpies, and Proletarian Mothers: Commemorating Female Participation," I explain how writers and artists used memories of October 1934 to mobilize women in gender-appropriate ways and to carefully delineate female social roles. The struggle for political power after October quickly became entangled with thinly disguised fears over alterations in the gendered order and the disruptive effects that these had on society. I argue that commentators on both sides resorted to conventional images of women in war in order to counteract the unsettling notion of a politically active woman. Chroniclers often simply referred to women in the most general sense and reduced the struggles of individual female protagonists to caricatures; conservatives argued that the revolt changed women into vicious killers, while pro-revolutionaries employed the imagery of motherhood to inspire leftist unity. Each side used the representations of women in order to divide the political and social world into two sides. In much of the chapter I concentrate on the evolution of imagery depicting the activities of Aida Lafuente, a young woman who took up arms to fight on behalf of the insurrection. Despite her role as a combatant, however, the pro-revolutionary commemorations ultimately portrayed her actions within traditional gender stereotypes.

In the final chapter, "The October Revolution in Democratic Spain," I explore commemorations of the revolt following the death of Franco and the subsequent transition to democracy by revisiting the major themes prevalent in commemorations prior to the Civil War. I use the examples of the martyrs of Turón and Aida Lafuente to argue that the Manichean divisions so important to previous representations had been replaced with a desire to show tolerance. Unlike the period immediately following the insurrection, commemorations of the murdered clerics now focused on their image as model Christians without linking them explicitly to a conservative political agenda. In addition, descriptions of the dark events stressed compassion and forgiveness over strident calls for militant action. By the end of the twentieth century Lafuente had come to represent progressive democratic politics, and her appeal remained largely as a nonthreatening icon of the political left. While the memories of October 1934 still had the potential to illicit an emotional response, they no longer inspired the outrage and violence that in the 1930s had such tragic consequences.

THE REVOLUTION OF OCTOBER 1934

On the morning of 4 October 1934 the veteran socialist leader Teodomiro Menéndez sat on the train from Madrid to Oviedo comfortably dressed in a gray jacket and hat. He was no stranger to trains, having long been the director of the Unión General de Trabajadores (General Union of Workers, UGT) railroad syndicates in the north. Menéndez's labor experiences had also accustomed him to strikes and confrontation, and he had spent at least a quarter of his life in prison because of such conflicts. Nevertheless, by 1934 he represented one of the more conservative factions within the Spanish socialist movement, and he vehemently disagreed with the growing radicalism of his party and union. Although it is impossible to know what he thought as he made his way through the spectacular mountain valleys that mark the passage from the south to Asturias, hidden in the band of his hat was a set of instructions to begin the "revolutionary general strike."[1] The journey of Teodomiro Menéndez helped put into place the events that culminated in civil war less than two years later. The uprising began shortly after word had been received, and it did not end until military units had forcibly occupied the province of Asturias and defeated lesser actions in other parts of the country.[2] The repercussions of those two weeks created a fierce battle over the commemorations and meanings of the revolt, and it was these conflicting interpretations that polarized politics and society and triggered the broader conflict in July 1936.

The direct causes of the October revolt included both economic and political factors. The effects of economic depression, along with the inability of either liberal or conservative administrations to improve conditions, led to a belief among many that only radical solutions would alleviate the suffering. In addition, the leadership of major leftist groups, especially the socialist movement began to publicly endorse radical action to both improve living conditions and counter the perceived threat of an authoritarian seizure of government.[3] The election of a conservative administration determined to liquidate the reforms of the Republic's first two years was combined with a growing unity movement among revolutionary groups to produce a series of confrontations that culminated in the revolution of October 1934. Ultimately it was a series of mutual pressures, actions, and demands that propelled a large part of the working class toward revolution.

THE EFFECTS OF ECONOMIC CRISIS

The Spanish economy entered the decade of the 1930s facing three fundamental challenges: the effects of the Great Depression, a lack of investment capital, and an unproductive and inefficient agricultural sector.[4] It was the inability of successive administrations to effectively deal with these issues that contributed first to the revolutionary insurrection of 1934 and ultimately to civil war. Although the worldwide depression of 1929 affected Spain comparatively less than it did other European nations, the economic slowdown still created significant problems. Important areas such as exports, emigration, and foreign investment proved especially hard hit. The closure of export markets meant industrial and manufacturing concerns had to rely on internal demand, an area that had never been well developed. Not only did Spanish goods fail to find a home in foreign lands, but the export of human capital also slowed. This lack of movement, along with the economic problems in general throughout the world, caused a reduction in the amount of remittances from immigrants previously established abroad, thereby creating financial hardship for many who depended on these moneys. Furthermore, the shutting off of the safety valve of emigration left depressed areas with larger numbers of unemployed laborers.[5] Total unemployment throughout the country rose steadily during the Republic, rising from 446,263 in 1932 to 703,814 by April 1934.[6]

In agriculture, the economic difficulties caused by the Great Depression only added to the twin problems of an undercultivation of land and an overabundance of landless laborers.[7] The advent of the Republic in 1931 gave hope, especially to the peasants and laborers, that these problems would soon be definitively solved. Although the newly established Republican system was not responsible for the initial problem of the Depression, many continued to blame the government, and the lack of concrete solutions led to increasing social and political tensions. According to Edward Malefakis, "The miserable lot of the day laborers under the *latifundia* system ensured that they would protest; their powerlessness to improve their condition through normal channels ensured that this protest would assume violent forms."[8] The desperate situation of the agricultural workers increased the radicalism of that sector and in turn influenced the direction of the labor organizations that organized them.

The coal and iron industries, both of which entered into a serious decline during the 1930s following a wartime boom in production during the years 1914 to 1919, dominated the industrial economy in Asturias. As Adrian Shubert notes, "The period 1919–34 saw the most sweeping changes in the history of coal mining in Asturias, all of which were detrimental to the worker, forcing him to work longer and produce more while earning less."[9] These changes in the industrial economy of the region largely resulted from rising costs, declining production, and a significant reduction in product demand. In the coal business, these problems were not new, as factors such as low internal demand and high transport costs had plagued the industry almost from its inception.[10] The new social benefits passed during the first two years of the Republic, such as the seven-hour workday and paid vacations, increased the cost of coal production, although mine owners had previously been able to compensate for these increases by raising prices.[11] The equation began to change because, despite the fact that the industry was largely shielded from external economic factors, its fundamental structural flaws left it vulnerable to economic depression. The rising price of labor was not the only contributor to higher production rates, for increased material costs and rail tariffs pushed up the cost per ton at least seven pesetas between 1929 and 1933, while the price per ton rose by just over four pesetas during the same period.[12] Changes in governmental investment lowered internal demand for Asturian coal. In contrast to the grand public-works projects of the Primo de Rivera dictatorship of the 1920s, which had inflated demand for coal, the Republican government funneled money toward education, social legislation, and the agricultural sector. The artificially high demand for coal and steel previously fueled by government spending thus ended abruptly during the 1930s.[13] The largest industrial consumers of coal, including railroads, merchant marine operations, and metalworking all reduced demand significantly between 1931 and 1932. In 1931, for example, the firm Altos Hornos de Vizcaya consumed nearly all of the coal produced by the Sociedad Hullera del Turón, but the next year it purchased only half of total production.[14] Both workers and owners responded to these changes with demands for a protected internal market: Spanish coal for Spanish industry. In addition, management hoped to lower the costs of production by reducing labor expenses, which led them into conflict with an increasingly desperate and dispirited workforce. The electoral victory of the conservative forces in November 1933 ensured that these owners would now have the upper hand, and in the eyes of many workers this change signaled the ultimate failure of the Republican system.

THE ROLE OF THE PARTIDO SOCIALISTA OBRERO ESPAÑOL

The actions of the Partido Socialista Obrero Español (Spanish Socialist Workers Party, PSOE), its national trade union (the UGT), and its youth organization, Federación de Juventudes Socialistas (Federation of Socialist Youth, FJS) during 1934 can be traced to a change in policy resulting from the electoral defeat of November 1933. Owing to a deterioration of relations at the local and national levels, the socialists withdrew from the coalition government they had shared with moderate Republicans since the advent of the Republic in 1931.[15] The leadership of the PSOE decided to contest the upcoming elections without electoral partners, despite the recently passed legislation that favored such coalitions. The result was a disaster for the PSOE, as the conservative bloc led by the Confederación Española de Derechas Autónomas (Spanish Confederation of Autonomous Rightist Groups, CEDA) emerged victorious and thus denied the socialists a share of political power for the first time since the beginning of the Republic.[16] The electoral defeat signaled a fundamental change in Socialist Party policy, and the leadership soon began publicly calling for revolution.[17] From a meeting of the PSOE-UGT executives on 25 November 1933 came the first call to "rise up" in order to defend the Republic from what the party called "the forces of reaction." The declaration was not meant to signal a mass rising but rather was issued as a warning to conservatives that the socialist organizations would mobilize at the first provocation. The exact definition, however, of what actions constituted a rightist provocation, or what the party's call to "rise up" entailed, remained unclear.[18] The vagueness of these conceptions had been a continuous problem within the socialist movement since at least the 1920s, and the coming of the Republic had only exacerbated them. At its heart the issue was the fundamental conflict between the PSOE's wish to support the Republic and its desire to implement a purely socialist form of government.[19] The historian Santos Juliá has argued that the PSOE had two separate conceptions of revolution. The first included a belief that the declaration of the Republic and the ouster of the monarchy constituted a revolution in government, and through the democratic processes of this Republic the PSOE could gradually introduce a socialist society. The second form of revolution allowed for a seizure of power, but only when it became clear that the proper functioning of the Republic had been compromised by conservatives.[20] In contrast to the organization's leadership, the working-class rank and file often made little distinction between parliamentary and revolutionary actions since they favored results above theory.[21] After the disastrous electoral loss in November 1933, only the revolutionary track seemed a viable option for the socialist movement.

Despite these conclusions, not all socialists agreed that the time had come to disavow parliamentary cooperation in favor of a revolutionary uprising.[22] These interparty conflicts also grew out of the intense personal rivalries between reformers and revolutionaries within the PSOE. The resignation and removal of many reformers from key leadership positions at the end of January 1934 temporarily resolved the strife but did not end it. The most significant change was the substitution of Francisco Largo Caballero for the reformist Julián Besteiro as head of the UGT. Largo Caballero, by this time also head of the PSOE, consolidated his control over the entire movement, and his followers, known as *caballeristas,* took over key posts within the union's largest affiliate, the Federación Nacional de los Trabajadores de la Tierra (National Federation of Agricultural Workers, FNTT), as well as in the important Madrid section of the PSOE.[23] These substitutions meant that from this point on the maximalists dedicated, at least on paper, to a revolutionary seizure of power controlled virtually the entirety of the socialist movement. In accordance with the radical outlook of the leadership, the socialists constituted in February 1934 a revolutionary committee charged with organizing the insurrection. Largo Caballero presided over a group that included many of the most hardcore revolutionaries within the movement, such as the FJS leaders Santiago Carrillo and Carlos Hernández Zancajo.[24]

By February 1934 the socialist movement within Spain had become increasingly dedicated to effecting political change through armed revolution. However, neither this new radical orientation nor the level of actual commitment to revolt was unanimous within the organization, and important questions and debates still raged regarding the timing and purpose of the revolution. In addition, a growing rift was developing between the intentions of the leadership and the growing radicalization of the rank and file, particularly in the FJS and UGT. Many leaders hoped to use the threat of insurrection to gain concessions from the conservative government, and these largely vocal revolutionaries remained less than fully committed to an actual revolt. The distance between membership expectations and leadership intentions proved especially significant in revealing Largo Caballero's fundamental lack of resolution, who despite his inflammatory language never fully committed to a genuine revolt. The difference between his idea of revolutionary brinkmanship and the goals of the workers and youth widened over time, and during the next seven months these tensions continually resurfaced in response to political and economic factors and ultimately helped to cause the failure of the October revolution.[25] Internally, the PSOE spent most of 1934 responding to political and social crises rather than actively plotting revolution. The real and perceived provocations of the conservative government along with the growing radicalization of the rank and file propelled the PSOE, and the workers movement in general, toward the events of October 1934. Despite public threats of revolution and the existence of a planning committee, half-heartedness and conflicting priorities characterized the revolutionary plotting of the Socialist Party. Even as the organization of the rebellion stalled, the leadership of the PSOE remained publicly committed to revolution. The language of revolt emanating from the national committee led many rank-and-file members, as well as conservative observers, to believe that the Socialist Party was unanimously committed to organizing an insurrection. Rather than taking effective measures to prepare the party for revolution, however, the executives simply encouraged the growing radicalization of the membership, and together they stumbled down the road to revolution.

THE CONSERVATIVE REACTION

Following the election of 1933 the CEDA emerged as the largest single party in parliament, but until October 1934 they had chosen not to enter into the government and instead supported an administration led by the Radical Republican Party.[26] Nonetheless, owing to their predominance in the Cortes it was the CEDA who generally took the lead on legislative matters. The actions of the conservative government that helped trigger the October revolution can be grouped into two categories: lack of enforcement of previous reforms, and perceived threats of a dictatorial takeover followed by a fundamental modification of the Republic. Almost since the right's electoral victory, and perhaps even before, large landowners had easily found ways to ignore or subvert the agricultural reform legislation passed by the Republican-socialist regime. In the countryside, the situation of rural laborers grew increasingly desperate as unemployment in some provinces skyrocketed to nearly 50 percent. The grave situation could not be easily mitigated, as few social programs such as unemployment compensation existed to relieve conditions. Soon laborers became disillusioned with the slow pace of reforms and the remarkable intransigence and callousness of landowners. The workers' pleas for relief were answered with cries of "eat the Republic!"[27] and their desperate attempts to feed themselves were met with violence and prosecution.

In addition to the casual neglect of reform legislation, the administration supported by the CEDA also threatened to rescind many provisions. In December 1933 the leader of the party, José María Gil Robles, outlined his group's determined opposition to the reforms promulgated during the Republic's first two years. He demanded revision of religious decrees and launched an all-out attack on social legislation. Gil Robles called for the repeal or modification of some of the most significant legislative reforms of the agricultural sector. Although the effectiveness of the measures in al-

leviating the economic hardship endured by the landless laborers was un-
even, they nevertheless represented an attempt to redress the oppressive
socioeconomic conditions. In the minds of leftist politicians and workers,
the neglect and seemingly imminent removal of these regulations symbolized the dismemberment of the Republic itself. Over the next several
months the government slowly implemented the new policies, with the
most significant changes coming in spring 1934. On 4 May the legislature
repealed the original provisions of the land appropriations bill that allowed
for the redistribution of property, and on 24 May it abolished the municipal
boundaries law that had aimed to alleviate unemployment.[28] The latter
action, coming as it did on the eve of the harvest, enabled landowners to
bring in low-paid workers from Portugal and other regions within Spain.[29]
The importation of cheap labor combined with the desperate economic
situation described above contributed to the growing radicalization of the
rural laborers and especially the socialist FNTT.[30]

As the government began dismantling the social and economic legislation erected during the first two years of the Republic, fear and alarm grew
among leftist groups. The rise of fascist states in Italy and Germany led many
to believe that the CEDA planned a similar takeover in Spain. The most
ominous development came in early 1934 with the eradication of the Socialist Party and the installation of a Catholic authoritarian regime in Austria. This seemed especially relevant to Spain owing to the popularity of the
CEDA, Spain's own Catholic party. The actions, pronouncements, and publications of Gil Robles and others often fed these anxieties. The CEDA never
truly became a fascist party like those in Germany or Italy but its vague
loyalties to the Republic made it suspect: as Stanley Payne notes, "Though it
was committed to legal, nonviolent parliamentary tactics in practice, the
CEDA's cherished aim of constitutional revision seemed to point toward a
more authoritarian and corporative Catholic republic."[31] The leadership of
the CEDA often walked a thin line between Catholic conservatism and outright fascism. Gil Robles attended the Nazi rally at Nuremberg in 1933 and
studied the propaganda and electioneering techniques developed by the
German party. During the campaign of fall 1933 the CEDA employed many
of these techniques, including an overwhelming blitz of radio, press, poster,
and film advertisements. In addition, the conservative papers printed stories
favorable to Nazi policies and praised the actions of Dollfuss in Austria.[32]

The actions of the CEDA also at times revealed both appreciation and appro-priation of fascist models. In April 1934 the youth section of the party held a mass party rally at the symbolically important royal residence, the Escorial. Up to fifty thousand supporters cheered the leader (*jefe*), Gil Robles, as he mouthed antiparliamentary slogans.[33] Later, in September, a similar event took place at Covadonga, the symbolic location of the beginning of the medieval Christian reconquest of Spain and a site closely linked to twentieth-century monarchical nationalism.[34] Gil Robles reflected this symbolism during his speech when he called on all those assembled to "impose the idea of authority on all social classes."[35] To many observers, these actions seemed like deliberate attempts to intimidate the opposition and to emulate the trappings of other authoritarian movements and govern-ments. Indeed, the conservative youth group also adopted a salute modeled on those of parties in authoritarian nations.[36]

The CEDA also used other methods, aside from political rhetoric and spectacle, to hint at a more ominous purpose within the government. A cabinet shuffle in February 1934 removed several moderate politicians and replaced them with conservatives. The most significant change was the appointment of the ultraconservative Rafael Salazar Alonso as minister of the interior. In early March 1934 he declared a state of alarm and ordered the closing of many leftist centers belonging to the Partido Comunista de España (Spanish Communist Party, PCE), Confederación Nacional de Tra-bajo (National Confederation of Labor, CNT), and FJS.[37] Salazar Alonso also attacked the political power of the PSOE by suspending or removing almost two hundred socialist mayors and city councils, primarily in the southern regions of Badajoz, Cáceres, Alicante, and Jaén.[38] These actions seemed to be a deliberate effort to erode the power of the socialist movement and to create a regime with virtually unchallenged power.

THE RADICALIZATION OF THE SOCIALIST LEFT

The combination of internal changes within the Socialist Party leadership discussed above and the actions of the CEDA and the government fed the growing radicalization of the socialist movement. The developments also exposed a dramatic separation between the largely vocal posturing of the organization's leadership and the more genuine revolutionary fervor of many rank-and-file affiliates as certain sectors of the party, notably the FJS and the UGT, became more committed to an armed rising. This change in orientation of the largest leftist party drew the PSOE closer to other, more consistently revolutionary, parties such as the Marxist Bloc Obrer i Campe- rol (Worker Peasant Bloc, BOC). The results of this political shift away from legal parliamentary opposition toward combative struggle created a series of violent incidents during 1934 that culminated in the October revolution. Just as the pronouncements and actions of Gil Robles and the CEDA revealed an ambivalent loyalty to the Republic, the responses of the PSOE and its leadership toward the system of government proved equally ambiguous. The key figure in the perceived radicalization of the socialist movement was Largo Caballero. Although he had been a reformist union bureaucrat during his years in the socialist movement, he began to mouth increasingly radical and revolutionary slogans, primarily in an attempt to strengthen his position vis-à-vis other factions within the socialist leadership.[39]

The tensions within the leadership had first dramatically manifested themselves publicly during the Torrelodones Summer School for Socialist Youth in August 1933. Each of the three figures competing for leadership of the movement, Julián Besteiro, Indalecio Prieto, and Largo Caballero, gave speeches at the institution. The first to speak was Besteiro, who cited the historical development of the party and stressed the need for continued reformism and gradualism. Prieto spoke on the following day and appealed to political pragmatism by stating that the PSOE was in no position to take power unilaterally. He urged listeners to defend the Republic from rightist attacks and to prepare for the day when conditions enabled the movement to install a socialist regime. These essentially reformist speeches did not sit well with the increasingly radical leadership of the FJS. Hoping for a more revolutionary message, the organizing committee headed by Santiago Car- rillo issued a late invitation to Largo Caballero. Although he did not advo- cate an immediate revolt he nevertheless made his message clear: "We have two roads: the legal struggle and the illegal struggle. We say we prefer the legal struggle, that we want to triumph using the legal struggle . . . And if they won't allow us? Ah! well then we'd have to use other methods."[40]

The growing radicalization of the rank-and-file membership manifested itself in the violent struggles carried on in spring and summer 1934, which were characterized by strikes as well as by street fighting between fascist groups and the FJS. The responsibility for these clashes rested with the leadership of the FJS and the FNTT, while the highest party officials including Largo Caballero largely opposed these measures. The FJS had only recently begun to exercise a strong influence on the direction of the socialist movement. The growing power of the group was in part due to the apparent failure of governmental participation and the rising numbers of youthful affiliates; by 1934 the FJS had as many as fifty thousand members.[41] The youth had little connection to the bureaucratic unionism that had dominated the ideological development of the socialist movement and instead looked to the Russian revolution as a model.[42] They agitated for the immediate and violent takeover of the government and the installation of the dictatorship of the proletariat: "The mission of the working class in general is to conquer political power, exercise it dictatorially and wholly and totally transform economic, moral, ethical and artistic conditions."[43] By April 1934 the moderate elements of the youth group had been definitively removed from positions of power within both the executive committee and the organization's main periodical, *Renovación*.[44] Throughout the spring and summer the socialist youth kept up the invective of revolution not only through the pages of their periodicals but also through concrete action on the streets. During this period the FJS militias engaged in a series of ongoing fights and shootings with fascist youths.[45] The socialist committee formed in February 1934 to organize the revolution recognized the need to create an armed militia ready to seize power when the appropriate moment came, and the responsibility for organizing these groups soon fell to the FJS. To this end the youth group created lists of those ready to "take to the streets" when the need arose, and according to some accounts at least six thousand members in Madrid alone were registered. These figures, as the events of October would reveal, neither accurately represented the organized strength of the militias nor recognized the scarcity of arms and ammunition.[46]

Socialist attacks on the members and property, including clubs and newspaper kiosks, of Spain's two fascist groups, the Juntas de Ofensiva Nacional Sindicalista (Groups of National Syndicalist Action, JONS) and Falange Española (Spanish Phalanx, FE), began in late 1933 and escalated during the first part of 1934.[47] Soon the fascist groups organized squads to protect newspaper vendors, and when the student leader Matías Montero Rodríguez was assassinated on 7 February 1934 they began actively fighting back. The actions reached a peak during June when a young *falangista* was killed during a brawl with socialist youths. In retaliation a group fired shots at a gathering of socialist youth, killing Juanita Rico, who was subsequently memorialized as the first victim of fascism in Spain.[48] These attacks helped establish an atmosphere of violence that served to heighten the level of sociopolitical tension in Spain and to radicalize and harden followers of all ideological stripes.

ALIANZA OBRERA

The conservative government's continued rollback and nonenforcement of agrarian reform legislation combined with economic hardship to create an agitated and desperate class of rural laborers. Not withstanding the intransigence of landowners and the outright hostility of the government, the socialist FNTT, as the largest rural workers' union, still attempted to negotiate within the system established during the first two years of the Republic. In doing so, the union made frequent appeals to the Ministries of Labor and the Interior to enforce agreements. The legal approach continued even though the leadership of the FNTT had been in the hands of caballeristas since early in the year. Nevertheless, as the crisis reached a peak near the beginning of the summer harvest, the FNTT made plans to strike. Although some within the government reacted positively to the demands, and real progress was achieved during negotiations as a result, the hostility of Salazar Alonso ultimately doomed the bargaining. He continued his assault on the Socialist Party by breaking up union meetings and arresting prominent activists. Eventually negotiations broke down and the FNTT set the strike date for 5 June 1934; it was to be a legal strike and not the signal for an armed insurrection.[49] Despite previous revolutionary pronouncements, the UGT executive committee balked at supporting the strike, and after heated debate it refused to issue calls for a general strike of all workers. Without the support of its own national organization, the FNTT strike was doomed to failure. Salazar Alonso cracked down hard on the strikers by arresting more than ten thousand and by removing more socialist mayors and town councils.[50] To many contemporaries (and, later, historians) the refusal of the UGT, led by Largo Caballero, to support the land workers revealed the fundamentally reformist character of the executive committee. The socialist leaders feared that the strike would provoke a fearsome repression that would weaken the socialist movement and strengthen the conservative hold on power. In many ways these fears proved true as the strike broke the UGT's single largest affiliate and rendered the FNTT ineffective until 1936. The government also moved further to the right during summer and fall 1934, while at the same time the revolutionary ardor of some socialist leaders, especially Prieto and Largo Caballero, began to cool.[51] According to Paul Heywood, the peasant strike had two important effects on the party: first, the recalcitrant attitudes of the rightist government and its brutal response to the strike seemed to prove the authoritarian ambitions of the regime; and, second, it underlined the need for cooperation between all worker groups to effectively counter this threat.[52]

The Socialist Party's lack of governmental power; the growing radicalization of the youth; and the lessons of the failed strike encouraged a rapprochement with other worker organizations. Official negotiations with other parties began in January 1934, but the push toward worker unity had started nearly a year earlier. The PSOE, despite its position as the single largest working-class organization, never emerged as the leader of efforts aimed at cooperation between revolutionary organizations. Rather, it was a former schoolteacher from Catalonia named Joaquín Maurín, and his party the BOC, who led the call for an Alianza Obrera, or Worker-Alliance.[53] Maurín began his political career as a syndicalist within the CNT, and he even held a leadership position within the organization. After disagreements on whether the CNT should actively support the Bolshevik revolution, members of the group ousted Maurín from the executive committee in 1922, and he eventually left the organization. By October 1924 his newly formed breakaway organization, favoring a form of communist syndicalism, affiliated with the PCE. Soon, however, Maurín began to resent the communist's increasing bureaucratization, and this issue, combined with personal animosity between Maurín and the leader of the PCE, led to tensions between the two parties. Eventually these conflicts came to a head, and the PCE executive committee, with the usual charges of being a tool of the reaction, voted to expel Maurín's organization in June 1930. The merger of this group with another small dissident communist organization led to the formation of the BOC in November 1930.

Although the BOC started slowly, with its original membership at around seven hundred, it soon began to increase affiliation largely at the expense of the CNT by winning over former anarchist locals at Gerona, Tarragona, and

Maurín's hometown of Lérida. Despite the growing rivalry between the two organizations, the BOC still believed that the CNT remained the best vehicle to initiate a revolution. However, this view changed as anarchists began physically assaulting members of the BOC and violently disrupting the group's meetings. The series of failed anarchist revolts in 1933 effectively dispelled Maurín's belief that any of the existing worker organizations alone could effectively initiate revolutionary change.[54] By summer 1933 Maurín's organization had ceased its verbal attacks on the socialist organizations and began agitating for some form of cooperation. This change in attitude toward the PSOE resulted from a growing disillusionment with the CNT, the rise of Hitler and Mussolini, and the growing power of conservative forces within Spain. Originally, the BOC appealed to rank-and-file socialists, believing them to be more open to cooperation as well as more radical in general. During the elections of 1933, the BOC urged its members to vote socialist, and the two organizations even formed an electoral alliance in Barcelona. After the conclusion of the elections the two local groups, along with several other small organizations, signed an agreement to form the first Alianza Obrera on 9 December 1933. Local branches of these organizations soon followed, with similar pacts being made throughout Catalonia.[55] In an attempt to create a nationwide system of Alianzas Obreras, Maurín traveled to Madrid in January 1934 to meet with high-ranking socialists, including Largo Caballero. Less than a month later, after he had solidified his control of the movement, Largo Caballero publicly announced PSOE support for the Alianza Obrera. This outward sign of cooperation, however, hid the dramatic differences of opinion that remained between the two groups. The BOC viewed the Alianzas as the Spanish equivalent of the Russian soviets; that is, workers' groups that would form the vanguard of the revolution, seizing power and organizing a Marxist state with the participation of all parties. The socialists meanwhile, saw the Alianza Obrera merely as a way of organizing divergent groups in support of the revolution. This conflict of opinion prevented real and meaningful cooperation in most areas, and the Alianza soon became merely a liaison committee between the groups' leaders.[56]

While relations between the PSOE and BOC improved by 1934, the other major worker groups, the PCE and CNT, remained adamantly opposed to any cooperation. From December 1933 to August 1934, the PCE actively discouraged the formation of an Alianza Obrera. They continued attacks on all other parties, calling the socialists "socialfascists," the anarchists "anarcofascists," and members of the BOC "communist renegades." A pamphlet published in summer 1934, titled "Alianza Obrera? No! United Front! This Is the Answer," illustrated the communist position. The authors called the Alianza Obrera an agent of the counterrevolution whose goal was to confuse laborers and sabotage the one true workers' organization—the PCE.[57] Meanwhile, the CNT objected to the inclusion within the Alianzas of the PSOE as well as of former anarchists, known as *treintistas*.[58] The February 1934 national congress of the CNT, held in Barcelona, opposed the formation of a workers' alliance and any type of revolution contrary to anarchist principles. They feared that the Alianza Obrera would be used for strictly political rather than revolutionary ends, and they maintained a belief in revolt based on spontaneous popular mobilization: "The revolutionary unity of the Spanish proletariat . . . has to be realized in the street in the moment of battle and at the margin of political action."[59]

In the majority of Spain the call for a nationwide movement of united workers' groups under the banner of the Alianza Obrera fell largely on deaf ears, but this was not the case in Asturias.[60] As early as January 1934 the Asturian sections of the BOC had been campaigning to create an Alianza Obrera within the mining regions. Although the successful agreements reached in Catalonia gave the group some prestige, the BOC generally lacked the size and influence necessary to organize worker cooperation, and their efforts, despite later claims, failed.[61] Instead the Alianza Obrera in Asturias resulted from negotiations between the CNT and UGT. The local federation of the CNT had expressed an interest in cooperation at a regional meeting of the organization held in January 1934. The anarchist executives, led by José María Martínez, thought that the situation in the country was right for an alliance, and only by joining together could the organization retain some say in the nature and course of the impending revolution. They exhibited a clear "political pragmatism" and immediately began negotiations with the UGT.[62] These discussions with the socialist union directly challenged the position of the CNT leadership established at the group's national convention. That the Asturian regional organization was willing to reject the pronouncements of the national committee reflected not only pragmatism but also the effectiveness of UGT vocal revolutionism. The increasingly radical position of the socialist movement following their withdrawal from the government and the electoral defeat favorably impressed the leaders of the CNT. This again demonstrated how the radicalism of the socialists combined with rank-and-file mobilization and fears of a rightist takeover to increase the revolutionary potential of the working classes. The negotiations reached a successful conclusion and the two groups signed an agreement forming an Alianza Obrera in Asturias on 31 March 1934.[63]

Enthusiasm for the pact, however, was not unanimous in either the CNT or the UGT. Sensing a need to justify their actions, the Asturian CNT soon published an apologia for the agreement. They maintained that the time had come to leave aside organizational rivalries and past conflicts in order to defend against attacks from conservative forces. In a rare case of self-reflection, the anarchists acknowledged the past mistakes of the movement and recognized that they alone could not create a revolution: "We do not have sufficient means to destroy the capitalist State in a single rebellious gesture."[64] At a regional conference of the CNT held in Gijón on 6 May 1934, many local sections challenged the executive on the question of the agreement. After fierce debate, the existing leadership retained majority support, even though a national CNT congress held in June 1934 reiterated its earlier policy against the Alianzas and dismissed the idea of cooperation with the UGT. The decision on whether to discipline the Asturian regional for violating this policy was shelved until a meeting scheduled for October (which then was never held).[65] Dissension within the Asturian CNT continued almost up to the eve of revolution, as intransigent locals again questioned Martínez and his supporters. In September, at another regional gathering, thirty delegates voted in favor of Martínez's position, six voted against, and seventeen abstained, while acceptance of the Alianza Obrera was even closer: thirty-nine delegates voted in favor, thirty-five against, and four abstained.[66]

The PCE, following a change in Comintern policy, reversed course and joined the Alianza Obrera only weeks before the outbreak of the October 1934 revolution. Apart from a shift in strategy, the adherence of the PCE also represented practical considerations in the hope of increasing the organization's membership and influence.[67] An analysis of the political situation within Spain led many PCE officials to conclude that a revolutionary uprising was immanent, and they had also witnessed the growing popularity of the

Alianza Obrera among rank-and-file workers. In addition, effective demonstrations, in Madrid and Asturias, of the Alianza's strength convinced the communists that not joining was to risk being left out of the revolutionary process.[68] With the Alianza Obrera in place and the CEDA demanding representation in government the stage was set for the revolutionary uprising of October.

THE COMBATS OF OCTOBER

The trigger for the revolutionary uprising was a cabinet reshuffle that, for the first time, led to CEDA members holding governmental ministries.[69] Many leftists viewed this as the first sign of an eventual takeover of the government and the installation of an authoritarian regime by the CEDA. Despite the existence of a socialist planning committee, the multiparty Alianzas Obreras, and although the entry of the CEDA into government had long been viewed as the event that would signal the start of the revolution, concrete plans for the rebellion scarcely existed. Stanley Payne characterized the national state of revolutionary organization as ranging "from feeble to nonexistent."[70] In Madrid the socialist youth had been unable to generate either the mass mobilization of militias or make important connections with police and military forces. In addition, they failed to adequately distribute the few weapons they had accumulated and even refused the help of other worker groups in organizing the uprising. As proof of the lack of concrete action and the indeterminate response offered by the party leadership, they had again followed legal norms and informed the government of the impending strike twenty-four hours in advance.[71] Therefore, in the capital and most important city of the Republic the revolt degenerated into a series of sporadic and desultory gunfights. The arrest or flight of key leaders, including Prieto, Largo Caballero, and Carrillo, further reduced the effectiveness of the revolt in Madrid.[72] In Barcelona the local government, or Generalitat, led a brief civil rebellion culminating in a declaration of independence of the "Catalan State within the Spanish Federal Republic." The refusal of local officials to distribute arms to workers' groups and the lack of CNT participation, however, ensured that the rebellion could not last. Indeed, after a brief show of force by the local military commander, the rebellion ended. Some fighting broke out in other areas of the country such as Catalonia and Albacete, but government forces soon quelled these uprisings as well.[73]

The revolution truly prospered only in the province of Asturias, as worker militias attacked police and other governmental outposts and fought a spirited campaign against the army troops sent to quell the revolt. As the CEDA prepared to enter the government the situation in the province grew exceedingly tense. The worker parties, knowing the moment for revolt was at hand, awaited confirmation of the rebellion. By the morning of 5 October the word had come to begin the general strike.[74] In some areas, local militias did not feel the need for official confirmation and began assaults on government posts on the night of 4 October.[75] One such attack occurred in Turón, where members of the four-thousand-strong communist union attacked the offices of the local mining company, disarmed the guards, and continued the assault on the nearby Civil Guard post. Once the call to revolt had been issued, fierce battles broke out in many locations, especially those with highly organized workforces. In Mieres, the groups led by Manuel Grossi and Fernando Solano Palacio captured the police barracks and the city government building, while similar incidents occurred in the towns of La Felguera, Nalón, and Aller.[76] The early success of the revolutionaries resulted in part from the cautious and defensive deployment of government forces. The small, isolated garrisons of police and Civil Guard were easily cut off, surrounded, and reduced.[77] In response to these events, Minister of War Diego Hidalgo asked General Francisco Franco to coordinate the repression from Madrid while the command of the troops in the field went to the liberal general Eduardo López Ochoa. Franco disagreed with the appointment of López Ochoa on political grounds, and he called on his close friend Colonel Juan Yagüe Blanco to lead the elite troops soon to arrive from Morocco.[78] These troops consisted of elements of the Spanish Foreign Legion as well as units composed of native Moroccans, called Regulares.[79] This move, and the hard-line approach taken by Yagüe toward the rebels in general, proved to be one of the most contentious decisions of the campaign.

Despite some early success, particularly in the outlying villages where the worker organizations enjoyed high numbers of affiliates, the revolutionaries found that they had underestimated governmental strength in the larger areas, including the cities of Avilés, Gijón, and Oviedo. Although striking workers surrounded the city council building in Avilés, they had virtually no hope of capturing it because, in addition to being outnumbered by the defenders, they could attack with only twelve rifles. In Gijón, the largest city of the province, the results proved to be catastrophic for the rebellion. Despite a high number of affiliates and a strong commitment to the Alianza Obrera, the CNT lacked arms and ammunition. To counter the presence of over five hundred police and soldiers stationed in the city the anarchists could only properly equip seventy rebels. Due to these numbers they failed to launch an assault during the first several days of fighting, thus losing the crucial elements of surprise and military initiative. Instead, the rebellion in Gijón evolved into a siege as the revolutionaries barricaded themselves into the working-class neighborhoods of the city, most notably Cimadevilla, Tremañes, and El Llano. Soon ships arrived to reinforce the government troops, and the cruiser *Libertad* began shelling areas controlled by workers. After a few days the government recaptured Cimadevilla and more reinforcements arrived, including the African troops led by Colonel Yagüe. By 10 October, the last barricades in El Llano had been taken and the fighting in Gijón ceased.[80] The early defeat of the rebellion in Gijón proved to be one of the most decisive factors in the ultimate failure of the revolt in Asturias, because it enabled the government to hold the port while bringing in additional forces.[81]

In the provincial capital of Oviedo, however, the fighting generally favored the revolutionaries. The original plan of the revolt had been to quickly seize Oviedo and then rapidly spread outward throughout the province and beyond.[82] Isolated and disorganized attacks began in the city on 5 October, but these early actions proved ineffective. As in other cities the governmental forces withdrew to several strongholds within the city and attempted to blunt the advance of the revolutionary militias. In general the rebels were well armed, and they even brought in artillery after the capture of the arms factory in nearby Trubia. For several days the fighting raged, and although the revolutionaries controlled most of the city they proved unable to reduce all areas of resistance.[83] The continued fighting in Oviedo kept the best-equipped rebel forces tied up in the city and prevented them from effectively organizing resistance to the advancing army. The military forces proceeded toward the capital in three main columns: from Galicia in the northwest under the command of López Ochoa, from Gijón in the north under Yagüe, and from the south through León under General Carlos Bosch. The rebels countered with barricades across the highways and by unleashing volleys of dynamite taken from the mines. The latter tactic proved extraordinarily effective in delaying the soldiers—as much from terror as from military potency. In the south, the miners from Mieres, using dynamite to its full effect, trapped Bosch's men in a valley and forced a stalemate. In other areas the rebels ambushed the columns, delaying their progress, and only a lack of ammunition prevented them from pressing the advantage.[84] The slow but steady approach taken by López Ochoa brought him into conflict with Yagüe, who accused the general of taking unnecessary risks and being too soft on the rebels.[85] Nevertheless, by 10 October the military forces stood less than three kilometers from Oviedo, and by the 12th they had recaptured the nearby arms factory. The following day, Yagüe's troops moved into the city and assaulted the train station and the church of San Pedro de los Arcos.

By 12 October the revolutionary leaders had decided to withdraw from the city. Like many aspects of the revolt, the retreat was disorganized and helped limit the effectiveness of the remaining militias. A few of the most radical fighters continued the struggle, organizing a new revolutionary committee. Now, however, the army outnumbered the rebels by ten to one, and the revolutionaries' supplies of arms and ammunition became dangerously low. Military troops controlled all of Oviedo by the end of 14 October, but sporadic fighting still took place in outlying regions, including Villafría and San Lorenzo.[86] The withdrawal continued into the south of the region but the advance of the army could not be halted. Although resistance had virtually ceased by 17 October, the official surrender did not take place until after a meeting between rebel leader Belarmino Tomás and General López Ochoa on 18 October. The general demanded the immediate surrender of all militias and the cessation of hostilities. Tomás made few demands, accepted the general's conditions, and announced the surrender from the balcony of the Oviedo city hall.[87]

The death and destruction resulting from the revolutionary uprising was extensive. The exact number of fatalities, however, is difficult to ascertain, in part due to the nature of the fighting but also because a thorough, even-handed investigation never took place. The official government compilation published in 1935 declared that almost one thousand buildings had been destroyed, including fifty-eight churches, twenty-six factories, and an extraordinary seven hundred and thirty public buildings.[88] Famous structures damaged or destroyed included the university, Campoamor Theater, and the cathedral in Oviedo. Debate raged over who was responsible for this destruction, with some blaming the rebels and others the government forces. In most cases the damages resulted from active combat and because the structures, particularly the government buildings, had been at the focus of the fighting.[89] The official government figures listed the number of killed as 1,051 revolutionaries and 321 government forces, with another seven declared missing.[90] Another contemporary source listed figures only for the action in Asturias, stating that 940 citizens were killed along with 256 government troops.[91] Recent historians, including Paco Ignacio Taibo and Stanley Payne, generally agree that the figures listed at the time undercounted the fatalities of revolutionaries, although not significantly. They argue that the number of revolutionary deaths could not have been less than 1,100 and might have been as high as 1,200 throughout the country. They also advocate an increase in the fatality figure for governmental forces as totaling nearly 450 across Spain.[92]

Even as the gunfire and explosions ceased, another fierce struggle began. This conflict, however, was not a war fought with bullets and bombs but with words and symbols. In the commemorations that followed the events, accurate counts of the dead ceased to be important; instead, partisans of both sides emphasized the horrors of the insurrection and repression. The deaths of clerics during the revolutionary commune and the execution of rebels in its aftermath spurred the creation of martyrologies dedicated to memorializing the fallen heroes. By providing horrible examples of what could happen should their opponents prevail, the texts served to excite tensions and motivate political action on both sides. The result was an increasing atmosphere of tension, which divided Spain into the opposing forces of good and evil locked into a struggle for the future of the nation. The imagery helped eliminate the possibility of political moderation, and ultimately it triggered the Civil War in July 1936.

SACRED BLOOD

The Martyrs of Turón and Conservative Politics

On 5 October 1934 a group of rebels broke into the De La Salle Brothers school in the south-central Asturian village of Turón.[1] The occupants had received word earlier that morning that the revolutionaries were detaining priests and other religious figures, and thus after celebrating mass with a visiting Passionist priest, the eight brothers returned to their rooms to pray and await the seemingly inevitable confrontation. The rebels who entered the school declared that they were searching for weapons hidden by the "fascists" of Juventud Católica Española (Spanish Catholic Youth, JCE) a nominally apolitical youth organization that regularly met at the school.[2] After the search turned up no weapons, the revolutionaries commandeered the school grounds and removed the nine clerics to the village's Casa del Pueblo. Since the start of the insurrection the building had been used as a jail, and the men from the school were placed in a room with other prisoners. A few days later, members of the local revolutionary committee, including an ex-student of the brothers' school, visited the prisoners. The men informed the clerics that they were in protective custody because overzealous members of the revolutionary commune might wish to harm them.[3] Again the prisoners were left alone, until after midnight on 9 October when several armed men appeared telling the prisoners to prepare to leave the Casa del Pueblo. Like true martyrs, a later account claimed, the brothers and the priest knew in their hearts that "they were going to give their lives on the altar of their faith."[4] Their short journey ended at the gates of the town cemetery, where they were brought inside and forced to stand near freshly dug graves. A witness later reported that both rifle and pistol shots "cut down the lives of these true soldiers of Christ."[5] The martyrs of Turón, as the nine men soon became known, were not the only religious figures killed during the October revolution, although they were probably the most well known. Indeed, following the insurrection the men became quite famous, and crowds of people gathered to see the funeral procession of the eight De La Salle Brothers when their bodies were moved to the order's national headquarters for burial.[6]

Just as the physical presence of the murdered clerics attracted large numbers of people, conservative writers hoped that the textual and visual imagery of martyrdom could mobilize support for their political programs. The idea of martyrdom had particular resonance during the 1930s, as notions of religious sacrifice and redemption fused with extreme political nationalism to create a powerful force that favored violence over democracy. Such sentiments, although generally stripped of denominational Christianity, had become commonplace after World War I in nations such as Germany and Italy.[7] While undoubtedly influenced by the theories and imagery from those nations, Spain had been developing its own unique mixture of fervent Catholicism wedded to radical conservatism since at least the late nineteenth century, but it was only in the twentieth century that such ideas reached their apex. In part this movement was a reaction to broader trends toward modernization and secularization, but it was also a direct response to growing, and increasingly hostile, anticlericalism. Anticlerical violence simmered throughout the early twentieth century, and it exploded with great force during Barcelona's Tragic Week of 1909.[8] The next major outbreak erupted with the proclamation of the Republic in 1931, when a series of church and convent burnings began in Madrid but quickly spread to other parts of the country.[9] What made the October 1934 revolution different was the scale of the violence directed against the Catholic Church, especially the brutal slayings of thirty-four religious figures, including the nine clerics at Turón. In comparison, the incidents of 1931 caused no deaths, and only three individuals had been killed during the Tragic Week.[10] By 1934 many

Catholics and political conservatives viewed the persecution of the clergy and the destruction of church property as the nightmarish culmination of the Republic's program of secularization. For the first time, the horrific scenarios of violence aimed at the Catholic Church and its members that had been a part of extremist rhetoric since the latter half of the nineteenth century finally materialized during those two weeks in October.[11]

The commemorations of the martyrs killed during October 1934 helped divide Spaniards into "good" and "evil" beings, with the former presented as individuals who embodied the traits most prized by conservative society while the latter appeared as dehumanized creatures bent on destruction. At a time when popular religiosity was declining, the examples of those killed for the faith could be used to inspire living Catholics, especially the young. As they had throughout the history of the Catholic Church, the martyrs were seen as exemplifying the finest characteristics of believers, including the willingness to make the ultimate sacrifice on behalf of the faith. Politically, the martyrologies fit nicely into the longstanding discourse on the need for Christians to protect the Church from those who would destroy it, especially forces from outside of Spain such as the Marxists and the Freemasons.[12] The martyrs also served as a vehicle for eroding the boundaries between religion and politics, since the ideologies and the organizations so often overlapped. In the conservative literature, defense of religion became fused with the defense of the nation, and being a good Christian was equated with patriotism. Although the parties of the Republican right also utilized this rhetoric, it was the forces of the radical right, especially the Alfonsine monarchists, who most successfully combined the religious and political messages. After the intense rhetoric of 1935, the victory of the Popular Front seemed to presage another revolt where atrocities such as those committed in Asturias would be multiplied tenfold. The imagery of the October revolution radicalized elements of the political right and helped justify violent action since many now argued that the only clear way to protect the Church and the nation was the intervention of the armed forces. The possibility of a legal rightist opposition had evaporated, and the most violent and reactionary vision of the conservative movement had emerged victorious. This polarization ultimately joined with existing tensions to speed a confrontation, and the resulting cultural atmosphere of violence and revenge ensured that the dispute would become a civil war.

THE POLITICS OF CONSERVATISM DURING
THE SECOND REPUBLIC

The advent of the Second Republic left the Spanish Church and loyal Catholics in a politically difficult position. For centuries the Church had been closely linked to the monarchy, and unlike the king, who quickly fled into exile, it could not simply abandon the nation as political winds changed direction. In addition, the Church had been an enthusiastic supporter of the dictatorship of General Miguel Primo de Rivera, and as a new political system came into being the ecclesiastical authorities found themselves on the defensive without a coherent plan for responding to the drastically altered landscape. Among both clergy and lay Catholics, feelings toward the Republic ranged from strong hatred to passionate approval. The latter attitude, however, remained a distinct minority, and as a result it had little influence within the larger body of the Church. The reaction of the Church leaders has been described by the historian Mary Vincent as "carefully worded respect and clear foreboding."[13] Official policy, known as accidentalism, argued that the Church had little invested in the precise form of government as long as its rights and prerogatives were protected; the hierarchy refrained from outright condemnation so long as the "essential" Catholicism of the nation was preserved.[14] The popular animosity toward the Church, however, posed a distinct challenge to its policies. In the history of modern Spain, periods of dramatic political and social change often led to renewed bursts of anticlericalism.[15] Physical attacks on the Church began shortly after the proclamation of the new Republic. On 11–13 May 1931 a series of churches, monasteries, and convents were damaged and destroyed by anti-clerical riots. For the Church the inaction of administration officials seemed far more ominous than the actions of the mobs. To many believers the slow response of the police and the fire units during the attacks, and the lack of a concrete response by the government afterward, proved that the Republic was determined to physically destroy the Church in Spain. The church burnings of May 1931 also planted seeds that later prevented the formation of a moderate political party that was both Catholic and Republican. This occurred because both the president of the Republic, Niceto Alcalá-Zamora, and the minister of the interior, Miguel Maura, responsible for security at the time of the burnings were moderate Catholic Republicans.

The disorganization of the Church and its supporters left the organization poorly situated to contest the Republic's first elections. The Catholic
right had not previously needed a mass movement established specifically to
defend Church rights. At the end of April 1931 the Vatican sent instructions
to top Church officials in Spain declaring the need for Catholics to ensure
that only candidates willing to "defend the rights of the Church and social
order" be elected to the constitutional assembly.[16] While the letter did not
clearly suggest the formation of a political party, it did call for an organization that could contest elections. The first step in generating a national
movement was the creation of Acción Nacional (National Action, AN) in
April 1931.[17] The group refused to name itself as a party, instead declaring
that it was "an organization of social defense" designed to work within the
legal Republican system. The founder of AN was Ángel Herrera Oria, the
editor of Spain's largest Catholic daily newspaper, *El Débate*, and leader of
an elitist and extremely influential lay organization called the Asociación
Católica Nacional de Propagandistas (National Association of Catholic Propagandists, ACNP).[18] At the same time that he headed AN, Herrera also led a
nonpolitical Catholic group called Acción Católica (Catholic Action, AC).
Founded in the late nineteenth century and officially recognized by the
Vatican in 1903, AC strove under the leadership of the clergy to mobilize lay
people toward the creation of a Catholic culture distinct from liberalism and
modernism. By the advent of the Second Republic most of AC's broader
goals remained unrealized, but it had blossomed into a national organization
that included groups for women and young people.[19] The close connections
between the religious organization AC and the political organization AN
went beyond the leadership of Herrera. Although it did not officially endorse any political organization, including AN, Church leaders provided
both material and moral aid to the fledgling party. At the beginning clerical
officials often allowed church buildings and residences to be used for AN
gatherings: indeed, the movement was officially launched on 26 April 1931
at a meeting of the ACNP's Madrid chapter in the Jesuit residence at Chamar-
tín de la Rosa.[20] In many places supporters of AN, as well as its youth and
women's sections, were drawn from the local Catholic organizations. The
groups often shared cultural activities, including summer courses and excur-
sions designed to mobilize the next generation of Catholic youth.[21] In
addition, the leadership of both groups was virtually identical and usually

included several members of ACNP.[22] This double or even triple militancy helped AN to organize rapidly, and within two years it had become the largest confessional party in Spanish history.[23] It also tended, despite official declarations to the contrary, to explicitly link the Catholic Church to a specific political party. To show the impact of Church connections on the rapid development of AN, we can compare its rise with the fortunes of the Derecha Liberal Republicana (Liberal Republican Right, DLR) party. The latter, despite the support of prominent national politicians, was never able to establish a strong local base, in part because it lacked the unofficial support provided by the Church.[24] The connections between conservative mass politics and the Catholic Church help to explain why commemorations of the events of October could simultaneously have both religious and political meanings. The personnel, meeting places, and messages of conservative politics and Catholic values became virtually inseparable. Even the boundaries between conservative political groups could be fluid. María Rosa Urraca Pastor, for example, while affiliated with the Vizcayan chapter of AP also headed the women's section of the Carlist party and had been president of the Bilbao chapter of Acción Católica de Mujeres (Women's Catholic Action, ACM).[25]

The results of the first national elections demonstrated the electoral weakness of the conservative parties when voters returned a center-left government determined to limit the special position of Catholicism within the Spanish state. Only five seats were won by AN and overall the opposition parties garnered a mere fifty-four seats.[26] These results assured that the parties with a strong Catholic identity, whether in favor of the Republic or against it, would have little power to contest the anticlerical measures of the soon-to-be-drafted constitution. Following the disastrous showing in the elections, conservative groups began to regroup and reorganize. In 1932 a Republican decree forced AN to abandon its original name and to reconstitute itself as Acción Popular (Popular Action, AP). Soon thereafter AP joined with a number of other conservative groups to form the Confederación Española de Derechas Autónomas (Spanish Confederation of Autonomous Rightist Groups, CEDA) in February 1933.[27]

Although the CEDA came to represent the largest Catholic party, there were many within the organization who rejected the group's implicit acceptance of the Republican system. At first the monarchists of both Alfonsine and Carlist leanings joined AN, as it was the only organized group that opposed the center-left coalition of Republicans and socialists. Soon, however, many became disillusioned with AN's policy of accidentalism, and those individuals left to form more intransigent parties.[28] The two largest and most influential organizations became Renovación Española (Spanish Renovation, RE), which supported the return of the deposed king Alfonso XIII, and the Comunión Tradicional (Traditionalist Communion, CT; or Carlists) which supported a pretender to the throne.[29] The entry of the CEDA into the government in October 1934 left the monarchists in a difficult position. On the one hand they hoped that a rightist government would be able to undo the reforms of the previous administration and possibly lay the groundwork for an authoritarian state and ultimately the return of the king. On the other hand, the radical right feared that by entering the government in a legal way the CEDA was helping to consolidate the Republic.[30] Instead these groups opposed the entire concept of a republic, and from the moment that the king fled the country they began plotting ways to bring it down. The commemorations of October 1934 helped overcome resistance to such ideas from the mainstream conservative movement and led to the widespread rejection of legal opposition that culminated in the military uprising of July 1936.

THE RELIGIOUS MOTIVATIONS OF COMMEMORATION

The events of October occurred at a time of spiritual and physical crisis within the Spanish Church, and historically the political and cultural importance of martyrs often peaked at times of real or perceived difficulties.[31] Beginning in the nineteenth century, popular religiosity began to decline, particularly among intellectuals and the working class. Attendance at mass was down, especially in urban areas, and a Jesuit who studied the matter remarked at the time that the Church was fast becoming a strictly bourgeois affair.[32] One purpose of the martyrologies designed to commemorate those killed in 1934 was to provide lessons and models for other Catholics. The writings highlighted the example of the martyrs by contrasting their qualities with those of the revolutionaries. They created a series of dichotomies that ultimately revolved around good versus evil, human and animal, Spanish and "anti-Spanish." In this way, conservatives argued that the insurrection had revealed the true nature of the struggle underway in Spain: it was a battle for the souls of individuals as well as the soul of the nation. The martyrs killed during October 1934 came to represent the true values of Catholic Spain while also providing the necessary sacrifice for the redemption of both the faith and the nation.

The battle for the souls of individuals waged by the Church was fought in two areas: education and values. Although conservatives of all stripes abhorred many of the provisions of the new constitution, perhaps the most alarming was the effort to end Catholic education. Resistance to legislation aimed at curtailing religious instruction served to mobilize conservatives into taking political action in defense of the faith and in opposition to the Republic. When legislation was introduced that would place limits on Catholic education, the government was flooded with petitions and the Church hierarchy issued a letter condemning the new law.[33] The campaign also served to mobilize women in large numbers. The line between politics and religion blurred as women were encouraged to disobey laws banning religious schools. The conservative press celebrated as martyrs those women jailed by the government for refusing to pay fines related to their civil disobedience.[34] The Church viewed education as a fundamental part of its ability to inculcate proper religious and civic values in young people, including discipline and obedience, precisely those qualities commemorated in the martyrologies from October 1934. A textbook on the history of Spain published by the De La Salle Brothers denigrated the Republic and praised the values inherent in the traditional social hierarchy, including the monarchy.[35]

Many of the martyrs of Turón were seen as exceptional teachers, especially in the instruction of catechism. Brother Cirilo-Bertrán, the leader of the community, was a "model religious figure" whose skill at teaching the catechism led students to travel extra kilometers for instruction, despite the fact that a secular school was much closer to their homes. The book *Los martíres de Turón* declared that Brother Julián-Alfredo might have become one of the greatest teachers in Spain, and even an ex-student of the school who participated in the insurrection praised the abilities of its faculty.[36] The stress on the educational abilities of the slain clerics reflected the Church's preoccupation with maintaining its virtual monopoly on Spanish education. As religiosity began to decline in the nineteenth century, education became an important element of plans to reverse the decline and maintain the hegemonic cultural and social position of the Catholic Church. Thus the number of new religious schools increased dramatically, especially those run by orders like the De La Salle Brothers. In the 1870s only a single community of the brothers existed in Spain, and they educated fewer than three hundred pupils. At the inauguration of the Republic in 1931 there were 149 schools educating thirty-two thousand students.[37]

Throughout the martyrologies published after the insurrection, the dead were presented as ideal heroes who represented model Christians. The authors of *Asturias roja* (Red Asturias) proclaimed that they published the book in the hopes of illuminating the glorious words and deeds of those who were victims of the revolution of October. They initiated the project soon after the insurrection in order to render homage to the dead and to provide an example to those still living. By reading the story of their lives and deaths the authors claimed that the reader became closer to the miracles of grace provided by God.[38] Francisco Martínez, the sibling of a slain priest, also glorified the sacrifice of the dead and emphasized how they exemplified the values of Christian Spain. In *Dos jesuitas mártires en Asturias* (Two Jesuit Martyrs in Asturias) he recounts the good deeds performed by the two martyred Jesuits during their lives, and he supplements the account with eyewitness testimony and photographs.[39] In addition to telling the story of his brother's death, Martínez memorialized the dead cleric with a poem titled "To Father Emilio Martínez, S.J., Martyr of Christ the King." Written by Angel Usoz, the verses describe the humility and faith of the slain priest as well as his good works.[40] Another text, *Los mártires de Turón* (The Martyrs of Turón), begins with brief biographies of the nine murdered clerics, which are presented in a fairly straightforward manner and include careful notation of their dates of birth and final vows as well as a brief history of their work up to 1934. The book describes each of the clerics as having a series of virtuous qualities, many of which are common to nearly every biography. One brother, for example, is described as "simple without ordinariness, humble without meanness, helpful without dejection, affable without excessive flattery, serious without arrogance and energetic without harshness."[41] The martyrs of Turón also embody popular religious devotion: one had not missed a day of communion in six years and another said fifteen decades of the rosary nightly.[42] Six of the nine men held a particular devotion to the Virgin Mary, and the Passionist priest, Father Inocencio, had even managed to obtain a small piece of her cloak as a relic.[43] The text points out that nearly all of the slain men had a special dedication to their vocation and declared their willingness to do whatever the Church superiors ordered them to do, even if it meant leaving Spain. Brothers Benito de Jesús and Marciano-José had even expressed a desire to be martyred for the faith if necessary. The former, in a letter to his parents written soon after the establishment of the Republic in 1931, declared that if martyred he would "come to heaven and [his] enemies would go to hell."[44]

According to the texts, the clerics personified qualities, notably discipline and obedience, especially valued by the Church and conservative political groups. The books sometimes articulated the language of discipline and obedience in military terms. Brother Ancieto-Adolfo stated that despite the anticlerical measures of the Republic and its attempts to disband the religious orders he continued being a soldier under the orders of "Captain Jesus."[45] The author Ramón Rucabado characterized all of the religious figures killed during October as "the white army of the martyrs of Asturias, who praise God from his ranks and regiments."[46] The choice of language created a dichotomy that had political overtones, since the "white army" with its monarchic connotations stood against the "red army" of revolutionaries who were responsible for the killings. Rucabado also quoted an older work on martyrdom declaring that "martyrs are witnesses . . . to the distinction between good and bad, and the separation of light and darkness."[47] The militaristic language helped bridge the gap between religious belief and political action. The choice of words also alluded to historic forms of crusading Catholicism when the interests and goals of the Church and state were perceived as inseparable. In the aftermath of the October revolt, many believed that such ideas had never ceased being true and that the Republic, by attempting to separate them, had failed to represent the authentic character of the nation. Conservatives would soon argue that the time had come to renew the spirit of the nation by again taking up arms to save the Church and, by extension, the nation as well.

The trope of martyrdom could also be applied to lay victims or even to places that had suffered for the good of the nation. The celebration of the people who resisted the revolt, usually members of the police or the military, further illustrated the blurred line between religious and political imagery.[48] Jenaro G. Geijo's *Episodios de la revolución* (Episodes of the Revolution), commemorated the deaths of the Civil Guards and soldiers who had been killed during the fighting. Although they were not religious martyrs, the author still employs religious imagery in referring to them. Indeed, Geijo dedicates his book to those professionals who were wounded or killed while completing their "sacred mission" during the insurrection.[49]

In addition to memorializing the martyrdom of Civil Guards, Geijo characterized the city of Oviedo itself as a martyr.[50] Such imagery also emerged as one of the central themes of Gil Nuño del Robleda's fictional treatment of the revolt called *¿Por qué Oviedo se convirtió en ciudad mártir?* (Why Was Oviedo Converted into a Martyr City?) He describes the slain clerics as men of "morality, virtue, [and] austerity,"[51] and he claims that forty thousand well-armed "savages" entered Oviedo and immediately began to demonstrate their "hatred of the city."[52] The author uses the theme of martyrdom to dehumanize the revolutionaries by accusing them of willfully destroying the city, and he compares the actions of the revolutionaries to the Jews who allegedly killed Jesus. By depicting the conflict with such overtly religious imagery, Nuño del Robleda converted the rebellion into something more than a conflict over political power or economic justice. Indeed, he states that during the invasion of Oviedo, "the revolutionaries had a terrible enemy in our beloved Jesus of Nazareth."[53] The rebels became inhuman Jewish creatures determined to obliterate the city of Oviedo, but as they overcame the resistance of the police and Civil Guard they encountered a more powerful foe: Jesus himself. The imagery thus associates the destruction of the rebellion and the redemption of the city with a messianic figure. Later, the author praises the true liberators of the city, the armed forces led by Colonel Yagüe.[54] The symbolic connection between Jesus, the "terrible enemy" of the insurrection, and the military reinforces the messianic vision of the army as the only earthly force able to resist the revolution.

Another celebration of place, this time of the province of Asturias as a whole, appears in the poet Casimiro Cienfuegos's *Elegía de Asturias y otras poems del dolor trágico de España* (Elegy for Asturias and Other Poems of Spain's Tragic Pain).[55] The centerpiece of the book is the eponymous poem dedicated to the province. Cienfuegos paints a picture of ruin by describing the actions of the rebels as a "bloody orgy" of "demented fury." He lists the buildings, works of art, and other objects destroyed or damaged during the insurrection. Nevertheless, despite the carnage the province had survived to inspire renewed action in defense of the nation. The poem metaphorically likens the province of Asturias to Jesus by describing the region's symbolic death and resurrection.[56] The imagery further has an overtly political message as Cienfuegos wrote of an impending conflict in which the true Spain would be restored; it was the historic Spain whose strength and unity came from Catholicism, and it was a nation closely linked to the monarchy. In addition, it was the historic nation unified, according to tradition, by the armed forces of the reconquest. Just as the knights of the Middle Ages forged a united Spain during the struggle against Islam, so too would the modern-day knights of the armed forces re-create a unified nation again purged of foreign, non-Christian elements. The final stanza of the poem reiterates the themes of sacrifice and redemption while concluding on a triumphal note:

> You, unhappy beloved homeland,
> martyr of Spain, Asturias wounded,
> by the seven piercing daggers
> of this week of monstrous passion;
> you, who for all Spain endured
> and who tore your innards
> for the unity of Spain,
> look all of Spain is speeding
> to aid in your relief
> to restore the blood that flowed
> and to cure the wounds that you won
> in the sad campaign.
> Your body remained bloody,
> wounded and vulnerable,
> but your soul was intact.
> Very soon, rested and strong,
> you will be prepared and ready
> to, in return for today's favor,
> be present, as always, in front
> of the restoration and reconquest
> of that Spain of immortal memory,
> the only Spain that the world knows:

the Spain royally crowned
that fills the annals of History;
the Spain of Auseva,
with whom Pelayo was reborn in the Cave;
the great Spain, heroic and respected,
the Spain of honor and of glory.
Already the Cross of Victory
Is unearthed![57]

The Cross of Victory, originally made of wood and later encased in gold, supposedly led Pelayo's forces to the victory that began the historic reconquest of the peninsula. During the twentieth century, and by the time of the Republic, the symbolism of the cross and of the cave of Covadonga had become exclusively the domain of Catholic nationalists. As such, it was closely associated with the monarchy, and liberals largely had failed in their attempt to transform the imagery into something that could reinforce a secularized vision of national identity.[58] Indeed, by the 1930s the imagery was linked to a very particular political outlook: "The national identity implied in the act of commemoration would be the traditional one— Catholic, monarchist, and aristocratic."[59] In the aftermath of the October revolution, invoking the triumphant symbolism of the Cross of Victory and the reconquest represented a call to action. The poet hoped to enlist Catholics and Spaniards into the new reconquest, one that would destroy the secular forces that threatened the unity of the nation and restore a conservative, monarchical regime.

DEHUMANIZING THE ENEMY

If the martyrs commemorated in conservative texts personified the best qualities of Spaniards, then the revolutionaries who killed them exemplified the worst aspects. In fact, according to many conservative accounts the actions of the rebels who murdered the clerics revealed that they could not be true human beings let alone loyal Spaniards. Conservatives used anti-revolutionary imagery to outline a clear distinction between good and evil by describing their enemies in inhuman terms. The dehumanization of political opponents created a system of good victims and evil perpetrators and allowed for the strongest possible measures to be employed against them. The psychological process of creating and defining enemies in times of social tension allows for the reduction of anxiety by eliciting feelings of fear or anger.[60] Such feelings may have helped undermine resistance to the use of political violence. Stories about people outside of the local community can also become generalized, as the characteristics and actions of a few are attributed to an entire group.[61] Such a process seems to have occurred following the October revolt, as the brutal activities of some individuals in Asturias became descriptive of all members of an adversarial political group. The stories of atrocities helped create and reaffirm a shared identity by distinguishing between those within and those outside of the community. While descriptions of Marxism and other enemies of the right had long included references to the bestial nature of their adherents, the revolution of 1934 provided for the first time concrete examples and images that could validate those stereotypes. The gruesome imagery of the martyrologies, combined with other more extreme allegations, demonstrated the truthfulness of what, up to then, had generally remained simple caricatures. The commemorations of those slain in the insurrection helped bridge the gap between hollow rhetoric and political action. Loyal Spaniards would not be killing fellow citizens, but instead would be defending civilization from rampaging hordes that wished to destroy all that the nation held sacred.

The main text of Geijo's *Episodios de la revolución* details the events of the revolt in all parts of the country. Stories of heroic resistance offered by the forces of the government receive special emphasis, but acts of barbarism committed by the rebels are also featured prominently. One of the most explicit acts of cruelty was the murder, by "revolutionary hordes," of Civil Guard Lieutenant Fernando Halcón Lucas. In grisly detail Geijo relates how after killing the lieutenant the rebels cut off his legs and placed dynamite in his mouth. The author uses these techniques both to shock the reader and to lend more credibility to his text through sheer detail, explaining that these actions and others like them, including the destruction of important buildings, were the result of "Marxist hate."[62] Such language reinforces the imagery of martyrdom, since a hatred of religion on the part of the killers is one of the key elements in determining if those who are murdered can be called true martyrs. Geijo's efforts at communicating meticulous accounts of the brutal events also include the copious use of photographs. The text contains photos of the author at various key points described in the text, such as in front of a café where, he states, the Civil Guard mounted a vigorous and heroic defense. There are also pictures of individual victims and heroes of the revolt. Geijo intended to contrast the viciousness of the revolutionaries with the heroism and sacrifice of the government officials; his photos provided a human face for both the acts of suffering and the heroism related within the text. He contrasts the individualized victims with the anonymous revolutionary hordes that committed the atrocities. Some of the images, such as the wives and children of guardsmen killed during the fighting, seemed deliberately chosen to elicit the maximum amount of sympathy from the reader.[63]

The book *Episodios de la revolución en Asurias: Los Pasionistas de Mieres (Asturias) y la Revolución de Octubre de 1934* (The Passionists of Mieres [Asturias] and the Revolution of October 1934) begins with a dehumanizing portrayal of the revolutionaries. The book characterizes the rebels as full of more rancor and perversity than the authors believed possible to exist in the human heart. The writers call the hammer and sickle a sign of hate and the revolutionary call of the UHP (Unión de Hermanos Proletarios; Union of Proletarian Brothers) an augury of death.[64] *Los Pasionistas* also describes the imprisonment of fourteen clerics and the murder of three by recounting the killings in gruesome detail, including photographs of the exact locations of their deaths. At times the authors dwell on the cruelest aspects of the events, perhaps with the hope of inciting a reaction of outrage and disgust in the reader. The first death occurred as a rebel attacked his victim with a knife while the cleric begged for mercy with his hands held up. The "macabre spectacle" ends as the perpetrator violated the body with eighteen stab wounds. The authors recount the life of the victim in glowing terms, but describe the unnamed attacker as an inhuman creature.[65] The book describes how revolutionaries used a garrote to kill another priest and reports that the brutal slaying produced a great loss of blood. The section on this victim also includes an enthusiastic biography of the cleric, as well as his portrait and an image of the location where his body was discovered.[66]

One chapter of *Los mártires de Turón*, titled "Exhuming the Bodies," contains graphic descriptions of the clerics' deaths as well as detailed descriptions of the condition of the corpses. According to the text, many of the dead had been mutilated, decapitated, or severely disfigured, making positive identification difficult. A photograph of a large hammer, allegedly used by the rebels to crush the dead men's skulls, accompanies the text. Finally, the author recounts the funeral and burial of the martyrs in extravagant detail and illustrates the story with numerous photographs.[67] The pamphlet *Terror: El Marxismo en España: Revolución de Octubre de 1934* (Terror: Marxism in Spain: Revolution of October 1934) lists the "assassins" and "thieves" who led the rebellion. It often describes the events in extravagant terms; for example, by highlighting city streets filled with cadavers and neighborhoods of destroyed buildings. The text reports incidents where people are killed merely for fleeing a city because they are old, sick, or members of the clergy. The pamphlet focuses special attention on the abuse and murder of three young women by a group of rebels.[68] In these ways the authors hoped to illuminate the inhuman nature of the revolutionaries by removing the economic and political motivations of the revolt and focusing simply on acts of cruelty. The imagery depicts a hellish scenario of death and hatred, one that is a direct result of the revolution. Such representations tried to show that the true aims of leftist politics during the Republic were nothing less than the destruction of Spain.

POLITICAL MOTIVATIONS

Soon after the defeat of the insurrection, commemorations of October 1934 began to be used to rally political support. The book *Asturias roja* made a direct appeal for political action on behalf of the Church by urging readers to support Acción Católica. The authors hoped that the blood of the "martyrs of the faith, of the Patria, of civilization" would not be spilled in vain but would engender a movement to save the nation.[69] The political symbolism in the work of the poet Cienfuegos is related to his close connections with the major conservative politicians of Asturias. His poems about the events of October were first recited at a meeting of Acción Popular in March 1935. At the start of his text he praises the support he had been given by the Marqués de la Vega de Anzó, whom he describes as a generous man with a "fine spirit." In addition, he dedicates the poem "Song of Blood" to the aristocrat. The poem celebrates the honorable victims of the revolt along with the noble forces that subdued the rising. It also contains political references that reflected the monarchist preferences of the poet's aristocratic patron. The opening verses characterize the revolt as "a wind more violent than that of the Frond," while the final line of the poem ends with "Viva

Spain!"[70] The Marqués de la Vega de Anzó played an important role in conservative political circles and had a close relationship with both Francisco Franco and the CEDA leader José María Gil Robles.[71] The Marqués served as an elected representative during the 1934 assembly of AP in Madrid, and he was involved in the negotiations among conservative parties about a possible electoral alliance in January 1936. In fact, the first meeting of the top-level leaders was held at the Marqués's residence in Madrid.[72] Although involved in AP, Vega de Anzó had clearly not abandoned his monarchist sympathies: the ultraconservative monarchist journal *Acción Español* offered a prize in his name for the best work advocating an antidemocratic system in Spain.[73]

Another poem in Cienfuegos's collection, titled "Dies Irae," was dedicated to José María Fernández Ladreda, whom the poet called "the soul and eloquent voice of Asturias in parliament following the tragic, monstrous villainy of the heartless ones [revolutionaries]."[74] Ladreda had long played an important role in Asturian conservative politics. He served as mayor of Oviedo during the Primo de Rivera dictatorship and directed the powerful regional section of AP. Despite AP's official policy of accidentalism, Ladreda was among those in the party who challenged that line of thinking, and he remained a committed monarchist. In general, the Asturian section of AP was known as one of the groups most dedicated to returning the king. Although Ladreda supported a stronger promonarchist cast to the organization, and even contributed to *Acción Español,* he nevertheless remained a part of AP. When the CEDA was formed in 1933 he served as a regional member on the board of directors and was elected to the Cortes in 1933 and 1936. He also understood the value of propaganda, and early on he had been among those who urged the organization to effectively coordinate efforts nationwide. Just four months prior to the Asturian revolution, Ladreda took over the editorship of the region's largest paper, *El Carbayón.* Significantly, the man he replaced, Maximiliano Arboleya, was one of the leading proponents of progressive social Catholicism. As a priest and distinguished theologian, Arboleya strongly resented the new editorial line, calling it "vulgar" and "partisan." In fact he felt that the paper's coverage of the October revolt and subsequent repression was so harsh as to provoke crimes of retaliation once the Popular Front took power in 1936.[75] In January 1936 Ladreda was listed as the director of the youth journal *JAP* although this designation was probably done simply because his parliamentary seat made him immune from prosecution or fines. The principal financial backer of both *El Carbayón* and *JAP* was none other than Marqués de la Vega de Anzó.[76]

COMMEMORATIVE IMAGERY IN 1935 AND THE ELECTIONS OF FEBRUARY 1936

During 1935 the conservative parties dominated public discussion of the October events, as the country remained in a state of war, including press censorship, until April 1935. Even then, the state of war was not lifted in all provinces and many remained subject to extraordinary limitations on the ability of groups to publish or hold public meetings. Furthermore, the CEDA and the Radicals controlled the government and used their position to reinforce anti-revolutionary imagery.[77] Overall, the events of 1935 proved decisive in creating a vision of a nation under siege by revolutionary hordes with only the sword of the army and the shield of Catholic faith to protect Spain. Celebrations of the armed forces and the government began even before the insurrection had been suppressed. On 7 October 1934 the Falange Española (Spanish Phalanx, FE) organized and led a march in support of the government. The event began with only three hundred marchers carrying signs with slogans like "Long live the unity of Spain!" but the group soon swelled well beyond the original number. Although technically illegal owing to the government's declaration of a state of war, the march was not halted by the security forces. Eventually the crowd convened at the front of government buildings in the Puerto del Sol where José Primo de Rivera, leader of the FE, declared, "We, first a group of guys, and later this multitude you see, wanted to come . . . to give you thanks. Long live Spain! Long live national unity!"[78] During 1935 a public appeal for donations in favor of the forces that defeated the revolt resulted in a collection of over sixteen million pesetas. The vast majority of funds went directly to the army, which distributed them among the troops and also to the families of soldiers killed during the fighting and to those wounded.[79]

Another factor that reinforced conservative depictions of the October revolt was the trials of those accused of participating in crimes and atrocities. The proceedings, generally held by military rather than civilian courts, continued throughout 1935 and drew enormous press coverage.[80] The judgment on those accused of the killing of the martyrs of Turón, for instance, took place in June and resulted in thirty-five men receiving life sentences and four facing the death penalty.[81] Trials were held in the months immediately following the insurrection, as well as in each month from May to December 1935, and took place in many areas of the country including Madrid, Asturias, Vizcaya, Alicante, Catalonia, León, and Albacete. The hearings also included charges against prominent leaders such as Ramon González Peña (February), Manuel Azaña (March and July), Javier Bueno (October), and Francisco Largo Caballero (November).[82] The results of the trials and the media coverage that accompanied them meant that the images, and especially the crimes committed during October, were constantly in the public sphere. Nearly every month produced new stories of atrocities, and the geographic distribution and fame of some of the accused ensured that they received national attention. In this way it was the most brutal aspects of the insurrection that undoubtedly received the most public attention, and the coverage may have helped shape perceptions of the revolt as a vicious, mindless assault on innocent victims.

The rhetoric of the monarchists, both Alfonsine and Carlist, in the aftermath of October 1934 focused on two themes: the horrors perpetrated by the rebels and the perceived weakness of government efforts at repression. The goal of the first stream was to convince "rightist opinion to identify the republican regime with a situation of disorder and social chaos."[83] The Carlist press eagerly published all stories of the atrocities committed by the rebels, even though a special commission sent to the region refused to confirm or deny the truthfulness of the claims.[84] All forms of propaganda were employed to these ends including both verbal and physical violence on the floor of the Cortes. Even while the revolt continued José Calvo Sotelo slapped one deputy who accused the government of being too harsh while another prominent monarchist called for "executions and garrotings . . . as many as are merited and necessary."[85] For many on the radical right, the system of democracy itself was too intrinsically weak to defend the nation or to punish those who threatened it. For the Carlists, the inability or unwillingness of the CEDA to crush those perceived as responsible for the revolt drove relations between the groups to an all-time low.[86] After the October revolt both the Alfonsists and the Carlists courted military conspiracy by creating propaganda designed to foster a climate favorable to such a coup.[87] They argued that it was not the administration that had defeated the revolt

but rather the armed forces and despite the privations of the military reforms conducted during the first biennium, the army still remained strong
enough to save Spain.

Although the attitude of FE and its leader José Antonio Primo de Rivera
toward violence was at times ambiguous, the group nonetheless employed
the bellicose and martial rhetoric that characterized rightist propaganda following the October revolt.[88] The FE syndicalist Manuel Mateo, in a speech
given at the Cine Madrid during a large gathering of the party on 19 May
1935, insisted that the time had come for a new political revolution. As he
told party members, "We are not against the Socialist revolution [of October 1934] because it was violent; all revolutions are violent, we are violent.
We are against the Socialist revolution because it is sterile."[89] It was around
this same time, mid-1935, that the FE began seriously planning a coup d'etat,
and party leaders tried hard to enlist the active support of the military.[90] José
Antonio reiterated this stand on the eve of elections in 1936, writing that his
group would contest the power of the Socialist Party in all areas: "Against
this [socialist] politics, another politics; against this society, another society;
against this revolution, another revolution."[91]

The revolution of October became the centerpiece of propaganda for
both the left and the right during the electoral campaign of 1936.[92] The
CEDA's imagery focused on two main themes: "Against the revolution and its
accomplices" and "Vote Spain!" The desire to reduce complex issues into a
simple dichotomy of good versus evil had long been a feature of the CEDA's
propaganda. Developed in part from its Catholic roots, the CEDA's members
believed that the party was involved in a battle between good and evil and
that no one could remain neutral.[93] The CEDA approached the elections
with an enormous amount of confidence and with a well-organized and
well-financed party machine. Their propaganda efforts employed the latest
in modern campaigning techniques, including radio broadcasts, electric
signs, mass rallies, and the use of aircraft to quickly travel the country. The
overwhelming majority of materials produced made some reference to the
revolution, and at times the flood of materials was nothing less than extraordinary. In Madrid the party used comprehensive lists to mail over five
hundred thousand notices, one to each registered voter. They produced
forty different flyers, of which they distributed over fifty million. The organization published almost four million pamphlets and almost three million

posters.[94] One flyer claimed that "Spain was closing its doors" to Marxism, Masonry, and sectarianism. Another poster depicted a stern-faced Civil Guard member with a rifle over his shoulder. The caption declared him to be "always at the service of order" and urged viewers to "Vote Spain!"[95] Perhaps the most famous piece of electoral propaganda was the enormous billboard erected in the center of Madrid that featured Gil Robles.

A comprehensive example of how the revolution was incorporated into electoral propaganda was Acción Popular's booklet *Terror*. In an opening exhortation the authors ask if the reader could still vote for the revolutionaries and their supporters after examining the contents of the pamphlet. The text continually repeats this message, often in even stronger terms, inquiring of voters if they wish to return a leftist government "so that it can again form the assassinating, pillaging horde" of the revolution. This echoed one of the major conservative slogans from the period, "Against the revolution and its accomplices." The authors of the pamphlet continue by telling readers that, among other things, the future of religion in Spain hinged on the results of the upcoming election. *Terror* framed the events of the revolt to highlight attacks on religion and challenged citizens to support their defense of Catholic values. In this way, the commemorations served to further separate Spanish society into those who would destroy religion and those who would protect it. This version divided the world into victims and perpetrators by employing the familiar language of religious martyrdom, as well as appealing to the repulsion and anger of readers. The characterizations established a social and cultural duality, in which the two sides struggled for survival, where one side was good, virtuous, and human while the other was evil, immoral, and not human. This duality helped justify the imprisonment and killing of those who threatened the survival of those perceived as good and pure. In a speech given in Toledo during the campaign, Gil Robles played on the fears of revolution expressed in pamphlets like *Terror*. More importantly, amid chants of "Long live the army!" and "Long live General Franco!" he seemed to allow for the use of violence in defense of the nation: "Those who unleash winds of chaos will reap storms of blood."[96]

The rhetoric of aggressive action in defense of the Church had appeared in conservative discourse even before the events of October. One source justifying the use of violence could be found in Aniceto de Castro Albarrán's *El derecho a la rebeldía* (The Right to Rebellion). This work, written by a canon of the cathedral in Salamanca, was published in early 1934 and had the approval of the Church censors. Its text is essentially a philosophical justification for violent revolt. In the epilogue, titled "The Reality of Spain Today," the author condemns the actions of the Republican-socialist government by calling them "a barbarous blow to the rights of the Church, to the grave moral interests of the Patria, [and] to the most sacred rights of thousands of conscientious Spaniards."[97] The perceived abuses of governmental power placed Catholics in an ambiguous position toward the state. In his text Castro Albarrán announces that loyal Spanish Catholics had an obligation to defend the Church against state aggression. He applauds the actions of conservative politicians who used parliament to loudly protest abuses. Nevertheless, he declares that stronger methods of resistance exist, and he asks rhetorically if the time had now come to employ them. Castro Albarrán argues that historically the Church protested in two ways: through martyrdom and through armed revolt. He employs the well-known golden age drama *Fuenteovejuna* to justify revolt, even against legally ordained powers. He also draws on historic examples, including the reconquest and the war against Napoleon to defend the just use of violence. Castro Albarrán seamlessly joins the defense of the Church with that of the nation by declaring that "Spanish history is a perpetual war of independence."[98] These patriotic examples demonstrate that the real threat to Spain came from outside influences that had corrupted Spaniards and led them away from the true faith. Throughout his text Castro Albarrán stops short of explicitly advocating a violent response, but near the end he states that the conclusions and examples of the book should be "concretely" applied to the contemporary political situation.[99] In the increasingly polarized atmosphere after October 1934 Castro Albarrán's message fit with interpretations of the revolt, while the endless repetition of the bloody crimes committed by the rebels seems to authenticate his stance. After the events of October, the movement had its martyrs; now it needed to find its heroes.

One of the most vocal proponents of martial Catholicism in the aftermath of the October revolt was the best-selling author José María Carretero, who wrote under the pseudonym El Caballero Audaz (the Bold Knight). During the period 1934–1936 Carretero authored a series of political commentaries with titles such as *La Agonía de españa* (The Agony of Spain), *Traidores a la Patria* (Traitors to the Patria), and *1935: Un balance de vergüenzas políticas* (1935: A Tally of Political Embarrassments).[100] According to the author, the texts were written "in defense of a politics of justice, order and Spanishness."[101] In each he intimates that only a violent response could protect Catholic Spain from future attacks similar to the October revolt. Like Castro Albarrán, Carretero declares that the Republic had proven unable to defend private property and, in fact, that state power had been used to create a "regime of terror and violence."[102] In response to this threat Spain needed to rely on its historic defender: the Catholic Church. Christianity, he argues, had long served to unite Spain in defense of national sovereignty against foreign invaders, and this unification had been created through the blood sacrifice of its people. For Carretero, combative Spanish Catholicism was an indisputably positive force: "For the faith, Spain has made wars and dominated worlds; for the faith, it has heroes and martyrs."[103] He declares that the time had come to return to this martial form of Catholicism and to definitively abandon any kind of participation in the political system of the Republic. The obstructionist tactics of parliamentary deputies and other legal means in defense of the faith had failed. The October insurrection proved that violence had to be met with violence: "The error of the Spanish church was to substitute [the] generous combative ardor of true Catholicism for the cunning, hidden, evasive strategy of the Jesuits."[104]

For many conservative writers, the authors of attacks on the Church and on Spain itself were foreigners.[105] Such attitudes help explain why so many viewed the military as the only force able to defend the nation from this foreign invasion. Carretero repeatedly designates international Marxism and Masonry as the driving forces behind the insurrection.[106] Although present throughout the period, Carlist anti-Semitism increased markedly as the Republic seemed to gather strength. The press warned about an "invasion" of Jewish refugees from Hitler's Germany and referenced the historical "crimes" committed by Jews against Spain. One writer called Judaism, communism, Masonry, and death the Four Horsemen of the Apocalypse.[107] Similar accusations appeared in *Antiespañolismo: Marxistas y separatistas contra España* (Anti-Spanishness: Marxists and Separatists against Spain), written by Victoriano Navarro González under the pseudonym Pyrene. In this work the author proclaims that Masons, Jews, Marxists, and fascists had joined forces to destroy Spain, solely because of the nation's historically strong support of the Catholic Church.[108] Russian communists, aided by Masons and Jews, remained the most potent threat to Spain. He calculates that fourteen thousand Jews lived in Barcelona while working to undermine the economy of the nation, and he further insists that they had financed the October revolt in order to "seize the economy of the country and destroy the Christian morality that they hate so much."[109] *La revolución de octubre de 1934* (The Revolution of October 1934), published in two volumes by Ignacio Núñez, also stresses the role that Masons and Jews played in fomenting revolt in Spain. The work declares the insurrection to be a war in favor of atheism and against Christ: "It was the determination of Marxism, united with Jewish Masonry to destroy Catholic Spain, to make her a guinea pig in which to experiment with the paradisiacal delights of another Soviet Russia, to uproot the faith and religion of the soul of Spaniards."[110]

Mauricio Karl's *Asesinos de España: Marxismo anarquismo masonería* (Assassins of Spain: Marxism, Anarchism, Masonry) declares that the forces of international Masonry and the Jews had directed the assaults on Spain. He paraphrases a passage from Adolf Hitler's *Mein Kampf,* stating that "only knowledge of Masonry—slave to Judaism—provides the key to understanding the true proposals of Socialism."[111] According to the author, many of the leaders of the October revolt, regardless of political affiliation, were Masons. The author alleges that the Masons hoped to destroy God, the Church, and the Spanish nation. As Spain was on the verge of being eliminated as an independent nation by these foreign invaders, he calls upon true patriots to organize resistance.[112] Karl felt that after 1934, leftist forces had again begun amassing strength in a new attempt to destroy Spain. He charges that proper Spaniards had been drugged into inaction through political participation and that existing solutions no longer worked. He further believed that, despite almost being destroyed by the reforms of Azaña, the army would restore order to Spain.[113] The author P. M. Vélez, in *La revolución y la contrarrevolución en españa: Antes y después de la batalla electoral* (The Revolution and Counterrevolution in Spain: Before and After the Electoral Battle), expresses similar beliefs, writing that he was confident that "God has blessed our propaganda." He argues that God and the army had defeated the October insurrection and that in order to defend the nation in the future, conservative forces needed to unify.[114]

The electoral campaign waged by the radical rightist groups in early 1936 reached new heights in hyperbole and hysteria. Not only did they attack the Popular Front, but in many cases they ridiculed the CEDA and other moderate conservatives. They accused the CEDA of maintaining a system that allowed the revolutionary parties of October to contest elections and possibly even come to power. Although they criticized Gil Robles and the CEDA, they reserved the most scathing invective for the leftists. Calvo Sotelo stirred up fears of continuing revolt and argued passionately that only the army could save the nation. Within Carlist propaganda, "no effort was spared in recapturing the horror of October 1934 and in linking the Popular Front with revolution."[115] Another theme of CT's propaganda was the notion that the electoral battle was also being waged for the future of religion in Spain. One pamphlet ordered followers to "appear in church and give to God your poor heart, and in the voting booth, the altar of the nation, deposit on election day your valiant and pious vote, to the defeat of the infernal revolution and to the triumph of holy religion."[116]

Although the CEDA had put together an impressive political machine with a massive propaganda effort, the result of the elections was a disaster. The Popular Front emerged with a solid majority, and the CEDA's policy of full participation in the Republican system seemed now to many to have been a grave mistake.[117] Following the results of the elections the Alfonsines wasted no time in laying the blame on the CEDA for the victory of the Popular Front. The organization of RE was in shambles as members fled the country and the group's newspaper was first banned by the government and then had its offices burned. The CEDA was accused of destroying the conservative movement while in government and allowing the forces of the revolution to again come to power. Calvo Sotelo still had one podium, the floor of parliament, from which he could not be censored. In the months prior to the start of the Civil War, he became the most eloquent and visible spokesman for the radical right. His goal was "to raise with dramatic denunciations the sensation of civic insecurity and breakdown of the democratic system, with the goal of strengthening the conviction of many soldiers on the urgency of an armed intervention." To accomplish this task he received letters from all over the country that reported not only atrocities but also the names and movements of prominent leftists.[118] Carlists too viewed the victory of the Popular Front as a prelude to revolution. Ever since the October revolt they had proclaimed that the movement was ready to launch a pre-emptive strike once revolution seemed immanent. After February 1936, that time had apparently arrived, and Carlists began plotting a coup almost immediately. Only the discovery of a cache of counterfeit Civil Guard uniforms prevented an uprising originally scheduled for spring. Eventually Carlist plotters made contact with the leader of the military plot, General Emilio Mola, and they participated eagerly when called upon in July 1936.[119]

CONCLUSION

The texts of the political right employed martyr imagery to validate a position of martial Catholicism and to conflate protection of the Church with defense of the nation. Although commonly employed by all rightist groups, the harshness of the rhetoric varied by time and by organization. The CEDA attempted to use such language in order to reinforce its power through the normal electoral process, but the actions and discourse of the group, especially during 1935, often seemed to reveal a less than firm commitment to constitutional legality, especially in light of international events in Germany, Italy, and Austria. During the February 1936 electoral campaign Gil Robles and the CEDA confidently predicted a sweeping victory that would finally enable conservatives to modify the Republican system. They employed largely negative imagery that concentrated on the threat posed by the revolutionaries, but this message failed to capture the votes needed to prevent the Popular Front from coming to power. For many rightists the defeat represented the failure of legal means and seemed to herald a repetition of the revolutionary horrors that had filled public discourse since the end of 1934. Over the next several months the actions of the Popular Front government and the spontaneous reaction of many in the cities and countryside seemed to validate the notion that a new revolution was in process. The disorder and chaos of the events of spring 1936, however, did not alone cause the Civil War because nearly all of the conservative groups had begun plotting revolt immediately following the announcement of the electoral returns and before the level of strikes and disorder had truly escalated. The conspirators, for various reasons, had been unable to muster enough support as long as it seemed that the CEDA might achieve its goals through the ballot box alone. Once that no longer seemed possible, they began actively organizing for an insurrection. Because the constitutional Republic had proven unable to protect religion and prevent the revolutionaries from undermining Spain, many rightist commentators argued that the democratic process had been irreparably broken and that a new form of government needed to be implemented. Although the conservatives disagreed on the precise format for the new state system, they unanimously agreed that the army was the instrument to implement the new order. The fusion of religious loyalty and secular patriotism provided a powerful motivation and justification for an armed response. By denouncing the revolutionaries and those who supported them, the commemorative imagery of October 1934 encouraged violence and gave conservatives the dispensation to carry it out. The key to these plots was not the events of 1936 but rather the commemorative imagery that had filled the airways, streets, and meeting places during the previous year.

"YOUR COMRADES WILL NOT FORGET!"

Revolutionary Martyrs and Political Unity

The insurrection of October 1934 is considered a grand failure when measured by the goals advocated by the revolutionary committees that seized power in various Asturian towns. Within two weeks the rebels had been decisively defeated, thousands of militants had been arrested or had fled the country, and the organizations that sponsored the revolt faced censorship and the closure of political and social centers. The local government (Generalitat) in Barcelona had been humiliated and its leaders were imprisoned. The insurrection had even failed in its stated aim of preventing members of the Confederación Española de Derechas Autónomas (CEDA) from assuming positions within the government. Despite this bleak assessment, just fifteen months later the forces of the revolutionary left and their Republican allies won an electoral victory and once again ruled democratic Spain. This dramatic turn in political fortunes can be attributed in large part to the left's successful manipulation of revolutionary commemorations. The components of the imagery included visions of defiant glory, but ultimately they focused on the suffering and death incurred during the repression that followed the revolt. Like the conservative organizations discussed in the previous chapter, pro-revolutionary groups employed the framework of martyrdom to commemorate the insurrection and mobilize political support.

The sacrifices and horrors endured by revolutionary martyrs served as both example and inducement for future political and military actions. The success of martyr imagery in generating assistance helped mobilize diverse social groups and contributed to the electoral victory of the Popular Front in early 1936.[1] In the eyes of many radicals, the suffering of the prisoners and their families would be rewarded in the end with the final victory of revolution, an idea that echoed traditional martyr literature where eternal glory is bestowed on those killed for their beliefs. Supporters of the revolt thereby turned defeat into victory by proclaiming the insurrection of October to be a necessary step on the way to the ultimate revolution. For nonrevolutionary leftists the tales of torture and mistreatment spoke to the conservative administration's arbitrary and illegal abuse of power. Supporters of the Republic feared that the conservatives would use the events of October as an excuse to rescind the democratic principles guaranteed in the constitution. In addition, they clearly sympathized with the plight of the incarcerated rebels and, especially, their children. All of these strands combined to create a powerful political and social movement constructed through commemorations of the repression. Images of October 1934 also continued to be invoked even after the leftist coalition had assumed power. In the crucial period of spring 1936, many politicians recalled the horrors of the repression to validate or excuse the mounting numbers of strikes and land appropriations and the increases in political violence. These events, combined with the legacy of bitterness created by the suffering, ultimately joined with other existing tensions to speed confrontation, and the resulting cultural atmosphere of violence and revenge led directly to civil war.

COMMEMORATING THE REVOLUTION

In the period immediately following the events in Asturias, the leftists rapidly embarked on a deliberate campaign to commemorate the insurrection. José Díaz, the general secretary of the Partido Comunista de España (PCE), confirmed the purposeful appeal to remember the events of October 1934 and their crucial link to political action. In a major speech, titled "Forging the Arm of the Popular Front," delivered to antifascist groups in Madrid on 2 June 1935, he urged: "Do not forget that in Asturias remain many orphaned children of miners, many comrades in frightful misery. Do not forget that the Asturian proletariat was condemned to hunger by the counter-revolution. Do not forget that there are 25,000 comrades in jail. Do not forget that there are many persecuted heroes of the insurrection."[2]

The journalist Manuel Benavides, in his account of the revolt *La revolución fue así* (The Revolution Was Thus), declared that his main purpose was to record the truth. He wanted to ensure that society never forgot the horrors of the repression, and he hoped that this memory would ultimately serve to inspire the proletariat: "Day by day we kindle the memory of October and we stoke the flame of our hope."[3] Another author, writing about the murder of journalist Luis de Sirval, implored the Spanish people to "remember Casa Viejas, but do not forget Asturias!"[4] In a collection of verse called *La rosa blindada* (The Armored Rose), the poet Raul González Tuñón explained how a conversation with the communist leader Dolores Ibárruri inspired his poetry. The two met while she was leading a group organized to help the orphans of miners killed by the Spanish Foreign Legion and the African troops. Ibárruri told González Tuñón the "true" history of the revolt, the stories "of the heroism and martyrdom of the Asturian miners."[5] González Tuñón's stated goal for *La rosa blindada* was to create a revolutionary art that served the needs of the proletariat by commemorating the October revolution in verse. In one poem, he announced,

> Something remains in the vital air, something remains that remembers
> what had happened,
> something remains that makes us think of that which still has not
> occurred,
> something remains that tells us of something that will happen
>   tomorrow.
> One desires to scream: Your wives will not forget,
> your comrades will not forget,
> your poets will not forget![6]

This stanza demonstrates that the act of remembering the uprising of 1934 was both deliberate and political. The socialist leader Francisco Largo Caballero expressed similar notions in a speech during the electoral campaign of February 1936. He saluted those who remained in jail or in exile because of their participation in the insurrection, and he criticized the actions of the government during the repression. As Largo Caballero stated: "We will never forget those victims. The dead live with us. We will not abandon their widows or their orphans and we promise, before the Spanish proletariat and the whole world, to recover the memory of those that fell [and] to avenge them."[7] Thus the poet and the politician both created and solicited memory, exhorting people to remember and to act upon the lessons implicit in that memory.

The writers and artists who commemorated the revolt created texts and images that focused on the sacrifice and the heroic suffering of the victims of the repression that followed the defeat of the rebellion. The historical realities of the incidents I describe below can be difficult to determine.[8] Following the conclusion of the hostilities, governmental forces engaged in a wave of arrests and subjected prisoners to systematic torture. Thousands of militants were incarcerated, and although the precise number is impossible to determine, leftist propaganda would later claim as many as forty thousand.[9] Some allegations of beatings and mistreatment were verified by different investigations, including that by a moderate member of parliament named Félix Gordón Ordás. His inquiry uncovered evidence that numerous cases of torture and murder did indeed occur.[10] The government also tried a number of leaders of the revolution, including the prominent socialists Ramón González Peña and Javier Bueno—both of whom were sentenced to death. González Peña and Bueno, along with others who led the revolt in Asturias, remained incarcerated and under penalty of death until after the victory of the Popular Front in 1936. Despite the judgments of death imposed on many rebels, only two executions actually took place, the most notable being that of Sergeant Diego Vázquez Corbacho, who deserted his military post to become an important revolutionary leader.[11] Some historians have argued, however, that while official executions remained scarce, informal murders took place throughout the province. Bernardo Díaz Nosty estimated the number killed after the cessation of combat at around two hundred.[12] Not all of those killed had participated in the rebellion, however. The most celebrated murder of a noncombatant was the case of Luis de Sirval, a journalist killed by officers of the Foreign Legion. Reports of looting and misdeeds by the victorious soldiers were also well documented, although the only recorded punishment was the execution of four African soldiers.[13] Even if the chroniclers had just cause to feature the excesses of the government repression, the specific language employed to recount these events remained exaggerated and sensationalistic.

VICTIMS AND PERPETRATORS

The literature of the revolution focused on the deaths of individuals killed both during and after the revolt, as well as on the general stories of the atrocities. Some victims became living martyrs who were glorified for both their earlier and continued suffering for the revolutionary cause. These heroes of the revolution included many leading political figures, but eventually the entire mass of prisoners, refugees, and exiles became symbolic living martyrs. One of the most widely celebrated individuals was the socialist leader Ramón González Peña. Victor Salazar's *El presidiario número 317* (Convict Number 317) provides an excellent example of how the propagandists memorialized living martyrs. The organization of the text closely follows the traditional format of Christian martyrologies, including those produced by conservatives following the events of October.[14] The structure of these martyrologies generally includes a biography detailing the martyr's lifelong adherence to the faith, and then concludes with an account of his or her sacrifices because of that devotion. Salazar wrote that during his time in prison with González Peña he found the socialist to be "simple, noble and valiant"; an exemplar of everything that a true hero should be.[15] The author details González Peña's long dedication to the revolutionary faith and catalogues his lifetime of good works, emphasizing his generosity and commitment to the miners of Asturias. The text proclaims in quasi-religious terms that González Peña remained ready to give up his life for the cause and that he patiently awaited the "second coming" of the revolution. The concluding chapter elevates González Peña to a living sign of the revolution of October and recognizes him as a symbol of socialist unity. Salazar aimed to use the story of González Peña's life and actions during the rebellion not only to help unify the Socialist Party but also to attract the support of other revolutionary groups. Salazar claimed that the revolutionary slogan UHP had been invented by Ramón González Peña and signified *Union es fuerza* (Union is strength).[16]

The journalist Luis de Sirval emerged as another important martyr, but unlike González Peña he was neither a member of any revolutionary organization nor had he participated in the insurrection. His murder by soldiers of the Foreign Legion became a highly visible symbol of the cruelties perpetrated during the repression. The commemoration and debate of the case helped turn the public discourse, especially among the non-revolutionary sectors of the political left, away from discussions about the rebellion itself and toward the government's repression. Born Luis Higón y Rosell, Sirval took his nom de plume shortly after beginning his career in journalism.[17] Biographies written after his death portray him as a simple man who bravely sought to expose injustice through his publications. Politically Sirval favored the Republic, and he even ran for parliament as a member of a non-revolutionary republican party. After losing the election he resumed his career as a journalist at the left-leaning Republican newspaper *La Libertad*. According to published accounts, he resigned from the paper and started his own press agency when he believed that some of his stories critical of the conservative administration were being censored for political reasons. When revolution broke out in October 1934 Sirval grew frustrated at both the lack of information coming out of the province and the dubious nature of the stories that did emerge.[18] Following the conclusion of the fighting, he decided to journey to Asturias to report on the rebellion and its aftermath. Sirval traveled by train to the city of Campomanes and then made his way north to Oviedo. During his time in the province, Sirval published two reports that ran in various newspapers across the nation. The stories were generally evenhanded as they spoke of the terrible destruction caused by the revolt and the sufferings of the population, especially women, in its aftermath.[19]

Sirval later went to Oviedo in search of information regarding the alleged atrocities committed by members of the Foreign Legion. Eventually he was arrested, and after being interrogated by members of the Assault Guards he was taken to the police station and held along with several other journalists. Shortly thereafter, three officers of the Foreign Legion, Dimitri Ivanoff, Rafael Florit de Togores, and Ramón Pando Caballero, removed Sirval from the cell, took him to the central courtyard of the building, and shot him. When the soldiers faced trial for their actions they claimed that Sirval had been shot while trying to escape. At the end of the trial the court pronounced a penalty of six months plus one day in prison and a fine of fifteen thousand pesetas to be paid to Sirval's family.[20] The books written in commemoration of Sirval generally follow the format of martyrologies. They praise the qualities of the dead man while simultaneously vilifying the actions of the government. A poem published in Sirval's former paper, *La Libertad*, describes him in transcendent terms: "I want to remember you as you are—As you always will be!—happy and pure, dreaming of merciful Springs, casting your gaze toward the future."[21] Ignacio Carral declares at the start of his work that Sirval was a "peaceful, unarmed man, assassinated in prison by a representative of the government."[22] The author further states that he wrote the book not only as a token of the fifteen-year friendship he shared with Sirval but also to reveal how the government had abused its power in order to stifle dissent.[23]

The majority of revolutionary texts commemorate the revolt by detailing the sufferings endured by less-prominent prisoners than Sirval. The cover illustration of Fernando Solano Palacio's *La Revolución de Octubre: Quince días de comunismo libertario en Asturias* (The October Revolution: Fifteen Days of Libertarian Communism) shows a crowd of men with fists in the air, as well as a smaller drawing of men being shot down by rifles. These images represent the two faces of revolutionary commemoration, one emphasizing the solidarity and power of the rebels during the insurrection and the other exposing the violent repression that took place at its conclusion. The combination of images is also reminiscent of Goya's two paintings about the revolt and repression of 2–3 May 1808.[24] Several long sections of Solano Palacio's book examine the crimes of the government troops during the fighting and in the repression that followed. Solano Palacio lists tortures such as dislocated arms, broken bones, and other injuries. The author quotes in full from letters he received from the victims of these crimes, including one from a prisoner who had been beaten with rifles and other instruments by a gang of Civil Guards. In the end, the man lost multiple teeth, suffered a broken nose, and fractured several ribs. Despite these wounds he was again beaten, verbally assaulted, and forced to repeat "Long live Christ the King."[25] The similarities with the texts on the conservative martyrs are particularly striking here as both pro- and antirevolutionary literature use the same phrasing but with radically different meanings. Francisco Martínez, who tells the story of his brother's murder in *Dos jesuitas mártires en Asturias,* writes that the murdered cleric shouted "Long live Christ the King!" as he was shot.[26] The phrase had both religious and political significance; since the late nineteenth century Catholic devotional associations began to take on a more political character, and one of the most successful of these was dedicated to Christ the King. Further, *Acción Católica* (AC), the religious association closely associated with the CEDA, had since its founding asserted "the kingship of Christ in society."[27] The phrase thus became a regular part of conservative political meetings following October 1934, and it symbolized for many leftists the right's staunch resistance to the Republic.[28] In this context forcing a prisoner to make such a loaded statement could be read as an illustration of the left's broader fears of a conservative takeover. Solano Palacio intersperses his accounts of torture with photographs of the Moroccan troops and the Foreign Legion, which he describes sarcastically as "the forces that 'pacified' Asturias."[29] While some photographs vilify the governmental forces, others glorify the heroes of the revolt. Solano Palacio's book includes pictures of Sirval, González Peña, and Sergeant Vázquez, but special attention focuses on the anarchist leader José María Martínez, whom the author calls "the soul of the revolutionary movement in Gijón."[30]

Other accounts of the repression graphically illustrate the cruelty prorevolutionary writers accused the government of inflicting on prisoners jailed following the rebellion. The texts employ a wealth of gruesome detail in order to demonstrate the accuracy of the accounts by providing specific victims and methods of torture while also exploiting the potential for such stories to enrage and motivate the audience. Manuel Villar's *La represión de Octubre: Documentos para la historia de nuestra civilización* (The Repression of October: Documents for the History of Our Civilization), presents descriptions of the acts of repression in a very simple and straightforward manner. Villar delineates four major areas of repression: military invasion; repression directed by the Civil Guard; judicial actions; and the mistreatment of prisoners. Villar emphasizes two important points that became standard details in the literature of the repression; he places specific blame on the African troops for the atrocities of the army and he anoints the Civil Guard commander Lisardo Doval as the figure most responsible for the mistreatment of prisoners. During a general assessment of the tortures inflicted on prisoners, the author lists various devices and methods consisting, in part, of the following: "Twisting the testicles; applying fire to the sex organs and other parts of the body; tearing at the flesh of the hands and other members; employing the ratchet and the rack; beatings, with hammers, of the hands and knees; introduction of splinters under the fingernails and flesh of the fingers; spraying naked parts of the body with boiling water; scraping knees over small pieces of stone; simulating executions."[31]

Villar characterizes the force of the repression as stronger than anything previously experienced by the working class in Spain. In addition, he stresses that all leftist groups, including anarchists, socialists, and communists, shared equally in the suffering. This reinforced a unity of action; Villar proclaims that the victims should not be separated by political affiliation, for "they are all our brothers, flesh of our flesh, blood of our blood."[32] His choice of language echoes the biblical words of Adam after God had created Eve.[33] Although Villar was staunchly anarchist, he nevertheless framed his depiction of the agony of the miners with immediately recognizable and meaningful religious imagery. The selection of this verse emphasized the unity and togetherness of the revolutionaries, despite their adherence to competing groups. His decision to stress the political solidarity of the repressed prisoners is indicative of the time when the book was written. *La represión de Octubre* appeared before the elections of 1936, which ultimately benefited from a large anarchist vote. Villar's text encouraged support for the Popular Front without actually advocating political action or participation.[34] His actions placed the interests of the Confederación Nacional de Trabajo (CNT) and its members alongside not only that of the other worker parties, but of mainstream leftist parties as well. The efforts of Villar coincided with the Popular Front's deliberate strategy aimed at increasing anarchist participation.[35]

The booklet *Los crímenes de la reacción española* (Crimes of the Spanish Reaction) also outlines the gruesome atrocities committed during the conquest of the province and the subsequent repression. Produced by the Spanish section of the Comintern agency Socorro Rojo Internacional (International Red Aid, SRI), it was published on the first anniversary of the revolution in October 1935. The cover proclaims that inside could be found the truth about the events of the past October. Also on the front is a photomontage of both the victims of the revolt, here seen merely as corpses, and the reactionaries of the title: priests, soldiers, and the Civil Guard. The pamphlet details the cruelties and torments inflicted upon the prisoners themselves. These included three common methods of torture: the trimotor, the tube of laughter and Maria's bath. The trimotor consists of hanging the prisoner by the arms as though crucified, sometimes adding weights to the victim's legs. For the tube of laughter, guards forced the prisoner to run a gauntlet of men who beat him as he passed, and they often forced the victim to run several times in a row. Finally, for Maria's bath the prisoner is submerged in ice water and then beaten with rubber whips. While these three forms of torture were the most common, *Los crímenes* listed others. Sometimes the guards told the families of people killed during the revolt that a certain prisoner was responsible for that person's death, and then allowed family members to beat the prisoner. Like other texts, the authors also relate specific complaints from individual prisoners. In contrast to the images of anonymous perpetrators, the fallen revolutionaries become recognizable human beings. Juan Sabillo Salomón, for example, claimed to have been beaten with a gun barrel until two of his ribs were broken. Another victim, this time subjected to the trimotor, was Celestino Garcia from the town of Mieres.[36] Much as the conservatives had done, the text divides society into sympathetic, human victims threatened by anonymous, bestial criminals and defines the political process as a life-and-death battle between good and evil. The authors of *Los crímenes* focused on the Foreign Legion and Moroccan troops as perpetrators of the worst crimes and accused the government of deliberately sending the Foreign Legion to Asturias because of their notorious reputation for cruelty. They blamed the Legionnaires for committing previous atrocities in Morocco, and announced that "savages and evil doers" filled their ranks.[37] The text alleges that many crimes and atrocities inflicted on civilians had been committed as the troops recaptured Asturias, and it recounts stories of shops and taverns looted and innocent workers killed. Afterward the authors condemn the leading figures of the repression, including the commander of the military repression, General López Ochoa, as well as the Civil Guard officer Lisardo Doval.[38]

Another leftist tract that describes the horrors of the repression is *La represión en Asturias* (The Repression in Asturias). It begins by stridently proclaiming that the workers had always experienced repression and that recent incidents in Asturias were merely the latest incarnation. Furthermore, the authors maintain that the level of atrocities committed by the forces of reaction was unlike anything ever seen in the history of Europe.[39] The usual suspects, Doval, the Foreign Legion, and the Moroccan Regulars, receive most of the blame for crimes committed during the fighting and for the severity of the repression. In addition, the text charges that soldiers had accused the revolutionaries of murders that they themselves committed. The authors contrast the relatively good conduct of the rebels with the

ferocious actions of the army. According to the pamphlet, the revolutionaries only searched buildings suspected of containing guns or of hiding
troops, and they fired only on those who first fired on them, while the
"hyenas" of the military killed peaceful workers without provocation. The
pamphlet tells the story of one district of Oviedo, Villafría, where the in-
habitants remained largely peaceful and had not participated in the revolt.
The authors detail the brutish behavior of the Foreign Legion and the
Regulars as they rampaged through the area looting shops and assaulting
residents. The booklet continues by describing an attack on a home filled
with innocent refugees from the fighting. Upon entering the city without
resistance, African troops opened fire on the house, and the text dutifully
listed the victims: "Carmen Corral, 49 years old; her children Manuel, 29,
Luis 27, Rosario 20, and Laura 14. A neighbor, Josefa Rodríguez, who had
taken refuge in the house also died; she was 21."[40]

Throughout the pamphlet the authors refer to the forces of the government only as soldiers or in animalistic terms, such as hyenas. In contrast, the
accounts humanize the victims by giving them specific names and ages,
thereby making them more sympathetic in the eyes of the audience. The
booklet celebrates workers and other innocent people and describes their
lives in detail, while at the same time stereotyping the soldiers and labeling
them as simple killers. Once again, pro-revolutionary commemorations
created a duality between good and evil and asked readers to choose one side
or the other.

TRUTH AND CONTESTED MEMORY

The battle for the revolution did not end in the cities and hills of Asturias
but rather continued afterward as commentators and political parties fought
to establish the most convincing and true memory of the events.[41] Authors
of all political beliefs, in an attempt to provide meaningful commentary,
aimed to prove the veracity of their particular account. The contestation of
memory required that each writer somehow demonstrate that his version
was the correct and true one. These texts often denied having any other
motivations apart from exposing the truth of what had happened. By validating the accuracy of their claims, they attempted to ensure that their
memory became the dominant one. In order to prove the veracity of memory, both pro- and anti-revolutionary authors relied on two techniques. The

first was an emphasis on eyewitness testimony and direct reporting within Asturias; the second was the use of visual evidence, mostly in the form of photographs. By employing eyewitnesses, all groups claimed to record and disseminate what they believed to be the authentic memory of the insurrection. The leftist texts that emphasize the value of eyewitness accounts include Villar's *La represión de Octubre*. Villar stresses that the stories he told came from the victims themselves, or from reliable witnesses present during the events. The author thus attempts to build a collective memory of the repression on a foundation of individual recollections. Furthermore, he supplements this eyewitness testimony with observations and interviews conducted during an investigative visit to the province, in which he meticulously documented the statements of the victims by listing names, places, and dates. Photographic evidence, such as pictures of corpses as well as those of the victorious army troops, complements these descriptions.[42] The personalized accounts humanize the suffering of the prisoners and thus highlight the brutality of the repression. In addition, the wealth of detail testifies to the veracity of the account. All of these factors helped to create a more believable and effective memory of the events.

The prologue of *Los crímenes de la reacción española* asserts that the stories reported in the booklet came from family and friends as well as recently released prisoners. The authors state that they included in the text only those tales that could be confirmed, and they add that many of the crimes described had been uncovered through an investigation by a Republican ex-minister of government. They also claim that censorship made impossible a total knowledge of all crimes.[43] These declarations were made to assure readers that the memories they present had originated with the testimony of the victims themselves. The authors even claim to have exercised restraint and to have attempted to communicate only true facts. The main text begins by answering charges made in conservative newspapers regarding the actions of the revolutionaries, calling stories of mutilated priests exaggerated and accusing the government of using such reports to legitimize the repression. Even the photographic evidence produced by conservatives is questioned; the exhumation teams pictured in the conservative texts had allegedly searched in vain for the bodies of victims killed during the insurrection.[44] The reporter and author Manuel Benavides recognized the fact that the conflict over memory ultimately meant a struggle for political support. He charged that stories of revolutionary atrocities were being deliberately fabricated and disseminated by conservatives in order to outrage the middle class. By eliciting such feelings of horror, anti-revolutionary groups hoped to enlist widespread support for the oppressive techniques used during the repression. The author also accused others of using religious imagery to convince moderates that God was behind the forces of the army and against the revolution.[45] Benavides's text vigorously defends the actions of the workers and describes the crimes of the repression, arguing that reports of worker atrocities in the conservative press were both false and censored and that the destruction of church property was unintended and lamentable. He presents testimony that discounted many of the more outrageous crimes and claims that the killing of ecclesiastics during the revolution resulted from a specific history of repression by the church. The assassins had acted on their own and against orders from the revolutionary authorities explicitly forbidding summary executions. Other instances where clergy had been killed occurred only because those men had actively resisted the insurrection. Benavides denied the rightist accounts of the revolt and described his work as an attempt to finally publish the truth. He further declared that as a reporter he aspired only to faithfully record the events, and he judged his account to be more accurate than the others: "You now see the difference that exists between official truth and real truth."[46]

During January 1936 the left-leaning Madrid newspaper *La Libertad* continually published stories refuting the tales of atrocities that had appeared in the conservative press. The paper expressed outrage at what it characterized as a deliberate campaign to frighten readers and disparage all of the political left, including the nonrevolutionary parties. At the same time, however, *La Libertad* printed its own atrocity stories detailing allegations of mistreatment and murder during the aftermath of the revolt. On 4 February 1936, the paper even reproduced a letter sent to the editors by the families and widows of those killed in several small towns surrounding Oviedo. The signatories of the letter declared that the reporting done by the leftist press on the events of the repression in those towns was "totally truthful."[47] José Ruiz del Toro's *Octubre: Etapas de un periodo revolucionario en España* (October: Stages in a Revolutionary Period in Spain) also confirmed that the leftist authors consciously decided to contest the accounts of the revolt offered by the conservatives. Its author declares that monarchist and clerical newspapers had overstated the crimes of the revolt in order to justify the brutality of the repression. He even quotes General López Ochoa, commander of the military forces in Asturias, as having characterized the reports of revolutionary outrages as grossly exaggerated. The revolutionaries had not been filled with hatred, Ruiz del Toro reasoned, but instead fought for the attainment of an ideal—something totally lacking in the soldiers of the Foreign Legion and the Moroccan troops, who had no such scruples. The author calls the Civil Guard officer in charge of the repression, Lisardo Doval, the "Hyena of Asturias" and characterizes him as the "black soul" of the repression. The book includes stories of robberies, murders, and rapes perpetrated by the victorious government troops,[48] and it denounces the soldiers and leaders of the government forces while simultaneously emphasizing the heroic suffering of the proletariat.

THE POLITICAL VALUE OF MARTYRDOM

The construction of pro-revolutionary commemorations had an avowedly political purpose as the parties of the left hoped to unite people around the inspirational memory of fallen heroes. The outrage and horror arising from the graphic descriptions of suffering helped consolidate resistance to the conservative administration among both moderate and radical elements of the political left. Ultimately these groups came together with the formation of the Popular Front electoral alliance in early 1936.[49] In this way the political fortunes of the moderate left became tightly linked to that of more radical groups. For some pro-revolutionary groups, the valor of the revolutionary workers and the repressive actions of the government could also be employed to vilify and discredit the Republic itself. These groups believed that the October revolt and its aftermath demonstrated that only a determined and radical reform could properly deal with the threat of authoritarianism and implement a revolutionary utopia. The existence of these two commemorative themes, combined with the disturbances of spring 1936, helped to convince many conservatives that only the military could halt the seemingly inevitable march toward revolution; a revolution that would repeat the atrocities of October 1934, only this time on a national scale.

The publishers of the pamphlet *La represión en Asturias* advocated continued revolution despite the failure of the events of October. They wished to use the memory of the revolt to effect subsequent political events, believing that the lessons and sacrifices of October would ultimately speed the final victory of the proletariat. The text declares the Republic of leftist democracy to be a failure and then further states that only social revolution can solve the problems of Spain. It claims that democracy had not improved the condition of the workers but instead showed the contempt and violence that the forces of authority had inflicted on the proletariat. The pamphlet concludes by stating that the memory of the heroes of October would never die and, as such, provides a great inspiration to the future: "If the repression leaves one open wound in the heart of the proletariat, and a gigantic mountain of cadavers as a proletarian homage to the 'triumph' of Spanish Jesuit politics, it also is certain that something more important, more valuable, remains: it is the clear idea and the firm sense that all of the workers should have a single concern, a single cause, and when their desires are united for the fight against the enemy, capitalism, they are invincible."[50]

El romancero de octubre: Poesías de la revolución española (Ballads of October: Poems of the Spanish Revolution), a collection of thirty-five poems written by J. González Bayón in 1935, invokes both the heroic nature of the revolt and the suffering endured following its defeat. In the opening poem, "To the Reader," the author states in verse that he wishes to "be the spokesman / for the people that are suffering and silenced / . . . to say in this book / things that others will silence."[51] Later in the poem he calls himself a proletarian poet, a "red worker" whose factory is his verse. In this way, González Bayón hoped to contribute to the proletarian struggle by supporting the workers through poetry that commemorates the revolution of October and highlights the suffering of the working class. In other words, the poet celebrates the revolt as an event of both heroic action and terrible suffering. The poem "Sixth of October" commemorates the insurrection in order to provoke an appropriate response for the next great fight:

> Asturias is not defeated
> nor is Castile still defenseless:
> there is a red star
> that illuminates all minds.
> Bourgeoisie of Spain be afraid,
> of the coming unity of the armies
> of the proletarian class!

for in the immanent combat,

they will put you in the tragic sepulcher

that you deserve![52]

These lines demonstrate how the commemoration of the revolution often included a call to political action. In this case, the poet hoped to draw upon the glorious example of the Asturian miners in order to convince others to actively participate in the next uprising.

Texts that contain descriptions of suffering often end with specific political appeals. A pamphlet published in 1935, for example, called simply *¡Acusamos!* (We Accuse!), contains graphic descriptions of the repression. It offers the testimonies of over five hundred prisoners outlining their experiences of torture, including the use of devices such as the trimotor. The authors single out the Foreign Legion, Moroccan troops, and Doval as being especially vicious and accuse them of rape, robbery, and murder.[53] Such material is standard in the kind of martyr texts produced by the left, but *¡Acusamos!* also includes a political statement written by the Bloc Obrer i Camperol (BOC). The statement proclaims that the experience of October showed that worker unity and cooperation were the keys to victory. The pamphlet also offers a series of revolutionary slogans favoring cooperation: "Worker Alliance! United Front! Syndicate Unity . . . Political Unity!"[54] Other writings by BOC politicians reinforced these sentiments. In 1935 one of the group's leaders, Joaquín Maurín (under the pseudonym Mont-Font), published a pamphlet titled *Alianza Obrera*. In the pamphlet the author stresses the fact that only the unity of the revolutionary organizations had made the October revolt possible: "The Asturian revolutionary movement was the work of the Alianza Obrera. Its importance, its meaning, its heroism all proceeded from the Alianza Obrera."[55] The suffering and repression of the Asturian workers was used to support political unity and cooperation among the parties of the left. The book *Los crímenes de la reacción española* also ends with a direct appeal to political action by encouraging the reader to support SRI and the prisoners. The text declares itself to be in favor of unity of action between all leftist parties, including the CNT and PSOE. Only together, the authors claim, would the workers be able to resist the forces of fascism. By imploring all readers, regardless of political affiliation, to "venerate the heroes of October and all the martyrs of the revolution!" they appealed for unity in the name of the fallen revolutionaries.[56] In eliciting support for leftist unity the booklet anticipates the formation of the Popular Front and reflects the Communist Party's new interest in political cooperation.

The pro-revolutionary groups, especially the PCE, reinforced the message of the political pamphlets through works of fiction including novels and plays. The novel *Sangre de octubre: U.H.P.* (Blood of October: U.H.P.) is presented as the authentic story of the revolution narrated by a self-described simple miner, but the political aims of the book are not hidden. The story echoes official PCE policy toward its rival organizations, which at times remained critical but overall stressed the need for cooperation. Despite problems among the groups in organizing the insurrection, Alvarez Suarez wrote that by the third day all of the revolutionary parties were working together. Later, as he contemplated the lessons of the rebellion, he declared that only unity could illuminate the path toward a more successful revolt: "The blood of October screams for the union of the proletariat."[57]

Another example of fiction produced by leftist groups is Pablo Toucet's *El pueblo esta preso* (The People Imprisoned). As illustrated by the title, the drama reflects the belief that the conservative administration had overreacted in its repression of the revolution. The story centers around two men jailed following the revolt. Victor is young, unmarried, and prone to excited outbursts, while Pedro, an older married man, carefully guides and instructs his young friend. Despite the hardships of prison, Pedro tells Victor not to lose faith in the idea of a better and more just life. In an example showing the value of unity, Pedro describes how comrades on the outside had shown great compassion in helping his wife and child. In this play Toucet links two important dates as milestones in the people's desire for a better life: 14 April 1931, the advent of the Republic; and 6 October 1934, the start of the revolution.[58] The play associates the beginning of the democratic republic with the armed insurrection of October in order to press the claim that the revolt was merely an attempt to save democracy from the tyranny of fascism. The play follows the standard interpretation by the Socialist Party that the purpose of the revolt had simply been to prevent the formation of an authoritarian government and the destruction of the Republic. Indeed, the introduction of the play contains words of praise from prominent local socialist politicians, including the socialist deputy for Santander.[59]

As part of the memorialization process, many organizations formed groups with the express goal of remembering the events of October 1934. In reference to the first anniversary of the revolt in 1935, the Communist Party's trade union submitted to the Asturian section of the socialist Unión General de Trabajadores (UGT) a three-point proposal, as follows: to re-create the Alianza Obrera; to jointly commemorate the first anniversary of the October revolt; and to unify the two organizations.[60] The commemoration of the revolution thus provided the means for encouraging political cooperation. Another proposal for celebrating the anniversary of the insurrection, this time in 1936, was led by a group called the National Commission of Homage to October. The national committee of the group included prominent representatives of the PSOE, PCE, and UGT. In a circular addressed to the entire Spanish proletariat, the committee outlined plans for a ceremony of commemoration.[61] The committee proclaimed that the defeat of the revolution was only an illusion, and that in fact it had been successful in preventing fascist control of the government. Furthermore, Asturias had become a symbol of the proletariat's refusal to live in bondage. For these reasons, the committee wished to pay homage not only to those who fought and died in the revolt but also to those who suffered in the repression that followed.[62] The organization explicitly stated its purpose as an effort "to organize an homage by all the Spanish proletariat in honor of the Asturian workers for their action in October and to perpetuate the memory of their heroes and victims."[63] The goal of the project was to create and preserve the memory not only of revolution but of repression as well. It revealed how the commemorations of October 1934 had become focused as much on images of suffering and martyrdom as on examples of heroic revolution. The ceremony of homage itself would have taken place in Oviedo. It was to begin as a general demonstration complete with flags and banners declaring solidarity with the imprisoned revolutionaries as well as those who had been killed. Next, the crowds were to march up to the top of Mount Naranco and erect there a monument dedicated to "the insurrection and its victims." The circular ended by asking all individual groups to organize local events similar in nature and to solicit funds to build a suitable monument.[64] This was not, however, the only plan for erecting a permanent memorial to the workers of Asturias. In spring 1936 a group calling itself simply "October" also solicited funds for a similar project.[65] Although there was no monument per se, Luis de Sirval was memorialized by the renaming of a Madrid street in his honor.[66]

Such committees dedicated to sustaining the memory of suffering were fairly common in the years after the revolution. One such group, the Central Committee of Aid to the Prisoners and their Families, celebrated a national meeting in September 1935. Claiming governmental censorship, however, they did not publish an account of the event until February 1936. The meeting included sixty-eight delegates from thirty provincial committees, and the groups present included Republicans, Socialists, the PCE, and the BOC. The CNT had originally participated in some local committees but later dropped out and declined repeated invitations to attend the national meeting. The rest of the committee's pamphlet detailed activities of the local groups and listed funds donated both from within Spain and internationally. The local committee of the group in Murcia, for example, planned to sell commemorative stamps and hold a soccer match to raise money. Finally, the pamphlet announced that the diverse agencies to aid prisoners must unite, for a divided movement only caused harm to the workers. This clearly echoed the political slogans being espoused by the PCE in the months following October.[67]

The existence of multiple groups organized to commemorate the insurrection showed that political organizations were quite successful at rallying support based upon representations of the October revolution that favored repression and suffering. At a time when censorship and arrests limited active political association, the memorial groups provided an alternative means of organizing a population sympathetic to the goals of the October movement.[68] A proposal sent to the executive committee of the UGT from SRI in May 1935 contained hints as to how this process might have worked. The document stated that one goal of the commemorative movement was to create a network of volunteers and to establish local relief committees in all cities that lacked one.[69] These links, once in place, contributed to the mobilization of both economic and political support. In addition to keeping the organization of the workers' movement fairly coherent, these groups and actions may have attracted new members who sympathized with the plight of the miners. The creation of relief groups also allowed for the organizations to raise money from both national and international sources.[70] The organization of relief organizations had a direct political goal, and the dominant role of the SRI was in part a consequence of the lack of aid coming from international socialist organizations. The communists knew this and designed a campaign to take advantage of popular sentiment to improve their own position, especially relative to the socialists.[71]

The committees of remembrance and aid to the revolutionaries also functioned as political vehicles. As early as 6 November 1934, the executive committee of the PSOE discussed the need to form an entity in support of the prisoners. A few days later they received a proposal from the PCE suggesting a joint operation to help all those incarcerated after the uprising.[72] By 17 December the leaders of the PSOE and PCE had arrived at an agreement delineating the scope of action. Along with acts of solidarity came more general agreements on political cooperation that sought to help the prisoners through a national and international campaign. In addition, both organizations agreed to work jointly to reopen closed workers' centers; regain social improvements lost under conservative administrations; and continue the fight against fascism.[73] The decision to work together on improving the lives of prisoners was one step toward moving the parties closer together, because it provided a politically neutral and ideological ambiguous rallying point for the two organizations. The communist and socialist youth groups also worked together on the clandestine distribution of banned pamphlets and other publications describing the repression.[74] Joint activities such as these contributed to the ongoing negotiations toward the unification of the socialist and communist youth groups and trade unions. The youth groups combined in March 1936 while the UGT absorbed the communist syndicate in December 1935.[75] The memory of the brutal repression and the suffering of martyrs, regardless of political affiliation, helped make these mergers possible.

Ideas of cooperation had great resonance among the rank and file of the PSOE and UGT as stories of repression elicited a powerful reaction from the workers. The extraordinary response of the membership demonstrated the political effectiveness of the commemorations, especially those framed in the imagery of martyrdom. On 20 March 1935, for instance, PSOE leaders received a letter from the local organization in Valencia calling for a general strike if the government continued to mistreat prisoners.[76] Soon messages poured in from nearly every region in the country declaring that socialist locals had begun forming joint committees or were requesting permission to hold actions with other groups based upon the idea of helping those suffering from the repression of 1934. Often these meetings and demonstrations corresponded with discussions about forming new Alianzas Obreras. The executive committee of the UGT received messages of this nature from Valladolid (30 May 1935); Albacete, Guipuzcoa, Vitoria, and El Ferrol (6 June 1935); Asturias (27 June 1935); Málaga (18 July 1935); Catalonia (1 August 1935); and Ceuta (8 August 1935). The messages had a wide geographic distribution, demonstrating that this was truly a national movement.[77] The preponderance of correspondence showed a direct connection between the commemorations of October and the movement toward political cooperation. At times, some of the rank-and-file members of the union grew frustrated with the unwillingness of the organization's leadership to work with other groups. In April 1935 the UGT's Guadalajara federation sent an angry letter to Largo Caballero criticizing the committee's attitude: "To impede the workers from unifying and working together at all times is, simply, a betrayal of the revolution."[78] Despite the fact that the leaders of the PSOE and UGT continued their staunch refusal to support the formation of Alianzas Obreras, they did authorize joint actions in support of prisoners. By September 1935, the PSOE had agreed to form a committee with the PCE for the purpose of commemorating the anniversary of the uprising.[79] On the local level, an item in the bulletin of the Socialist Party of Madrid of March 1936 discussed its intention to form a project of homage to the Asturian workers. Along with providing funds to widows and orphans, the purpose of the undertaking was to "perpetuate the memory of its [the October revolution's] heroes and victims."[80]

Concern over the treatment of the victims, especially those in prison following the insurrection, became a central plank in the electoral program of the Popular Front. The first three points of the group's manifesto included amnesty for crimes committed before November 1935, restoration of workers fired or punished for political reasons, and reparations to those victimized by either the rebels or the forces of repression.[81] The issue of the prisoners also helped bridge the gap between the parties of the Popular Front and the anarchists who remained outside the electoral coalition.[82] During the electoral campaign of January and February, anarchists in Madrid held rallies against the death penalty and in favor of amnesty.[83] In the province of Asturias, the wish to free the prisoners emerged as the single most important part of the coalition's program. Prominent syndicalists believed that if the CNT continued its policy of abstentionsim, as they had in the previous elections, the organization itself might be destroyed.[84] They recognized that a Popular Front government offered them the best opportunity to reorganize and recover in the wake of the repression following the uprisings of 1933–1934.[85] The election results demonstrate that the participation of anarchists in Asturias was key to the defeat of the rightist bloc.[86]

Organizations formed to support prisoners and their families, or in favor of amnesty, were not exclusively the domain of the worker parties. Just days after the revolt, the newspaper *El Liberal* published notices about events and organizations designed to help the workers and their families. At least three organizations, two of which were affiliated with governmental agencies, solicited donations for programs aimed at alleviating the suffering of children. The third group, the Committee of Women against War and Fascism, was heavily influenced by the PCE but also included members of mainstream leftist political parties such as Izquierda Radical Socialista (Radical Socialist Left), Izquierda Republicana (Republican Left, IR) and Unión Republicana (Republican Union, UR). Their message appealed to "all persons with democratic and humanitarian feelings." Other events, including benefits on behalf of the children of Asturias, took place all over the country during the next few months and were sponsored by groups such as the Women's Association for Workers' Children.[87] In August 1935, a group calling itself the Pro-Amnesty Committee called upon the PSOE to join. Already affiliated with the group were mainstream political organizations such as Unión Republicana, Esquerra Catalana, Radical Socialista, and Izquierda Republicana.[88] A similar letter, signed by such luminaries as Victoria Kent, the first woman appointed to a top governmental position in Spain, and Ramón del Valle-Inclán, a well-known modernist author, was also sent to the UGT leaders requesting that the union send a speaker to an event scheduled to be held in Madrid.[89] Although the socialists declined to participate, the mere existence of a group including such a diverse coalition is important because it confirmed that the images of suffering had some definite role in bringing together a wide alliance of leftist groups. Although joining a pro-amnesty organization did not automatically entail any kind of direct political cooperation, it did provide a dialogue and opened the possibility for such cooperation. Ultimately, this movement toward unity combined with other sociopolitical factors to help form the Popular Front in January 1936. The blood of revolutionary martyrs nourished the seeds of political cooperation and created a solid pro-revolutionary bloc to contest the elections. The existence of this unified front heightened the political dichotomy and gave the impression that Spain was divided into two uncompromising forces that were contesting nothing less than the future of the nation.

ATTRACTING THE MODERATE LEFT

The actions of the government during the aftermath of the revolt provoked a strong reaction outside of the revolutionary organizations. In particular, many viewed the repression as an excessive abuse of governmental authority. While these individuals vigorously objected to the insurrection itself and generally did not share the aims of the revolutionary organizations that participated, they sympathized with the plight of those who suffered at the hands of governmental agents during the repression. Coming at a time when authoritarian and fascist regimes had achieved power in Italy, Germany, and Austria, fears of a breakdown in democracy seemed very real. The workers' organizations, particularly the socialists, viewed with alarm the events in other nations, especially the destruction of revolutionary parties and unions. These groups often justified the October uprising as having prevented the "fascists" from coming to power in Spain, and for nonrevolutionary leftists the fear of an authoritarian dictatorship could almost have been as great.[90]

According to the historian Manuel Aznar Soler, the repression in Asturias combined with other international and national trends to politicize many prominent writers and intellectuals who feared that an authoritarian regime in Spain would sharply limit artistic freedom. They also sympathized with the plight of the working class and viewed the revolt as an expression of desperation. Moderate cultural reforms initiated at the beginning of the Republic, such as the Misiones Pedagógicas, seemed to have failed, and after 1934 many artists and writers became openly sympathetic with more radical groups such as the PCE. Eventually, many of these artists formed a broad antifascist front in defense of culture and in support of the Popular Front.[91] An especially interesting case was that of Valle-Inclán, who at one point held a fund-raising dinner to express solidarity with those incarcerated following the October revolt. In a letter, he related that the evening held a "revolutionary aura" and that it was quite successful in raising funds for "our incarcerated friends."[92]

Fears that the CEDA would eventually destroy the integrity of the Republic permeated the political thinking of the left Republican parties. In April 1935 moderate leftist groups sent a letter to the government to insist that it lift the state of war in effect since October 1934. Among other things the groups demanded that the trials of political prisoners be "scrupulously legal" and that the workers who were penalized for striking be rehired. The document stopped short of demanding amnesty but instead stressed adherence to legal and constitutional procedures. The signatories included many of the organizations that later joined the Popular Front, such as IR and UR.[93] The author Consuelo Bergés criticized the actions of the government in Asturias after the revolt because she feared that the arbitrary use of state power would result in the loss of democratic freedoms. In a prescient example of political analysis, she discounted the possibility of fascism in Spain but acknowledged that present circumstances seemed ripe for an authoritarian dictatorship. Writing with a great deal of pessimism, Bergés describes the political discourse after the revolution as "a situation full of defects, empty of content and solutions, without power or reason."[94] She believed that eventually democratic freedoms would be curtailed by force and the Republic would cease to exist.

For many moderates, the murder of the journalist Luis de Sirval came to symbolize the excessive use of force by the administration in its repression of the revolt. The perfunctory trial of Sirval's killers and the relatively light sentence handed down by the tribunal provoked a letter of protest signed by many important cultural figures, including Miguel Unamuno, Azorín, Antonio Machado, and José Bergamin.[95] The actions of the court even motivated a response from a legal scholar who disagreed with the decision on technical grounds.[96] The importance of Sirval as a symbol of the repression crossed political and social boundaries. On the same day that saw a massive rally celebrating the Popular Front's electoral victory, the city's cultural elite honored Sirval's memory in a ceremony at the Ateneo. The event was organized by the "Sirval Committee," a group largely composed of writers and journalists such as Antonio Espina, José Díaz Fernández, and Ramón J. Sender.[97] Other writers used the case of Sirval to reinforce aspects of the pro-revolutionary campaign to create a memory of suffering based on the crimes of the repression. The book *Sirval*, by M. Alvarez Portal, includes a dramatic account of the reporter's final hours. According to the author, Sirval argued with strangers in an Oviedo restaurant about the actions of the revolutionaries. Unable to contain his outrage over the false horror stories being told about the rebels, Sirval purportedly exclaimed, "The revolutionaries fought bravely for a cause they believed was just . . . they committed no crimes. The truly frightening part of this revolution is what the people who are agents of the State have done."[98] When asked for proof of the crimes committed by government officials, Sirval produced his notebook and related the story of how Dimitri Ivanoff had shot eight people, including a young woman he called "Daida Peña."[99] Alvarez Portal contended that the three soldiers feared exposure and hoped to silence the journalist who "glorified the memory of a sublimely heroic Spanish girl."[100]

Members of revolutionary organizations certainly were not unaware of the outrage caused by the actions of the government, in particular the murder of Sirval. These groups hoped to use this indignation to their advantage by generating propaganda that emphasized the illegality of the administration's tactics. Moderate members of the PSOE, for instance, sought to celebrate the events of October while simultaneously appealing to non-revolutionary groups. In *La revolución española de octubre* (The Spanish October Revolution), the socialist Antonio Ramos Oliveira characterizes all true revolution as a defensive reaction to tyranny. By applying this definition he includes centrist Republican parties such as IR and the Izquierda Radical Socialista alongside the PCE, CNT, and PSOE as organizers of the October insurrection. He also called for the Republican parties and the workers' organizations to join together in an antifascist front.[101] The PCE also sought to appeal to Republicans by calling the insurrection an attempt to thwart fascism. As early as May 1935 the party instructed its speakers to call for the formation of antifascist blocs not only with the PSOE and CNT but also with Republican parties. The PCE's plan was clearly aimed at achieving electoral success as the party urged its members to criticize the abstentionism of the anarchists.[102]

The PCE did more than simply appeal for leftist support through the use of propaganda. The communist-led organization SRI largely financed the Agrupación de Abogados Defensores de los Encartados por los Sucesos de Octubre (Organization of Defense Lawyers for those Incarcerated because

of the Events of October). The group was not a revolutionary organization—indeed, its president was a Republican member of the Cortes Victoria
Kent. In a report from 1936, the group stated that out of a total budget of
64,734 pesetas, SRI had provided 64,156.[103] The association also organized
meetings, such as the one that took place in Madrid on 26 May 1935, in
favor of amnesty for all prisoners. The assembly included representatives
from Republican parties and the PCE as well as the moderate politician Clara
Campoamor, who represented the Association for Workers' Children.[104]
Following the victory of the Popular Front in 1936, the PCE propaganda
continued to reflect the themes of the brutality of the repression and the
need to appeal to nonrevolutionary leftists. In a speech before the Cortes,
Dolores Ibárruri listed the crimes of the repression and made direct reference to the killing of Sirval. Curiously, she did not mention any of the well-
known communist victims of the repression, and the journalist was the only
one specifically identified. Ibárruri's reference drew tremendous applause
along with an ovation by leftist deputies as well as the journalists who were
covering the proceedings. Later, a professional association of journalists
from Madrid delivered flowers to the communist leader in gratitude for
recalling the memory of Sirval.[105] Ibárruri's speech also illustrated another
facet of the ways leftists used the memory of October prior to the Civil War.
By the time she delivered the speech the Popular Front had already assumed
power; in fact, the group had been governing for several months and the
political atmosphere was becoming increasingly polarized and violent. During this time the right launched continual attacks on the government and
criticized it for escalating lawlessness and killings. These actions culminated
with the murder of the monarchist politician José Calvo Sotelo on 13 July
1936. Ibárruri accused conservatives of provoking violence and then coming to the parliament to complain about it. She noted how rightists had
been contributing to the atmosphere of political polarization through the
dissemination of false atrocities committed by the rebels: "You cultivate lies;
horrendous lies, infamous lies; you cultivate the lie of the rapes of San
Lorenzo; you cultivate the lie of children with their eyes ripped out; you
cultivate the lie of priest flesh being sold by the pound; you cultivate the lie
of Assault Guards burned alive."[106]

Ibárruri declared that the causes of the disorder could be blamed on the
actions of the conservative administration before and after October 1934.

She used revolutionary memories of the repression to justify the actions of the workers at the same time that she criticized attempts by the right to impose a different memory of the revolt itself. Ibárruri was not alone in using the events of October to justify the actions of the government and workers in spring 1936. In a speech given in May 1936 during a campaign for special elections in the city of Cuenca, the moderate socialist Indalecio Prieto also blamed much of the current disorder on the actions of the right during the repression. As Stanley Payne notes, the speech illustrated the difficulties posed by more moderate leftist politicians like Prieto. On the one hand, they needed to mobilize electoral support for their candidates, but on the other hand they wished to avoid excessively violent reactions.[107] Unfortunately they proved too successful at constructing a revolutionary memory of October 1934 built on a foundation of atrocity stories.

CONCLUSION

An examination of the pro-revolutionary texts produced in the wake of the October 1934 revolt shows that authors of the left sought to create a specific memory of suffering. They used culturally familiar imagery to detail the sacrifices of the fallen revolutionaries while at the same time urging their audience to take political action. In this way the memory of martyrs, both living and dead, could strengthen the cause to which they had given so much, namely the revolution. Leftist texts also responded to conservative writings that were attempting to construct their own politically useful memory of the insurrection. If judged by electoral success, then the pro-revolutionary forces clearly emerged victorious after February 1936. Both sets of memories, however, ultimately served to polarize the political landscape and harden the resolve of both pro- and anti-revolutionary forces.

The resulting Civil War, however, was not caused solely by the polarization of politics. The memories of October preyed on much more than fears of political defeat. Often the writers of accounts of the insurrection used gender to frame the events as something more than a political struggle. The imagery produced by both pro- and anti-revolutionary writers and artists depicted a conflict that involved the survival of the family and the nation. The commemorations helped create an atmosphere of Manichean division where only strong, virile men could protect passive women from rampaging hordes of foreign enemies.

GRANDSONS OF THE CID

Masculinity, Sexual Violence, and the Destruction of the Family

The cover of the pamphlet *La represión en Asturias* displays a figure wielding a bloody sword while hovering over a pile of bodies (see figure 1). Clothed in a military uniform complete with epaulets and medals, the figure also wears a papal crown. A swastika replaces its eyes and nose and the mouth is twisted into an angry grimace. The *tricornio* (tricorn hat) of the Civil Guard, the cap of the Foreign Legion, and the turban of the Moroccan Regulares sit atop the butt ends of three rifles plunged into the mound of corpses. Among the pile of bodies only one man and one woman, in the foreground of the image, are clearly visible. Red ink, indicating wounds, stains the man's chest and leg, and while one hand is clenched into a fist the other rests protectively on the woman's leg. The woman's arm cradles an infant, also splashed with red, and although her wounded chest is clothed, her raised dress and slightly parted legs reveal her pubic hair—also colored red to indicate blood. The gruesome tableau undoubtedly was designed to showcase the repression described by the title as well as to identify those responsible: the church, the armed forces, and the conservative administration. In the image the male figure, although not overtly identified as a rebel, expresses continued resistance through the clenched fist, long a symbol of revolutionary power. Meanwhile his other hand holds the

woman, thereby physically connecting them while at the same time estab-
lishing the man's protective responsibility toward her and the child. It is not
hard to imagine that the scene represents a family unit destroyed, though
not quite defeated, by the forces of the repression. The male corpse reflects
two aspects of masculine duty: to heroically resist the forces of reaction
(even unto death), and to protect women and the family.[1] The illustration
also reveals the consequences, including death, sexual assault, and the destruction of the family should the enemies of the revolt prevail.

For the creators of the pamphlet the picture clearly represented a pro-
revolutionary perspective, but the conservatives also employed masculine
imagery to mobilize action on behalf of their political programs. Most
authors who reported on the events of October 1934, regardless of their
political leanings, depicted the revolt as an almost exclusively male event.
The imagery of commemoration granted men a political agency that reinforced accepted notions of masculinity. The use of gender to frame the
commemorative imagery of the revolt heightened the emotional content of
such representations and turned a political struggle into something more.
Just as other national states had done since the nineteenth century, Spanish
commentators relied on masculine imagery to link the public and personal
worlds of male citizens and to build political coalitions.[2] Only political and
military victory could preserve and protect the private world of women and
the family from sexual assault and violence.

The conservatives used the representational schema of proper masculine
action to mobilize action on behalf of the nation, but for the leftists the
imagery promoted unity of action among pro-revolutionary forces. The
depictions of pro- and anti-revolutionary forces reflected different visions of
ideal masculinity based on socioeconomic status.[3] Rightist imagery in the
wake of October focused on showing the forces of order as powerful, virile
men who destroyed the opponents of the nation. For conservatives, true
masculinity resided in the expression of strength and power. A revolutionary
society therefore posed a serious threat since it advocated a substantial reordering of the economic and political structure of the nation. Indeed, the
October revolution had begun as a determined effort to deny the Confederación Española de Derechas Autónomas (CEDA) political power. Pro-
revolutionary writers and artists portrayed the rebels as exemplifying the
ideals of working-class masculinity. For laborers, manly virtue resided in

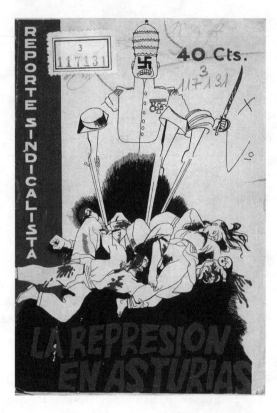

Figure 1
Cover of *La represión en
Asturias.* SOURCE: LABORATORIO
FOTOGRÁFIO DE LA BIBLIOTECA
NACIONAL DE ESPAÑA, 3/117131

the ability to provide for and protect women and the family rather than in
the expression of political or military power.[4] Although the leftist coalition
that emerged following the revolt was not exclusively proletarian, the imagery of pro-revolutionary forces remained centered on an idealization of the
working class.[5] The images of masculinity produced by leftists generally
showed the rebels as sublime protectors and providers; men who refused to
compromise these ideals even if it led to death and defeat.

Despite such differences, pro- and anti-revolutionary imagery overlapped by depicting the opponents of each as threats to both women and the
family. Men became either active defenders against the revolt or energetic
participants in the insurrection as a protective struggle against economic and
social repression. For both groups the violence of the rebellion provided the
impetus for national or fraternal unity as well as an opportunity to prove and
renew masculine virtue.[6] Since Catholic tradition linked the expression of
authority by men with their roles as heads of families, any threat to the
patriarchal model challenged the entire social hierarchy of power relations.[7]

Each side prescribed a vision of masculinity that required men to restore social tranquility through the protection of the gendered order and family unit. In this way both pro- and anti-revolutionaries depicted the struggle as a conflict over something deeper and more meaningful than politics or economics. By doing so they forced men into taking sides in the political struggle as the only way to prevent the other side from destroying the foundational elements of society. In addition, the explicit challenge to masculine honor encouraged some to greater levels of violence in defense of what they believed could best save society and the nation. At a time when fears of political and social upheaval had been growing, many people must have been drawn to extreme positions in an attempt to quell the gathering chaos.

GRANDSONS OF THE CID:
EXPLOITING TRADITIONAL MALE ROLES

Since at least the Middle Ages, warfare has played a key role in shaping masculinity as martial imagery linked the expression of manliness in war with virility and positive virtue. During the twentieth century, the experience of trench warfare during World War I helped reinforce the fundamental role that conflict played in the construction of masculine identity in Europe. Furthermore, the idealization of veterans as an elite group of hypermasculine battle-tested veterans continued into the postwar period. Many ultraconservative groups across the continent developed the image of the frontline soldier as a sharp contrast to the feminized politicians who led the nation to defeat and disorder.[8] In the aftermath of the October revolt, conservative commentators in Spain relied heavily on similar notions of masculinity linked to historical ideals of knighthood, especially the quintessential model for Spanish manhood, El Cid. After October 1934 the rhetoric of masculinity served to further divide and distinguish between the two forces that fought over Spain's future. Like their German counterparts following World War I, Spanish conservatives often contrasted the moral and sexual superiority of the armed forces with the effeminate weakness of their revolutionary enemies. Finally, much like the extreme German nationalists, the aggressive definition of masculine conduct privileged violent action over measured debate and helped legitimize the use of political violence by anti-revolutionary forces, including the military. Such notions had a long history in Spain, but by the turn of the twentieth century they held special relevance within the colonial army of Morocco where soldiers viewed themselves as the modern equivalent of medieval knights and their units adopted historical names such as El Tercio, an alternate title for the Foreign Legion. According to Sebastian Balfour, the Africanist worldview that emerged centered on a "cult of violence, redemption, death, and machismo" and many *africanista* officers saw their mission both as an extension of the historical process of empire building and as a means of restoring Spain to a position of world power.[9]

The October insurrection provided many rightists with an opportunity to showcase masculine values and to transfer them from the narrow confines of the colonial army into a frequent part of conservative political discourse.[10] Ultimately such imagery hardened attitudes and convinced many that only decisive action could prevent the victory of the revolution and the destruction of Spain. Mauricio Karl, in a book celebrating the actions of the victorious armed forces in Asturias, emphasizes that the suppression of the revolution was undoubtedly a masculine undertaking. He refers to the soldiers as "grandsons of the Cid" and true "sons of Castile," endowed with the characteristically male values of strength and courage. His description also paints the soldiers as authentic nationalists: "They felt Spanish blood in their veins, patriotic faith, the spirit of heroes, Castilian flesh, heart of the race, whole, strong, omnipotent and triumphal."[11] For Karl, the army stood for masculine virtue and respectable sexuality while the other side represented the blurring of gender identities and the consequent destruction of a weakened social and national order. In his book he announces with scorn that one well-known rebel "trembled like a common woman" when arrested.[12] True men, he implies, supported Spain and the forces of the counterrevolution while the rebels constituted nothing more than feminized traitors bent on the destruction of both the nation and traditional notions of masculinity. He further motivates extreme action by directly challenging the reader's manhood: "One cannot cry like a woman. One has to protect, and if necessary, die like a man."[13] Karl advocates political action by encouraging like-minded men to form a new anti-revolutionary front to protect the nation. This appeal reinforced contemporary gender roles that viewed combat and death for the protection of women and the nation as the domain of men.[14] Such calls to action echoed the feelings of some africanistas; in

June 1935, the military newspaper for Morocco, *África*, published a strident article that declared that Spain was under threat from the twin forces of Masonry and Judaism and only a movement of national defense could save the nation.[15]

Other anti-revolutionary writers disparaged the actions of their enemies by equating their responses to qualities perceived as feminine. José María Carretero, who wrote under the pseudonym "the Bold Knight," directly negated the masculinity of prominent leftists by labeling them "pseudo-men." In his work he describes the ignominious way in which after the revolt had failed the socialist leader Francisco Largo Caballero fled Madrid in a Red Cross vehicle, all the while denying "all blame, and protest[ing] in a womanly manner his innocence" of organizing the revolution.[16] In another publication, the Bold Knight repeats the charges against Largo Caballero by claiming that he was without "personal bravery."[17] The gendered invective continues as he attacks the Catalan rebels, describing one "who shook his musty feminine lion's mane in the air" while the "virgin separatist yelled hysterically his hatred for the unfortunate Motherland and ordered the raising of the singled starred flag."[18] By invoking traits generally assigned to women, the author portrays his political enemies as weak. Conversely, by default, those who defended the nation from these enemies embodied typically male characteristics. Indeed the Bold Knight characterizes the actions of the soldiers who defeated the revolution as a "virile action" in defense of the nation.[19] Such imagery demanded that men make a political choice to side with the masculine defenders of national unity or the feminized traitors who sought to destroy Spain.

The reaction of the armed forces to the revolution and the victory of the Popular Front also had a gendered aspect. Although opinions within the military were not homogeneous, many, especially within the army, saw the revolt as part of a general plan to weaken the nation's defenses. If some writers linked nationalism and the defense of the nation with manly virtue, then compromising the effectiveness of the military represented a direct threat to proper masculinity. In fact, military newspapers frequently expressed a dichotomy between the virility of the armed forces and the femininity of their opponents. Manuel Azaña, whose reforms during the Republic's first two years had earned him the hatred of the armed services, was by one publication called a sexual deviant and homosexual who was bent on the destruction of the military.[20] Another writer repeated the claim that reform had so weakened the armed forces that a bunch of female cooks instilled more confidence than a meeting of generals.[21] Much of the anti-revolutionary rhetoric produced in the wake of the October insurrection reflected attitudes that had been developing within the military since the nineteenth century. Of particular importance in the formation of "military nationalism" was the experience of the colonial wars in Morocco. The Foreign Legion and the Moroccan Regulars, who proved most effective in defeating the revolution, had originated in Africa. The founder of the Foreign Legion, José Millán-Astray, had a decisive impact on the ideological development of Francisco Franco and thousands of other like-minded soldiers. The ideas that emerged from the sands of Morocco fused with historical tradition and religious mysticism to form a worldview that ultimately helped launch the Civil War and lay the ideological groundwork for the Franco dictatorship.[22] Out of the furnace of colonial war came a vision of conflict centered on death. Although developed by Millán-Astray and his followers (including Franco) prior to the Republic, the October revolt and the propaganda that followed reinforced such notions and gave them widespread distribution. Nothing demonstrated the loyalty of a soldier and his patriotism better than his glorious death on the battlefield. The act often took on religious connotations linked with martyrdom as death in battle constituted, in the words of Geoffrey Jensen, the "redemption of the soldier through sacrifice for the *patria*."[23] In the aftermath of the October revolt the real-life stories of the martyrs of Turón and others must have resonated within the barracks. The imagery of martyrdom used to describe the clerics echoed ideas that had been emerging within the military. Even before the advent of the Republic, Millán-Astray invoked the symbolism of martyrdom to emphasize the similarities between soldiers and members of religious orders. In 1926, while a guest of Mussolini in Italy, Millán-Astray gave a speech in which he declared that monks "endure for the faith the same hardships that [soldiers] endure for the *Patria*."[24] General José Enrique Varela, an influential military officer and later a key figure in the anti-Republican group called the Unión Militar Española (Spanish Military Union, UME), also linked military and religious sacrifice in the aftermath of the failed military rising of 1932.[25] Following his arrest, Varela attacked the Republic by declaring that it had been overrun by communists whose goal was the humiliation of the army and the moral and physical destruction of Spain. Furthermore, Varela defended General Sanjurjo, the leader of the uprising, by comparing his arrest and persecution to that of Jesus Christ. Overall, Varela's statement, according to Balfour, "[represented] the military conspiracy within a Christian liturgy of persecution, sacrifice, and redemption."[26] The rhetoric linking religion and nationalism that appeared in the martyrologies of victims after October 1934 clearly echoed the attitudes of important military figures who together represented a diversity of conservative political opinions from monarchist to fascist. The ideas were not, therefore, exclusive to a particular political organization but instead superseded them. Later such ideas helped build the Nationalist coalition that emerged during the Civil War. The resonance of such beliefs in the wake of a genuinely revolutionary movement helped crystallize resistance to the Republic among many within the officer corps, and especially within the army of Africa. The intense use of nationalistic imagery infused with religious overtones characterized rightist depictions of the October rebellion. The extremist views that had formally been the domain of a small cadre of the military now became widespread within the civilian population. By giving such views legitimacy, conservative political parties helped create an atmosphere of intolerance and extreme polarization.

For leftist writers the notion of a combative masculinity appeared less frequently; instead, the imagery stressed the honorable male values of protection and sacrifice. Such ideas echoed the pro-revolutionary martyr imagery that emphasized the heroic suffering of the prisoners.[27] Although the imagery of helpless prisoners could be seen as a denial of masculine integrity, pro-revolutionary accounts instead linked the glorious sacrifices incurred by the rebels to virtuous masculinity. The values of protective masculinity did not preclude the expression of more martial qualities. The Cid personified such characteristics as he accepted exile with honor but made certain his family was protected during his absence. Although the Cid wept upon saying goodbye to his family, he still represented the paradigm of heroic masculinity: he could be both tenderly protective of his family and brutally effective on the battlefield. The story of the Cid also offered a contrasting vision of masculinity in the Princes of Carrión, who brutalized the Cid's daughters after marrying them and later proved themselves cowardly in battle.

The pro-revolutionary representations of October 1934 highlighted men as stoic figures whose self-control and dedication proved their great physical and mental strength. Such values were explicitly male and emphasized gender differences. As Alfonso Camín states: "Woman, the opposite of man, can not endure tragedies. She is more honey and wax than the dry metal and harsh fevers of [a gun]."[28] The expression of strength represented a set of ideals that equated masculinity with moral virtue, and it proved a valuable tool for mobilizing popular support when combined with the imagery of the revolutionaries as heroic martyrs. Fernando Solano Palacio's *La Revolución de Octubre: Quince días de comunismo libertario en Asturias* (The Revolution of October: Fifteen Days of Libertarian Communism in Asturias) contrasts the proper behavior of the rebels, who strove to protect women, with the dishonorable actions of the armed forces who refused women similar protection. One story describes how, before attacking the barracks in the village of Olloniego, the rebels allowed all of the women and children to be released unharmed. A similar act took place before the assault at Sotrondio.[29] For Solano Palacio, these revolutionaries had sublimely fulfilled their role as the protector of all women by not harming the wives of their enemies. The men followed a traditional male code that afforded women and children protection in times of conflict even if such actions became a military liability. At the same time women are relegated to their usual position as wives and mothers in need of male protection. In this way the author depicts a compassionate revolutionary force opposed by vicious reactionary troops. He uses categories of gender to create a moral divide separating the two groups who fought during the insurrection. By implication, this moral division corresponds directly with the two great political blocs that struggled for power in the aftermath of the revolt.

In contrast to the rebels' proper treatment of women, Solano Palacio presents stories calculated to highlight the brutality of the armed forces sent to suppress the revolt. He describes how the government's aerial bombardment of Mieres caused the death of many women and children who waited in line for bread. The women killed had been acting as proper women and mothers by risking death to provide nourishment for their children, and the bombs impeded them from fulfilling their assigned roles.[30] In all instances, the predominant function of the women was to be passive recipients of male protection or aggression. In order to highlight masculine roles, the imagery needed to maintain a strict sexual division of labor. Conservative political texts sometimes used similar anecdotes to illustrate the depravity of the revolutionaries. The pamphlet *Terror: El Marxismo en España: Revolución de Octubre de 1934* (Terror: Marxism in Spain: Revolution of October 1934), written by members of Acción Popular, alleges that bands of rebels indiscriminately shot defenseless people including the elderly and infirm women.[31] The writer Francisco Prada recounts tales of mutilated young people who lost eyes and limbs as a result of the rebellion. He blames such atrocities on the rebels, whom he refuses to call men and instead describes as beasts.[32] Such attacks on these vulnerable groups indirectly questions the masculine honor of the revolutionaries.

The decision of men to leave their families in order to participate in the revolt provided both pro- and anti-revolutionary writers with an opportunity to comment on the proper fulfillment of masculine duties. Similarities in the circumstances of the accounts reflected differing notions of male responsibility toward the family. Two poems by J. González Bayón express the belief that part of a man's duty was to provide for and, if necessary, defend his family. In "The Barricade," a man instructs his companion to remain home with the children while he goes off to fight. His sense of duty demands that he do what others are doing even if it threatens to kill him and disgrace his family.[33] Another poem in the same collection tells the story of a miner killed during the revolution. The man left behind an idyllic family, with two daughters described as the "most beautiful of all the girls at school."[34] In each poem the miner fulfills his masculine duties to protect and provide for his family, since participation in the uprising is viewed as a defensive action against social and economic repression. The worker feels an overriding duty to protect his loved ones, even if it means death. González Bayón also uses the poems to reveal how the forces of the reaction destroyed families through the wholesale slaughter of husbands and fathers.

The anti-revolutionaries told nearly identical stories but with the aim of vilifying the rebels. If protecting loved ones was a manly duty, then failing to do so called into question the masculinity of the individual. The book *Octubre rojo: Ocho días que conmovieron a España* (Red October: Eight Days that Shook Spain) explains how, just as in González Bayón's poem, a miner leaves his family behind to fight in the revolt. The man joins the insurrection over the protests of his wife and despite the fact that his children were suffering. As an explanation, the miner tells his wife that he has to go because it is a question of honor. The authors of the book describe the consequences of the miner's decision as follows: "If the red miner does not return he will carry on his back and on his chest a calendar page, it will be an untouchable page, one that will never be removed. It is the penal number: the page of the calendar is one of perpetual chains."[35] The text invokes the role of the man as protector and provider of his family in order to condemn the revolutionary because he turned his back on his masculine duties for the sake of what the authors viewed as a misplaced sense of honor. Rather than representing the miner as fighting to protect his family, as does the leftist text, the conservative writers view his decision as a rejection of his familial duties as a man. In addition, the authors deny the man a heroic death in the service of the revolt and instead show him as doomed to serve out his life in prison while his wife and daughters remained hungry and alone.

In addition to textual representations, the imagery reflecting the masculine values of strength and resistance was played out in the streets and public spaces across the country. Each side employed large-scale rallies and meetings in order to occupy public areas and dominate the geographic and symbolic space of the nation (see table 1). Just as the two sides engaged in a propaganda battle over the meanings and interpretations of the insurrection, they also contested the geography of Spain. The manipulation of crowds was seen by many European theorists and politicians as an explicitly gendered act. Research on the psychology of mass behavior concluded that crowds naturally became irrational and emotional—characteristics deemed to be typically feminine.[36] Male leaders could neutralize the chaos inherent in mass gatherings and channel their energies in politically constructive directions by exercising a kind of fatherly control over the crowd. One of the most successful manipulators of crowds during the interwar period was Benito Mussolini. Simoneta Falasca-Zamponi has characterized Mussolini's relationship with the crowd as one of "paternalistic dominance," and Il Duce himself once declared: "The mass loves strong men. The mass is female."[37] The large rallies held in the wake of October 1934, which were attended by tens of thousands of people, became a show of strength; a way to intimidate and dominate political opponents as well as an expression of masculine authority.[38] The effect of the meetings helped bridge the gap between language and action, as was the case on 27 October 1934 in Granada when the crowd at a rally in support of the government organized by the Juventud de Acción Popular (Youth of Popular Action, JAP) wanted to assault the headquarters of a leftist party but were stopped by the mayor.[39]

During 1935 the anti-revolutionary forces, due to their control of government, easily outdid the leftists in organizing demonstrations. However, during and after the Popular Front elections the pro-revolutionary groups also held a large number of meetings. The largest and most impressive rallies were held by the CEDA and its youth organization the JAP.[40] Although not a genuinely fascist organization, the CEDA deliberately employed methods of propaganda that clearly had been inspired by Italian models. By combining the determined use of mass meetings as political theater with the rhetoric and imagery of totalitarianism, the CEDA and its leader José María Gil Robles encouraged the belief among opponents that they were determined to seize power. Even some conservative rivals criticized the organization's adoption of fascistic language and symbolism. José María Carretero, the Bold Knight, attacked the emerging cult of personality surrounding Gil Robles when he declared that politicians were no longer "forged in the solitude of study or in the sacrifices of pilgrimage but rather in the tumult of assemblies and the bustle of the street."[41]

The CEDA deliberately chose the mass events to announce policy changes it knew would generate controversy. On 9 September 1934, Gil Robles announced during a JAP rally held at Covadonga that the party would soon be entering the government, an action that ultimately triggered the October insurrection. Furthermore, the locations generally held important historical connotations to Spain's reconquest of the peninsula or the imperial expansion.[42] Early in spring 1935 the CEDA held a series of meetings in various parts of the country that attracted a large number of supporters and featured flags, signs, and fiery speeches. At Salamanca on 24 March, for instance, Gil Robles discussed governmental initiatives to alleviate problems such as unemployment, but he also announced: "We are invincible."[43] Even if the overall tone of the speech was moderate, his strident language along with the radicalization of the JAP produced an image of an organization bent on seizing power. Less than a month after the spring meetings the JAP published a manifesto that had seemed to indicate the development of a cult of personality surrounding Gil Robles. The statement declared unconditional loyalty to the *jefe* (chief) and pledged "blind obedience to his com-

Table I Political meetings of 1935

Date	Place	Organizations	Numbers
Oct. 7, 1934	Madrid	FE and Others	300+
March 10, 1935	Zaragoza	AP/CEDA	
March 17	Armilla (Granada)	AP/CEDA	Large numbers
March 24	Salamanca	AP/CEDA	
April 7	Jaen	FE	
April 9	Madrid	FE	
April 11	Madrid	FE	
April 21	Seville	RE (?)—Calvo Sotelo	
April 30	Madrid	Madrid Socialists	>10,000*
May 3	Barcelona	FE	
May 12	Cordoba	FE	
	Guadalajara	Bloc Nacional	
May 19	Madrid	FE	6,000
May 26	Valencia	Manuel Azaña—IR	66,000
	Gijón	BN	
	Madrid	Agrupación de Abogatos Defensores de los Encartados por los Sucesos de Octubre and Asociación Pro-Infancia Obrera	
May 27	Uclés	JAP with Gil Robles	5,000
May (?)	León, Oviedo, Mota del Curevo (Cuenca)	FE	
June 2	Málaga	BN	
	Poplet	JET/CT	30,000
	Madrid	PCE	
June 15	Madrid	Socialists	
June 30	Medina del Campo (morning) Valencia (afternoon)	CEDA	50,000 70,000–80,000

Sources: Arrarás, *Historia de la Segunda República Española*, vol. 3; Souto Kustrín, *Y ¿Madrid? ¿Que hace Madrid?*; Azaña, *Obras Completas*, vol. 3; *New York Times*, 16 June 1935; *La Libertad*, 19 January 1936.

* In order to minimize attendance, the government only allowed the group to meet at Cine Paradiñas.

mands."[44] During the electoral campaign of 1936 the JAP produced slogans that echoed the fascist language of Hitler and Mussolini, such as that seen on a broadsheet featuring a modernist rendering of a soldier and airplane along with text declaring the need for a strong army and the slogan "All power to the JEFE." Other imagery also linked the need to give all power to Gil Robles with the perceived necessity of a strong military.[45] Considering that it was

Date	Place	Organizations	Numbers
July 7	Valencia	Radicals	70,000
July 15	Lasearre (Baracaldo)	Azaña—IR	
July 22	Riosa (León)	Military maneuvers with Gil Robles	
July 30	Chamartín de la Rosa (Madrid)	Socialists with PCE	
Aug. 1	(?)	PCE	
Aug. (early)	Santander, Vizcaya, Guipozcoa	BN	
Aug. 25	Baños de Montemayor	Radicals	
	Santander	Gil Robles—CEDA	
Sept. 1	Santiago de Compostela	JAP with Gil Robles	25,000
Sept. 8	Barcelona	Radicals	
Sept. 15	Madrid	Left	>5,000‡
Sept. 17	Valencia	Left (Azaña?)	
Sept. (?)	Vigo	Left	
Oct. 11 (?)	Madrid	Socialists and Left (?)	c. 100,000†
Oct. 14	Madrid	Socialists	
Nov. 3	Madrid	PCE	
	Montserrat	CT	30,000
Nov. 10	Villava (Navarre)	JET	8,000
	San Sebastián	BN	
Nov. 17	Madrid	FE	
Nov. 24	(?)	Basque Nationalists	
Nov. (?)	San Sebastián, Zaragoza, Cuenca, La Coruña	Left	
Dec. 19	Valladolid	CEDA	
Dec. 20	Madrid	CEDA	
Dec. 21	Plasencia	CEDA	
Dec. 29	Barcelona	CEDA	

‡ Meeting was an anti–death penalty rally sponsored in part by the Agrupación de Abogatos Defensores de los Encartados por los Sucesos de Octubre.

† Meeting was not organized; the crowds reportedly gathered spontaneously outside the hospital where Largo Caballero's wife was dying.

widely known that Gil Robles had studied the propaganda tactics of Hitler, the statements of the youth and of Gil Robles himself could only have reinforced doubts about the CEDA's commitment to the Republic. The actions of the CEDA and JAP may well have been a form of political brinksmanship, or they might have been a sign that the movement had an enormous amount of confidence in its political power, not only relative to the revolutionaries but also to the other conservative forces. The events also reflected the strength and power not only of the political movement but of its leadership as well. Coming as they did during a period when the pro-revolutionary forces were limited by governmental repression, the extremist language and actions served to escalate tensions by raising fears of an author-itarian takeover. Such fears could only have been encouraged when Gil Robles attended functions in his capacity as minister of war. A celebration put on by the city government of Salamanca in honor of Gil Robles and then president of the Republic Alejandro Lerroux on 23 June included a parade of military and Civil Guard units. At a later banquet, attended by 4,000 people, both men spoke about the need to save Spain from the revolu-tionaries. Another example came in July when the military, supervised by Gil Robles, conducted maneuvers on the border between the provinces of León and Asturias. Numerous officers known to be hostile to the Republic also attended the actions, and the site was deliberately chosen to send a clear message to any potential revolutionaries that a future insurrection would be met with military force.[46]

Other parties of the right also held their own rallies and meetings, al-though none could match the CEDA's in terms of size. The meetings of monarchists, Carlists, and fascists saw the most extreme anti-revolutionary and anti-Republican propaganda. The imagery of the extreme right served to equate the Republic with the revolution and to call for a fundamental reordering of Spain's political and social organization. Despite the continu-ing states of alert and of war that limited leftist activity in most parts of the country, the monarchist propaganda routinely declared that the revolution-ary forces had not been defeated and were already gathering strength for another attack on Spain. At a rally in Seville on 21 April 1935 the monar-chist leader José Calvo Sotelo declared that "the revolution is on a war footing," and he argued that the social order was already crumbling.[47] The speech reminded listeners that the revolution constituted something more than a political threat because it aimed to destroy the social fabric of the nation. Such invective continued during a series of rallies in May and June, at which speakers criticized the Republican system and continually warned of the impending revolution.[48] Although generally smaller than the other parties, the Carlist rallies made up for their lack of numbers with disciplined staging featuring cadres of uniformed male youths. At Poplet (Tarragona) on 2 June, for example, the Carlist organization, known as Communión Tradicional (Traditionalist Communion, CT), organized a meeting that attracted 30,000 people, including thousands of young people.[49] The presence of the increasingly militarized youth at the mass rallies combined with the anti-Republican message indicated that the Carlists had begun serious preparations for war.[50] The largest event held by the Carlists occurred at Montserrat on 3 November 1935. An estimated 30,000 people, including several hundred uniformed youth, heard CT's leader, Manuel Fal Conde, challenge the leftists: "If the revolution wants to lead us to war, then it will be war."[51] Throughout 1935, the Falange Española (FE) made attempts to increase its membership by disseminating propaganda and putting on its own meetings throughout the country. Although miniscule (the largest meeting was around 6,000 people) compared to those of the CEDA or Izquierda Republicana (IR), they were among the most strenuous critics of the Republic while at the same time promoting fears of another violent revolution.[52] The FE also played a key role in the development of the street violence that would ultimately help destabilize the Republic during spring 1936.[53]

On 26 May 1935 Manuel Azaña was the featured speaker at a massive rally held at Mestalla Stadium in Valencia. A reported 60,000–70,000 people gathered in what was the largest public demonstration of leftist politics since the October revolt. The rally followed the lifting of martial law only a few weeks before and occurred between attempts by conservatives to censure Azaña for his alleged involvement in the October rebellion. Although his speech was generally moderate in tone, he did warn against possible threats to the Republic by radical conservatives. The meeting elicited a strong reaction from the conservative press and raised fears of a rejuvenated left determined to launch a new revolt. The *New York Times* later reported that episodes of political violence resulting in the deaths of four people erupted in various parts of the country following the speech.[54] The government also followed the meeting by passing a law on 22 June 1935 prohibiting the public display of symbols of "political or social subversion" unless previously authorized by the administration. Although technically applying to all parties, enforcement was often left up to local officials who tended to favor conservatives during this period.[55]

The month following the leftists' meeting in Valencia, the CEDA held not one but two rallies in that same city. On 30 June 1935 Gil Robles began the day in Madrid but flew to a rally near Medina del Campo in the morning before returning to the capital for lunch. Later that afternoon he took off once more, this time headed to Valencia. The CEDA's leader first spoke at the bullring and later at the soccer stadium. As Gil Robles described the response: "Never had I heard acclamations so delirious or ovations so frequent and thunderous."[56] For good measure, the Radicals held a meeting in Valencia a week later that reportedly attracted some 70,000 people.[57] Azaña's Republican Left held at least two more mass rallies: at Camp de Lasearre (Vizcaya) on 14 July, and at Campo de Comillas (Madrid) on 20 October. In 1936, the former prime minister estimated the total attendance at the events, including the earlier meeting in Valencia, at 700,000.[58] Each meeting not only represented an attempt to rejuvenate the left and to forge a broad pro-revolutionary coalition, but they were also an expression of political strength. To the conservatives, however, Azaña's actions seemed nothing less than the reconstruction of the revolutionary alliance that launched the October revolt.

After the electoral victory of the Popular Front the left held numerous meetings, with the most spectacular taking place in Madrid on 29 February 1936. According to leftist accounts, the massive rally saw more than 500,000 turn out to celebrate the victory.[59] Since the announcement of electoral returns the capital had seen many different types of demonstrations, including speeches by released prisoners such as Ramón González Peña and Javier Bueno as well as a protest march by workers fired in the aftermath of the insurrection. Such events could only have confirmed the greatest fears of conservatives and reinforced the message delivered throughout 1935 that a new revolution was at hand. The grand meetings of both pro- and anti-revolutionary groups featured masses of enthusiastic supporters, raucous language, and strident imagery; as such, they undoubtedly heightened the polarization of the political landscape and stimulated political violence. This atmosphere of polarization was reflected even in the language used by political leaders: "Party members became known as militants or even militiamen; notices of political meetings became mobilizations; demonstrations became marches or rallies; leaders became 'chiefs,' and elections became electoral struggles, battle or fights."[60] Despite the impression of contemporaries, however, recent studies suggest that the level of political violence actually declined throughout 1935. Stanley Payne estimates that the number of political killings during 1935 was just 45 (including the two executions directly related to the rebellion), considerably less than the 178 recorded during the Republic's first two years.[61] It was not the numbers of violent events or their intensity that had changed following October 1934 but rather the perception of that violence. The rhetoric of martyrdom and masculinity highlighted even relatively minor incidents, and because the October revolt had provided concrete examples of where that violence might lead, it encouraged an active response.

THE REWARDS AND PUNISHMENTS OF PROPER MALE ACTIONS

The commemorative imagery of October 1934 exploited traditional notions of masculinity to encourage political polarization. The imagery dictated the proper attitudes as well as the proper actions expected of men. In addition to the prescribed characteristics demanded throughout the representations, the texts also described the rewards and penalties associated with the successful completion of male responsibilities. Both pro- and anti-revolutionary imagery rewarded men who properly upheld masculine values with the affections of women. The fulfillment of masculine duties earned men the physical affection and/or procreative rights to the women who became both witness and reward. The imagery reinforced the sexual virility of men and confirmed their primary role as the head of the family. The representations also posited the patriarchal family as an ideal and foundational element of a stable society. Attempts to reinforce the established family structure reflected the desire of both pro- and anti-revolutionaries to restore social stability during a period of increasing turmoil. At the same time that they listed the positive results of masculine actions, representations of the insurrection also described the horrific consequences when men failed to do the proper thing. Accounts of the revolt often contained brutal stories of sexual violence designed to frighten and cajole men into sympathizing with a particular position either for or against the rebellion. These images furthered the atmosphere of tension by invoking rape and the destruction of the family to defend a political position.

In *Caminos de sangre* (Paths of Blood) the conservative author Francisco Prada recounts numerous stories of men who did all they could to protect or provide for their families. He describes one man who left home seeking food for his hungry family, and after he did not return promptly his wife feared the worst until he finally arrived home wounded. Prada then continues by declaring that "the wife, with her sublime womanly love, cured him."[62] Gil Nuño del Robleda described his book *¿Por qué Oviedo se convirtió en ciudad mártir?* (Why Was Oviedo Made into a Martyr City?) as an homage to those who "liberated" Oviedo from the hands of the revolutionaries. A central storyline of the text concerns an engaged couple named Luis Gonzaga and Carmina Valle. On the day of the revolt Carmina had ventured into the city but failed to return and was feared captured by the rebels. Throughout the remainder of the story and during the worst fighting for the city Luis never ceases looking for the woman that "[the rebels] have stolen from me."[63] He demonstrates his heroism through his determination to locate Carmina and his refusal to stop looking despite the violence that overtakes the city. Luis even helps protect Oviedo by removing dynamite reportedly placed by the rebels as they fled. Eventually, with the help of Carmina's loyal dog, Luis finds her but not before she has been shot three times. Despite her wounds, she survives and the pair eventually marry and live together happily.[64] The story illustrates the rewards inherent in the successful conclusion of masculine duties. Luis demonstrates loyalty to his betrothed, bravery in refusing to give up the search even during the heaviest combat, and fearlessness in the way he removes the booby traps left by the rebels. By the end of the story the danger has passed and the couple is free to continue their lives together. The drama reveals that despite the hardships of the revolution the traditional family structure has survived—thanks largely to the exemplary efforts of the man. In many ways Luis proves to be an ideal man and model Spaniard, so he is rewarded with the prize of traditional matrimony.

Other accounts reveal how revolutionary violence could impair the creation of such family units. Prada's "The Bride's Veil Was Dyed with Blood" focuses on a young woman from a mining family who is about to be married when the revolt begins. Despite the fighting, she continues to plan the wedding and her mother and aunt busy themselves preparing her dress. However, a shot from random gunfire suddenly kills the young woman as she tries on the dress, and the author describes how her blood stains the "immaculate whiteness" of her gown. Soon afterward her fiancé returns to find her dead, and as he calls out to her he kisses the blood-stained veil.[65]

The white wedding dress has long symbolized the purity and virginity of the bride, and the veil has been linked specifically to the hymen. The literal staining of the bride's gown and veil perhaps metaphorically represents a sexual assault, which destroys both her honor and her life.[66] The revolutionaries thus contribute to the moral and physical destruction of the family as the young man laments not only the loss of his fiancée's life but also the symbolic loss of her virginity, represented by her blood-stained gown. The text implies that the man, having lost his future wife, is denied the opportunity of taking her virginity and eventually fathering children. The author highlights not only the suffering of the woman but also the helplessness of the man. The actions of the revolutionaries have impeded the proper consummation of both male and female ideals, and thus the task of preventing future revolutions enables men to protect the lives and honor of women.

The linking of the display of masculine values such as strength and bravery with the rewards bestowed by women also appears in the work of the pro-revolutionary poet Federico Gerard Ruffinelli. In a poem titled "Sign: Song of Asturias" he writes about the fighting during the revolution:

The miners made strong:
the troops are defeated,
the lips of women,
revolutionary flags,
know to kiss the valiant,
know to hate the Guard.[67]

Once again the physical affections of women reward the brave and the victorious. By necessity, the symbolism reflects a system where men fight and women wait to praise, heal, and above all witness the glorious struggles of men. Solano Palacio writes that the martyrdom of revolutionary men occurs in part for the protection and betterment of women's lives. These women incur a debt to their masculine protectors and repay it with both emotional and physical love. In addition, the actions of men on behalf of women invoke powerful feelings within women, arousing them to strong expressions of emotion. He writes that during the repression, "women, possessed with a feeling we could classify as ferocious, threw themselves around the neck of the victims of the reaction, embracing them between their arms, without seeing in the comrade anything but a martyr, to whom,

with their kisses, they wanted to in part repay past martyrdoms."[68] Through
suffering, men win the approval of women, thus validating their masculinity
both as the primary instigators of political and social change and as virile
attractors of women.

If the successful completion of masculine duties resulted in feminine
affections, failure to complete these duties implied a loss of those affections.
One conservative commentator played on these fears by describing the
cruel effects of the revolt. In the report "Life among Shadows!" Francisco
Prada tells the story of a young soldier blinded in the revolt. Although his
girlfriend and family comfort him, he remains despondent. The girlfriend
believes that they must stay together, but he proclaims that it is impossible
because she would eventually leave to marry a sighted man. She does not
reply, as though silently accepting the truth of his judgment. Finally the
soldier's brother laments that his brother will never again be able to see the
eyes of his girlfriend. More significantly he announces that "[my brother]
will not be able to see her or to know if some other man is looking at her!"[69]
The power to control who looks at her represents his proprietary and exclusive right to her, and his brother's statement infers that even if the young
couple stays together, the blind man will no longer be able to keep other
men from visually possessing the woman. By not being whole he is no
longer entitled to the affections of a woman, and he acknowledged this by
declaring that she will marry a man who can see—that is, a complete man.
The story demonstrates how commentators played upon masculine anxieties in order to invoke a judgment against the actions of the revolution.
However, it also contains positive elements that allow the soldier to rescue
his honor through his determined refusal to allow the woman to marry him.
Although the wounds inflicted by the rebels prevent him from fulfilling his
duties as a husband, he is able to restore his manhood through his decision to
forego marriage. The soldier is thus destined to live an austere and celibate
life, much like the Catholic saints that often were held up as examples for
young boys to emulate.[70]

IMAGES OF RAPE AND SEXUAL VIOLENCE

Depictions of the October revolt included horrible scenes of sexual assault
and rape. As with many of the atrocity stories that emerged after the revolt,
the veracity of the accounts can be difficult to determine with any certainty.

One of the most prevalent stories concerns the alleged rape and murder of three young girls by revolutionaries. According to the pamphlet *Terror*, a band of marauding rebels encountered three young women on the streets of Oviedo and brutally raped them.[71] Although the authors offer no specific details and mention the incident only in passing, the story is constantly repeated in the conservative press and even inspired parliamentary debate. In January 1936, the liberal newspaper *La Libertad* published a story that refuted the allegations of rape and murder. The paper declared that two of the so-called victims of the crime were in fact alive, and that the third was the communist revolutionary Aida Lafuente who died fighting in favor of the revolt. Eventually the newspaper printed a photograph of one of the young women along with a statement from her denying that she had been attacked.[72] The historian Paco Taibo has concluded that despite intense public pressure to bring those responsible to justice, no evidence ever emerged to verify the account, and thus in all likelihood the story was a fabrication.[73] Nevertheless, the idea of widespread sexual assault and the imagery depicting such crimes became an integral part of commemorations on both sides. Although the imagery of sexual assault, either real or imagined, has often been a feature of conflict, the large-scale dissemination of wartime propaganda in the twentieth century made such depictions more extensive. In *Women's Identities at War* Susan Grayzel describes the purpose of sexual violence in Allied propaganda during World War I: "The use of rape in wartime propaganda overwhelmingly inscribed women as passive, ultimately sacrificial victims, as the emblems of the traditional home and family that the war was presumably being fought to protect and preserve."[74]

The imagery of sexual assault in Spanish commemorations reflected similar aims; that is, to communicate to the male consumer the enormous threat posed by those perceived as enemies and to encourage decisive action against them. Perpetrators of sexual crimes revealed themselves as creatures unable to control their desires and so represented a threat to all virtuous women. The widespread existence of sexual criminals also threatened the survival of Spain itself since rape and other crimes served to destroy traditional notions of sexual behavior and family. The imagery combined with extensive reporting on political violence to reinforce the notion of a society that was rapidly spinning out of control. Incidents of sexual violence perpetrated against women and girls also became intertwined with notions of masculinity. Rape and

sexual torture can be used to assert masculinity and humiliate male opponents through the violation of "their" women.[75] Under the law, rape has
often been classified as a crime of dignity and honor, originally against that of
the male and only later that of the female herself; as Rhonda Copelon notes,
in societies "where rape has been treated as a grave crime, it is because it vio-
lates the honor of the man and his exclusive right to sexual possession of his
woman as property."[76] In this sense the accounts of rape and sexual assault that
emerged after October 1934 can be read as both a challenge and a threat. The
authors of such stories appealed to the notions of masculinity that demanded
that men protect women (and themselves) from the shame associated with
rape, while at the same time the horrifying stories of violence served as an
explicit warning as to what would happen should their enemies win.

Anti-revolutionary commentators commonly employed accounts of sexual violence to illustrate the threat posed by the revolutionaries. Mauricio
Karl, for instance, after exhorting men to join together against the rebels,
declared that if not defeated the revolutionaries would return to rape the
wives and kidnap the daughters of their enemies.[77] Other writings relied on
the threat of sexual violence to encourage people to resist the revolutionaries
by any means necessary. Gil Nuño del Robleda's novel based on the events of
the revolt includes a scene where four rebels break into the home of a young
woman named Marta. The men brandish a paper that supposedly gives them
the right to confiscate one woman. The author characterizes Marta as being
both spiritually and physically attractive; she is a simple, modest young
woman who does not need makeup to appear pretty. Despite her seeming
innocence she grabs a pistol in her "virgin fingers" and shoots the men dead
in order to protect her honor.[78] The vignette uses the setting of the home and
the danger posed to morally upstanding young women in order to demonstrate the nature of the revolutionary threat. Like other women, Marta had
leave to defend her home and her virginity in the strongest possible way
without compromising her moral integrity.[79] The story also illustrates that
many conservatives viewed revolutionary ideologies as a direct threat to the
gendered order. In this case, the rebels saw no problem in parceling out
women just as they redistributed wealth, food, and other property. In other
instances anti-revolutionary writers described how leftist ideologies advocated conceptions of "free love" that ultimately served to break down the
traditionally monogamous practice of marriage and the patriarchal family

structure that resulted from it. Even while the fighting continued in Asturias the magazine *Estampa* published a series of stories describing the insurrection. One declared that part of the revolutionary program had been the proclamation of free love, and under "the new socialist republic, men were free to pick women, without obligation to support them."[80]

The emphasis on the threat posed by revolutionaries advocating "free love" showed that for many conservatives the insurrection of October 1934 represented more than just a political revolt. In fact, concern over the moral state of the nation and the dangers posed by revolutionary ideologies reflected a broader anxiety over changing sexual norms. Although much of this disquiet centered on the increasing public role of women in society, during the 1920s and 1930s attitudes toward sexual behavior were changing in other ways.[81] Movements for sexual reform began under the dictatorship of General Primo de Rivera (1923–1930) but it was only during the relative freedom of the Republic that such ideas received widespread political and public attention. The efforts of the reformers helped bring about the Republic's divorce legislation and encouraged public debates over such contentious issues as birth control and abortion. In addition, many of the most vocal reformers were associated with political liberalism, and some had been elected to the Cortes.[82] The revolutionary leftist parties, especially the anarchists, also contributed to the growing effort to renegotiate sexual norms. In one sense the conservative alarmists were correct in that the anarchist movement did indeed view bourgeois morality as an obstacle to be overcome before a revolutionary society could emerge. The anarchist educators sought to empower individuals by teaching them to make their own choices about love and sexuality outside of the constraints imposed by society or the Catholic Church. Such messages seemed to have a widespread appeal based on the anarchist claims that publishers of novelettes whose plots centered on ideas of free love and liberated sexuality often printed between 10,000 and 50,000 copies per week.[83] The rightist attacks on anarchist notions of morality, however, revealed an ignorance regarding the substance of libertarian beliefs. As a result, the conservatives often misconstrued the purpose behind such policies. For the anarchists, free love relationships never implied the level of coercion or transferability that the conservatives alleged. Instead, free love equaled "a freely established relationship validated by reciprocal agreement rather than state ratification."[84] Therefore, what opponents feared most was the desire to remove the moral authority of the Church and traditional social norms and replace them with a society built on relationships between equal partners. Many conservative accounts of the rebellion highlighted stories of sexual deviance in order to equate the revolutionary program with a breakdown in traditional ideals of heterosexual relationships. The reports called on rightists to support those groups willing to protect society from the imposition of sexual values that they believed would ultimately lead to the destruction of the family and the nation.

The continued importance of traditional attitudes toward sexuality and the family helps explain why pro-revolutionary works often utilized the same imagery of sexual violence as that used by conservatives in order to encourage male reaction. In the book *La revolución fué así* (The Revolution Was Thus) Manuel Benavides describes how, during the brief fighting in Madrid, women carried guns and ammunition to the front lines despite the strong fire from government forces. After the revolt had ended, these women were arrested and forced to remove their clothing. Benavides called them "mistreated ones, offended in their sex, victims of the rabble that exhibited them naked in the police station."[85] While the author praised the actions of the women, the main purpose of the anecdote was to reveal the cruelty of the authorities. The decision to demonize the enemy is often a feature of wartime propaganda depicting sexual assault. Newspapers in the United States prior to the war with Spain in 1898 were filled with imagery depicting the rape of Cuban women by Spanish soldiers, and horrific visions of marauding German soldiers drawn as bestial creatures emerged as a common vision of World War I propaganda.[86] What makes the Spanish case unusual is that the revolution was a civil conflict without strong national, religious, or ethnic distinctions. Unlike later conflicts, such as the Balkan wars of the 1990s where rape has been prevalent, sexual violence could not be employed as an attempt to destroy the nation's culture or racial and religious purity.[87] The conservatives negotiated this difficulty by dehumanizing their opponents or by declaring the insurrection a product of foreign influence. The leftists often blamed the African troops and the soldiers of the Foreign Legion for the sexual crimes committed during the repression, since many of the soldiers were clearly foreign and, in the case of the Africans, racially and religiously distinct as well. Pro-revolutionary accounts often accused these groups of perpetrating the worst crimes of sexual assault and mutilation.[88] The poet Raul González Tuñon made such an accusation in a poem titled "Careful, the Tercio is Coming." The verses of the poem advise the reader to guard certain things from the soldiers:

> Man, look after your woman,
> worker, guard your home.
> Look the wolves are coming
> with the desert in their souls.[89]

Other verses reveal that no one was exempt from the threat: not a prostitute, a girlfriend, or a niece.[90] The poet ascribed to men the role of protector, and women became objects to be protected. Many of the sentences referring to women contain a parallel structure that links women to other male possessions and encouraged the man to guard all his property including the women. Such combinations begin with the first verse "Man, look after your *woman,* worker guard your *home*" as well as in subsequent verses such as, "*Prostitute,* be careful / that the scoundrels of the sand / do not invade your *home*" and "Priest, watch your *niece* / and the *treasure* of your coffer."[91] Solano Palacio also tells of soldiers raping girls and then killing them in front of their own family. He writes that "the Moors raped women and afterwards slashed their throats and cut off their breasts."[92] The purposeful mutilation of women's bodies, especially the breasts, represents the symbolic destruction of motherhood.[93] Solano Palacio asserts that by destroying and mutilating women the Moroccan troops demonstrated their contempt for motherhood and for society in general. After her visit to Spain in 1934 Leah Manning reported that a nursing mother was tortured "particularly upon the breasts" simply because her husband had participated in the revolt.[94] Pro-revolutionary imagery attempted to show that the actions of the soldiers represented a danger to the family and thus ultimately to the society that men were charged with protecting. González Tuñón's "Poetry in the Service of the Revolution" also depicts the African soldiers as rapists. The poet declares that "The Moors come to Oviedo / . . . killing Spaniards, / and raping their wives."[95]

The symbolism of the African soldiers, commonly referred to as Moors by both pro- and anti-revolutionary accounts, references a myriad of historical connotations. Asturias remained the only part of Spain not to be occupied by Islamic forces after the invasion of the peninsula in 711.[96] As such it could be argued that it was the only part of Spanish territory never to be "violated" by the continuing presence of Muslim populations and that it served as the birthplace of the Christian reconquest of the peninsula.[97] Leftist commentators often repeated this fact while denigrating the government's decision to employ the African troops as part of the repression. In his analysis of the insurrection, the socialist Antonio Ramos Oliveira declares that Pelayo himself would be shocked to see Moors at the gates of Covadonga. He then adds sarcastically that it was unfortunate that when the Christians got into trouble they had to be rescued by Muslims.[98] In *La represion de octubre* Manuel Villar offers photos of the African troops, including one with the caption, "The new Reconquest of Asturias."[99] During the electoral campaign of 1936 the Popular Front coalition used references to the use of Moors to denigrate the patriotic claims of the right. As one broadsheet explains: "They say that they are Spain and they brought Moors to Asturias to 'raid' the homes of upstanding Spaniards and to satisfy the most dirty and obscene appetites."[100] The passage contests the patriotism of conservatives by referring to those who it perceived as the true patriots: the honorable workers whose homes were threatened by the use of foreign soldiers. The term used for raid, *razziar,* refers to a practice common to Moroccan intertribal warfare whereby a village would be looted and razed as revenge or punishment.[101] The broadsheet also obliquely references the threat of sexual violence and perpetuates the myth of the African unable to control his passions.[102] At other moments such sentiments were not so subtle as when Solano Palacio declared that the rebels had fought against "the moors who came with desires for revenge, for blood and for sex."[103] Through the use of stories of sexual atrocities, pro-revolutionary groups tried to provoke a response on the part of male consumers. Such imagery used an appeal to masculine values and fears in order to encourage political action against the administration and conservative political parties.

Conservatives defended the use of African troops since these forces were readily acknowledged to be the best soldiers of the Spanish army. They were, in the words of Minister of War Diego Hidalgo, "prepared, expert in defense and ambush, hard and accustomed to the campaigning life [and] subject to the discipline of an iron hand."[104] The Muslim soldiers were trained and led by strong Christian men who no doubt served to "civilize" them, thus putting them firmly under the control of the state. Sebastian Balfour notes that the "colonial officers no longer saw Moroccan volunteers as foreigners but as part of the same Spanish military community."[105] The experience of colonial war had led to the creation of a dual image of the "good Moor" who collaborated with the Spanish authorities and the "bad Moor" who resisted them. The forces allied with Spain were often used to destroy the rebellious Moroccans who posed a threat to the colonies.[106] Following the October revolt it was the miners of Asturias who were portrayed as the "other" threatening the destruction of the nation. As such the pro-revolutionary forces deserved to be treated with the same methods of extermination previously employed against African rebels.[107] The use of the Foreign Legion also proved controversial given the unit's not unwarranted reputation for brutality. From its founding the Foreign Legion became known for a high level of viciousness both on and off the battlefield. Such attitudes were tolerated by the officer corps, which cultivated an ideology that centered on the "extreme brutalization of military life and the dehumanization of the enemy."[108] These attitudes became reflected in the unit's tactics, which called for a cautious strategy that involved occupying small areas of territory and, before moving forward, eliminating all resistance.[109] In addition to its penchant for terror, the Foreign Legion had developed a carefully cultivated vision of itself as the saviors of the Spanish military in Morocco. Such notions reinforced the idea common among africanistas after October 1934 that they had a special mission to save Spain. Indeed, the colonial army and its officers played a key role in the military uprising that triggered the Civil War in 1936.[110]

THE DESTRUCTION OF THE FAMILY

Texts about the revolution often contained graphic images illustrating the destruction of the family.[111] Mary Vincent has argued that a close connection developed between threats to gender roles and political power: "Disturbances in both gender roles and the prevailing moral order threatened not only individual families but also wider society and even the state."[112] Commemorations of October 1934 used representations of destroyed families to illustrate what happened when men failed to behave as proper men. The accounts demonstrated to readers and viewers that victory for their enemies could result in not only the deaths of loved ones but also the destruction of Spain itself. As the authors of the pamphlet *Terror* declared in 1936: the upcoming elections would decide the fate of "Spain, your family,

Figure 2
Poster distributed by Acción Popular: "Remember the orphans of Asturias, victims of the Revolution! Vote Spain. Against the revolution and its accomplices!" SOURCE: LABORATORIO FOTOGRÁFIO DE LA BIBLIOTECA NACIONAL DE ESPAÑA, CATÁLOGO CARTELES REPÚBLICA Y GUERRA CIVIL, 178

your dignity, your religion."[113] In part to illustrate this point, the text contains the story of Julia Fraigedo, a woman who died in the fighting beside her Civil Guard husband. Along with telling the story, the authors include photos of the couple's children standing in front of the building where their parents died. The photographs represent powerful and emotional visual evidence of how the revolt was able literally to destroy families.[114] During the election campaign of 1936, Acción Popular (AP) distributed a poster showing three young children dressed in black holding hands (see figure 2). The image and text remind viewers to "remember the orphans of Asturias, victims of the revolution!" The poster also includes AP's major slogan of the 1936 campaign: "Vote Spain! Against the revolution and its accomplices!"[115]

Similar imagery also appears in leftist electoral propaganda. Posters depicting the suffering families of prisoners emerged as a central part of the Popular Front's amnesty campaign during 1936. One poster shows a shadowy male image behind bars while a woman weeps in the foreground. The caption declares, "They are 30,000! Vote for Liberty!"[116] A campaign poster

Figure 3
Poster distributed by Partido Comunista de España: "To return the 30,000 prisoners to their families; to bring bread to the homes of the unemployed and repressed; vote Popular Front!" SOURCE: LABORATORIO FOTOGRÁFIO DE LA BIBLIOTECA NACIONAL DE ESPAÑA, CATÁLOGO CARTELES REPÚBLICA Y GUERRA CIVIL, 364

produced by the Partido Comunista de España (PCE) depicts a woman holding a baby in one arm while her other arm stretches out to vote; at the same time a priest, a businessman, and a nun attempt to hold her back. The three figures sit atop a bloody mound of bodies, and to the side is another woman with a child on her lap, weeping over a bloodied male figure lying nearby (see figure 3). The lower left of the poster where the enemies of the revolution sat is colored black, except where red has been added to indicate blood. In the upper right of the image is a crowd of people with banners indicating the political parties of the Popular Front. This part of the poster is colored red and displays the central message: "To return the 30,000 prisoners to their families; to bring bread to the homes of the unemployed and repressed; vote Popular Front!"[117] The image refers to the absent male householder who because of death or imprisonment is unable to protect his family. Instead the mother is forced to step forward and work to end the period of darkness and usher in the red dawn of a Popular Front government. The newspaper *La Libertad* included images of destroyed families among the

atrocity stories it published during January 1936. On 25 January the paper
ran two photographs: one of a girl who reportedly burned to death with her
parents, and the other of a young boy who was the only survivor of the fire
that killed his family.[118]

Textual imagery supported the visual graphics of the electoral posters.
The book *Los crímenes de la reacción española* (Crimes of the Spanish Reaction) accused the armed forces of shooting innocent people including
women and children. At the same time that it reproduced photographs of
children it claimed had been orphaned as a result of these killings it also
ridiculed conservatives for highlighting the children of Civil Guards killed
in the revolt. The organization that published the text, SRI, appealed for
donations by arguing that many of the orphaned children needed bread and
clothing.[119] In "The Orphans of the Revolution" González Bayón also
wrote about the sons and daughters of those killed during the insurrection.
His verses tell of the "thousands" of Spanish children

Whose little white hands are bathed in blood
When, among many dead they painfully search
for the body of parents who proudly fought
until surrendering their life with heroic valor.[120]

In the final verse the poet comforts the children with the knowledge that
the events of October help to enable a future victory.[121]

CONCLUSION

The representations of the October revolt relied heavily on imagery that
reinforced traditional notions of masculinity, emphasizing strength, sacrifice, and virility. Both pro- and anti-revolutionary imagery equated political
action in the aftermath of the insurrection with masculine virtue. Representations of the revolt sought to glorify the masculinity of supporters while
denigrating those who resisted. All groups illustrated the potential rewards
and penalties should men fail to live up to such duties. Men on both sides
who fulfilled their masculine role received the love and affection of women,
thus enabling the continuation of the patriarchal family unit. For the revolutionaries, the defeat of the insurrection led not only to political repression
but to brutal assaults on women and the family. The conservatives pointed
to specific atrocities committed by the rebels to reinforce the view that the

revolutionaries stood for nothing less than the destruction of Spain both morally and physically. This language also linked the Republican system with the insurrection, and by 1936 it seemed that elections had again allowed the rebels to take power. Many conservatives viewed the army as the one force in Spain capable of halting what seemed to be an inevitable march toward destruction. Masculine imagery had particular relevance within military circles, and many influential officers saw themselves as the heirs to a heroic tradition of knighthood. They felt that just as they imagined had been the case in the past, only the force of war combined with the power of faith could save the nation from destruction at the hands of foreign invaders. In the end it was the members of the military who decided that the threat posed by the Popular Front government could no longer be staunched through legal means. Eventually the masculine imagery of heroic sacrifice became an integral part of Nationalist symbolism during the Civil War and on into the Franco regime.[122]

HYENAS, HARPIES, AND PROLETARIAN MOTHERS
Commemorating Female Participation

The October revolution of 1934, like many periods of conflict, had briefly disrupted the normal functioning of society and highlighted tensions over the seeming fluidity of masculine and feminine ideals. Commemorations of the insurrection sought to restore stability through the expression of proper gender roles for both men and women. If the imagery called on men to live up to traditional notions of masculinity, the maintenance of a stable society also required women to fulfill their assigned roles. Increasingly, women appeared to be moving away from the values of domesticity and instead were taking on new, and more public, positions in society. The changes in Spain echoed larger European debates on the meanings and effects of women's shifting images and roles during the interwar period.[1] In many countries the disruptions caused by World War I had briefly undone traditional gender categories and helped to spark fears of a "gender crisis." During the postwar era, many people saw the restoration of proper gender roles as a prerequisite to the establishment of social, economic, and political harmony. The struggle between men and women threatened to return the nation to a period of conflict.[2] In similar ways, the commemorative imagery of October 1934 ultimately served to reinforce contemporary notions of proper feminine behavior. Commentators used representations of the insurrection to rearticulate conventional values and to claim that they alone could restore gender stability. Only the destruction of those who challenged the existing gendered order could properly ensure its survival.

Both pro- and anti-revolutionary commemorations employed traditional gender roles to mobilize political support in the aftermath of the revolt. In part these efforts represented the mirror image of commemorations designed to stabilize masculine roles by requiring women to fulfill their passive responsibilities as witnesses, victims, and rewards. Despite similar goals and a shared emphasis on standard gender roles, the forces of the right and left differed somewhat in the ways they employed such imagery. The conservatives presented the revolution as a malevolent force that turned women into horrible creatures who abandoned their true nature as mothers and caregivers.[3] The leftists hoped to inspire unity and dedication in both men and women by invoking the symbolic language of motherhood to create female heroes pledged to social and political reform. In addition, the revolutionaries used the youth and purity of female participants to demonstrate the moral and ideological superiority of their cause. The diffusion of imagery celebrating traditional images of womanhood allowed both sides to once again divide the political and social world into two opposing camps. For conservatives, the insurrection demonstrated the pernicious effects that revolutionary ideologies had on the clear and unambiguous gender roles that they believed formed the underlying foundations of society. All conservative groups agreed that powerful action needed to be taken against those who caused women to abandon traditional roles. Pro-revolutionary groups used images of motherhood and virginity as a way to organize a broad coalition that supported a leftist, if not always an overtly revolutionary, agenda. The representations portrayed the motivations of the insurrection and those who participated in it as morally pure, while those against the revolt became evil beings determined to destroy all who opposed them, including women. In these ways the depictions of women following the rebellion helped to increase the divisions within society as well as contributed to the volatile atmosphere that soon exploded into civil war.

DISCOURSE ON WOMEN'S ROLES
PRIOR TO THE SECOND REPUBLIC

Discussion about gender norms in nineteenth- and twentieth-century Spain focused on fairly predictable roles for women. The "correct" roles emerged through a cultural discourse that emphasized domesticity and established matrimony and motherhood as the highest aspirations. The pervasive cultural influence of the Catholic Church and its views on women further reinforced these standards.[4] The dominant image of women was the "Angel of the Home" or the "Perfect Wife."[5] During the first decades of the twentieth century, the social and cultural basis for women's subordinate role changed from religious to secular scientific considerations. The switch from traditional to "modern" explanations did little to alter the prevailing attitudes toward proper gender behavior. According to Mary Nash: "Biosocial thought converted gender identity and the cultural representation of women into a cultural myth that justified gender hierarchies, discriminatory values, and gendered social roles."[6] Domesticity remained the primary position, as biological determinism cemented the belief that reproduction was women's logical function. In addition, the medical establishment determined that women, through their original identity as procreators, remained more closely linked to nature. This belief manifested itself in the notion that rationality was not naturally a feminine trait. Such strictures perpetuated and enforced the traditional roles of women in society, and those who denied their biological identity as mothers therefore violated the scientific laws of nature. In this way, both traditional religious doctrine and modern secular medicine converged to enforce existing gender identities. According to these norms, any woman who challenged the existing gender paradigms risked disaster and deserved all punishments that resulted from her transgressions.[7] The gender hierarchies represented the foundations of society, and any deviation from these norms threatened to unleash social chaos.

Although images of women changed slightly in the 1920s, a fundamental reshaping of basic roles still did not occur. Until 1931, a married woman could not sell property, engage in business, or even hold a job without her husband's permission. The education of women focused on domestic abilities and comportment rather than on the skills necessary for public employment. As late as 1930 nearly 40 percent of women could not read or write, compared with just over 20 percent of men. Even when women were allowed to complete a primary education and attend college, they often matriculated in traditionally feminine disciplines. In addition, laws prohibited them from taking state examinations for careers such as judgeships and notary publics.[8] Despite the continued presence of conventional norms in the 1920s and 1930s, new generations of women began to challenge, either directly or indirectly, the old patterns. Increasing numbers of young women began to take on public roles previously unavailable to their mothers and grandmothers. These young women entered into the public sphere as workers, students, consumers, and political actors. Population trends reinforced these developments as women and young people made up an increasing percentage of the active population. During the time of the October revolt, the majority of Spaniards were female and the difference between the total number of women and that of men increased between 1921 and 1936. The unequal distribution of the population came at a time when many women, especially in the anarchist movement, began public efforts aimed at giving women greater control over reproduction. The public discussion of birth control, along with a general movement that attempted to shift the image of women away from that based exclusively on maternity, reinforced these trends.[9] In addition to these changes, young Spanish women became an increasing presence in society as the percentage of women under the age of twenty-five reached almost one quarter of the total population of the country.[10] Adolescents were more likely to work outside of the home than were older women, and over 20 percent of this age group were holding a job.[11] By earning money these women took on roles that traditionally had been solely the domain of men, thereby liberating themselves from dependency on a male head of household and directly challenging the male role as provider. In other nations where the decision to work was not usually done out of financial necessity, the income afforded women a degree of social liberty unknown to prior generations. Although the labor could be difficult, it provided women with a way of expressing economic independence. Education also offered young women a new public role. Between 1900 and 1930 the number of girls in primary and secondary school rose over 600 percent, and the percentage of illiterate women dropped by almost one-third. More women enrolled in universities, and the number of female students increased from 345 in 1919–1920 to 1,681 in 1930.[12] Other social and cultural factors reinforced the changes that brought more women into the public sphere. A new articulation of women's role as citizen-consumers brought many, especially of those in the middle class, into the streets and squares of urban Spain.[13] The changes of the 1920s and 1930s resulted in greater pressures on traditional norms, and when combined with the escalating political conflicts of the Republican period, these pressures only compounded the feelings of instability and tension.

WOMEN AND POLITICS DURING
THE SECOND REPUBLIC

Along with a substantial change in the political system of Spain, the advent of the Second Republic in 1931 inaugurated a series of dramatic social transformations.[14] Many groups and individuals began to push for a greater public role for women in education, labor, and government. One of the most important results was the granting of suffrage to women. Soon female deputies, representing both conservative and liberal parties, served in parliament, and for the first time a woman was chosen for a top administrative post.[15] Once women achieved the vote, organizations on the right and the left began campaigns aimed at increasing the political mobilization of women. The first attempt at the mass mobilization of conservative women can be dated to the formation in 1919 of Acción Católica de la Mujer (Women's Catholic Action, ACM).[16] During the Republic, ACM urged its adherents to protest the reforms of the first biennium, particularly those that challenged the public role of the Catholic Church. The group encouraged members to defy government orders against public religious celebrations and Catholic education. Supporters of ACM within the church hierarchy used strident rhetoric to inspire women to carry the fight against Republican legislation into "the street, in the plaza, in the town-council and in the parliament."[17] The large-scale presence of women actively involved in public debates created a paradox within the rightist movement. While defending the traditional role of women as homemakers and mothers, the women of ACM appeared to violate this ideal through their participation in political activities. By being outspoken public figures they seemed to contradict the conventional image of domesticity that they fought so hard to protect.[18] The goals of these organizations were not to provoke a fundamental change of women's roles, nevertheless some reshaping was an inevitable result of their newly found public voice.[19] Although it is difficult to quantify, the large-scale mobilization of women in groups like ACM clearly had an effect on the attitudes of both men and women. According to Inmaculada Blasco, the presence of women in the public world of politics "could modify perceptions, provoke contradictions in the most active militants, and, without doubt, disturb all within the families of those women thrown into the public sphere."[20]

The changing status of women, combined with a highly charged political atmosphere, led to shifts in the ways that political organizations responded to women. Following the elections of 1933 in which the conservative parties managed to win a majority of seats, these groups began to refocus the emphasis of ACM. Instead of visibly protesting Republican legislation the group's mission became one based on charity, especially among working-class families. The goals of ACM were twofold: first, to try to cultivate political support for the conservative parties among the working class; and, second, to channel the energies of women away from public activities that threatened traditional notions of domesticity. The primary vehicle of this switch was the 1934 merger of the ACM with the Unión de Damas del Sagrado Corazón (Ladies Union of the Sacred Heart) to form a new organization called the Confederación de Mujeres Católicas de España (Confederation of Spanish Catholic Women, CMCE). The shift in emphasis seemed to accomplish the goal of restraining women's activities, as membership in the new organization declined relative to the levels prior to the merger. In 1929, for example, ACM had 118,000 members, but by 1935 the CMCE registered only 61,354. New demands resulting from the merger led some leaders of the CMCE to resign from positions of authority within the larger conservative movement. Residual worry over women's public activities remained, as evidenced by one CMCE leader who cautioned women to participate in only one or two public events per year.[21] Young women, however, generally avoided such redirection and remained a growing presence in the political sphere as conservatives proved unable or unwilling to stifle their involvement. Even as adult enrollment in ACM declined and the organization shifted its focus away from overt political protest after 1933, membership in the Juventud Católica Femenina (Young Catholic Women, JCF) increased dramatically. In 1928 the group had 9,000 members, but by 1936 the number had swelled to 70,000; total adherents more than doubled between 1932 and 1935 when conservative political fortunes were at their highest. The youth organization provided young women with the means for being publicly active in a way not linked to charity or individual piety.[22] The continued activism of young women might have served to highlight the important changes that had been emerging throughout the twentieth century. The October revolt, therefore, occurred at a time when Spanish women were undergoing substantial changes in political and social status. At the same time, conservative organizations both welcomed and feared the growing enfranchisement of women. The commemoration of the insurrection demonstrated the negative effects that the emancipation of women could have on society and politics. The representations of women contributed to an already anxious situation regarding gender roles, and when combined with the escalating political tensions of 1935–1936 an explosive situation was created.

Although many revolutionary groups professed the equality of men and women, in practice they exhibited little difference in their actual treatment of women within the movement. In general, all social classes shared similar beliefs regarding the roles of men and women in society.[23] Marxist theories that privileged questions of class over those of gender informed much of the leftist imagery, and for anarcho-syndicalists "the anarchist utopia stopped at the front door."[24] Such notions only served to reinforce the standard vision of the patriarchal family dominated by the male head of household. Women's groups became part of the socialist movement as early as 1902, but they generally remained small and subordinate to the larger party. As more women entered the workforce, particularly in professions such as teaching and nursing, they also joined the unions in larger numbers. Despite their growing presence within the socialist unions, women often faced the open hostility of male workers who viewed them as competition.[25] Early in the Republic the Partido Comunista de España (PCE) had made little attempt to appeal to women, but the policy began to change in 1932 when the organization initiated limited efforts designed to attract female workers. In 1933 these efforts intensified with the creation of a Spanish section of the Committee of Women against War and Fascism, which also included socialists and Republicans. These efforts seemed to bear fruit as total female membership in the PCE's Asturian section rose from 330 in 1931 to 1,800 by 1937.[26] When, as part of the post-October repression, the government closed worker centers and arrested thousands of male militants, women began to take on important roles within the party and also within those groups agitating for the release of the prisoners or in support of their families.[27] Organizations formed to increase female activism shifted focus toward activities deemed more suitable to women. After the defeat of the October uprising, the Committee of Women against War and Fascism, for example, changed its name to the more traditional Pro–Working-Class Children Committee. In part this change reflected the attempts to slow the mobilization of women, but it also enabled the group to remain legal as the conservative administration cracked down on worker groups following the defeat of the insurrection.[28] The seemingly practical switch in name also indicated that pro-revolutionary groups remained committed to standard gendered representations as a way of encouraging support.

HYENAS, HARPIES, AND COMBATIVE WOMEN

The bulk of interpretations of the events of 1934 on both sides denied women an active participation in the crucial events of the rebellion and generally portrayed them as passive observers unable to defend their interests except in certain proscribed circumstances. The few instances when female-initiated violence was accepted often reinforced women's primary roles as mothers and caregivers and highlighted the general attitude disallowing such active heroism. Instead, more often than not, women who tried to seize an active role—a male role—in the historical events ceased being considered real women and were stripped of their femininity. The commentators explained that the actions of their opponents had forced women into abandoning their proper destiny. Women who dropped conventional responsibilities threatened the continued existence of the nation by subverting the system of traditional gender roles that formed the foundational elements of society. Although the evidence for high levels of direct military participation by women in the revolt is indeterminate, women sometimes took an active role in combative situations and violent confrontations. Nearly all stories allowing women an active stance, however, described circumstances where women fought directly to protect husbands or the home. In these situations recourse to violence not only was found acceptable but also was considered to be the natural reaction of a good wife and mother. The social discourse of domesticity expected a woman to maintain an efficient household, and her connection with child rearing enforced a strict separation of public and private spheres. Gil Nuño del Robleda repeats these notions in his text on the events of the rebellion: "God created women for something more than being sports champions, [he created them] to be Christian mothers who know how to turn a home into a place of personal happiness and to be blessed by heaven."[29] The defense of the home became one area where social convention not only allowed for violent action but also expected it as part of a woman's "natural" emotional composition.[30]

Many conservatives had previously defended the entry of women into active politics during the first years of the Republic by arguing that they had been thrust into that role as new reforms threatened the home. The defense of existing gender roles therefore took on a political cast as even moderate change provoked renewed anxiety over the fate of society. The challenge of the Republic constituted a direct threat to women's true nature as ordained by God. Participation in anti-Republican protest was therefore seen as a logical extension of a woman's natural duty to fiercely protect her home and family.[31] It was also viewed as a means of preserving social stability through the continued functioning of the patriarchal family unit. The belief that it was not only acceptable but required that women protect the home from outside threats appeared in many conservative texts commemorating 1934. Adro Xavier, for example, warned against the agitation of Marxist elements from outside of Spain and cautioned women to defend their homes from the "contagion" of communist propaganda.[32] In a celebrated case, several anti-revolutionary writers reported on the actions of Julia Fraigedo, a woman who died while fighting alongside her husband in the village of Ciaño. Her actions did not signify that she was unwomanly because her deeds personified the protective ideal of Spanish womanhood. Jenaro Geijo speculated that a simple reason prompted her extraordinary actions: love for her husband.[33] The pamphlet *Terror* also commends the actions of Fraigedo by describing how the couple died heroically together in combat.[34] The booklet implies that she was not being celebrated for defending the police barracks but rather for fighting and dying beside her husband. In these ways her actions could be attributed to the paradigm of the traditional gender roles of protective mother and spouse. The imagery motivated resistance to the perceived revolutionary threat continually referred to by conservative politicians in the aftermath of the October revolt. The invasion of foreign elements represented something more than a political struggle; indeed, it threatened the very foundations of Spanish society, including women and the home.

As with conservative treatments, some pro-revolutionary tracts gave women exception to act violently as long they defended home or family. In an article titled "Trinidad" the prominent Socialist Matilde de la Torre describes the actions of a woman whose husband had been arrested following the insurrection. According to the author, Trinidad Alvarez was at the time twenty-six years old and lived in Oviedo. De la Torre describes her as having "a slender little figure, strong, feline: eyes that sparkled; a sharp visage; a very red mouth with a double row of diamond-like teeth."[35] Alvarez's husband was, in the words of the author, an "innocent" worker who had been unjustly beaten by soldiers during the repression. The mistreatment of her spouse infuriated Alvarez, and after he named Sergeant Manzano as the most brutal offender, Alvarez set about on a campaign for revenge. First, she attacked Manzano in the street and fought with him until they were separated, but not before she had bitten him on the hand; later she discovered him in a bar and smacked him in the head with a bottle. On 21 February 1936 Alvarez learned that the sergeant was to be sent back to Madrid, and she felt that in so doing he might escape punishment for the crimes he committed against her husband. She accosted Manzano on the train and managed to delay its departure, after which he was forced to remain in Oviedo, presumably to face trial.[36] True or not, the story of Trinidad Alvarez sent a message that the actions of the repression would not go unpunished. De la Torre employs the image of Alvarez to depict the fury of a woman whose vigorous search for justice often took a violent form. Perhaps the author hoped to represent the desires of all women whose loved ones had become victims of the repression. Nevertheless, because her actions had been in defense of her husband, whom she believed had been unfairly victimized, her combativeness could be attributed both to her maternal nature and to her role as wife, thus exempting her from criticism. Despite sympathy for her subject, De la Torre still portrayed Alvarez as something not quite womanly. The physical description, with its emphasis on animal-like characteristics, implies a certain viciousness not generally considered to be appropriate for women. Trinidad's cat-like figure and her red mouth also reveal her to be a highly sexualized creature. These descriptions recall the notions that women were less able to think rationally and were more clearly defined by their physical natures.

While the conservatives allowed for aggressive action in defense of home and family, they viewed as something less than human the women who took an active role in the revolt for other reasons. The possibility that Spanish

women were indeed naturally capable of actively supporting and participating in rebellion posed a serious threat to social stability. Anti-revolutionary
texts aimed to minimize the risk by dehumanizing and defeminizing the
women of the revolt. Francisco Prada's *Caminos de sangre* (Paths of Blood)
contains a chapter titled simply "Women . . . ?" In it he examines the
character of revolutionary women and concludes that they cannot be true
women because they do not embody feminine characteristics: "To say
woman is to say piety and heart; it is to say mother!"[37] Furthermore, these
women violate the standard role of women as caregiver. As proof, Prada
relates one instance where women had been charged with providing food
and water to prisoners of the revolution. The women not only withheld this
sustenance from old and weak men but also cruelly taunted them.[38] For the
author, the values of piety and motherhood make up an integral and inseparable part of what it means to be a woman. Therefore, because adherence
to the revolutionary cause stripped women of these basic qualities, the revolt
represented a threat to established gender definitions and, by extension, to
the whole of the social order. A revolutionary text whose authors are listed
as the "Prisoners of Asturias" describes a remarkably similar set of actions.
According to this pamphlet, a group of Catholic women served as nurses to
wounded revolutionaries after the insurrection. The authors allege that
these women deliberately tried to kill the prisoners by giving them the
wrong medicine or by administering excessive doses.[39] Each of the stories
exposes the anxieties generated when women became involved in conflict.
Seemingly unable to control themselves, they embody the exact opposite of
traditional values as they preyed on the men they should have been caring
for; the cherished vision of women as caregivers is thus shattered under the
pressures of political conflict. Such characterization of the struggle reveals
that both pro- and anti-revolutionary writers feared the effects that a victory
of their opponents would produce in women.[40]

The magazine *Estampa* explained in a report that the deleterious effects
of the rebellion on the nature of women could have more atrocious consequences. A group of women in the town of Sama actively participated in the
revolt by ambushing a company of Assault Guards and stabbing them. The
women also killed priests, and afterward took the bodies to a butcher shop
and displayed them there.[41] For the magazine, these tales demonstrated the
effects of revolutionary fervor on Spanish women—that is, it turned them

into cruel murderers who seemingly delighted in killing. Francisco Martínez's *Dos jesuitas mártires en Asturias* (Two Jesuit Martyrs in Asturias) also proclaims the inhuman and nonfemale nature of revolutionary women; indeed, the author devotes an entire section to their actions. The chapter titled "The Revolutionary Woman" repeats the claim that for many conservatives the most frightful part of the insurrection involved the active participation of women. Martínez defines the natural attributes of womanhood as those of being delicate, emotional, and good. Then he argues that when women lack these characteristics a radical change takes place: they cease being women and instead became "hyenas" or "harpies" who take pleasure in spilling the blood of their enemies. His attitude could not be more clear when he states, "Woman is either a saint or an infernal abortion. There is no middle ground."[42] Again, he shows how conservative commentators viewed the revolution as a fundamental threat to the established social order, of which the assigned gender roles of men and women played a central part. Anti-revolutionary commentators sought to protect the gendered system of values and identities and its perceived importance as the foundation of social stability, while also denying women the ability to challenge the existing order. The efforts to crush the October revolt and any future uprisings allowed for the preservation of society. In this way, the desire to prevent the pro-revolutionary parties from achieving power was not simply a political matter but rather one where fundamental elements of society were also at stake.

Some pro-revolutionary texts described women's active participation in the revolt, yet still remained focused on traditional female roles. Fernando Solano Palacio writes how, during the final desperate fighting in Oviedo, a young woman ran out on the battlefield to retrieve wounded comrades. Despite the bullets that flew overhead and the bomb that landed nearby, she continued working with, in the author's words, "efforts inappropriate for a woman."[43] He sees the bravery of this woman as notable because her actions are those not normally attributable to women. In another section, Solano Palacio describes how some women tried to seize an active role in the fighting: "[They] put on the *mono* and picked up a shotgun and went from parapet to parapet, bringing food to the revolutionaries, animating them in the fight with words of encouragement, without fear of the bullets that whistled over their heads."[44]

Although Solano Palacio acknowledges that the women carried weapons, he never states that they actually used them during the fighting. The only actions specifically outlined are those of bringing food and encouraging the revolutionaries. Here, "revolutionaries" is taken to mean specifically and exclusively men, and in order to join them the woman had to symbolically become masculine by donning the traditional male work attire.[45] Perhaps this act allowed women the right to carry arms, even if the author never reveals whether or not they used them. Instead, the women continued in their allotted role as wives and mothers by bringing the men food and by serving as inspiration and encouragement—both actions that traditionally have been the role of women during warfare.[46]

PROLETARIAN MOTHERS AND THE ROSE OF OCTOBER

A poem by González Bayón, titled "The Barricade," shows how leftists used images of motherhood and purity to mobilize action on behalf of the revolutionaries. The piece opens with a woman asking her companion to stay home and not go off to battle. When he remains committed to the fight she refuses to leave his side and vows instead to follow him into combat: "My conscience commands / that I place my chest / before the shrapnel / as you will do, / for the same cause!"[47] Through this act she demonstrates extreme devotion to her husband, not unlike that shown by the conservative icon Julia Fraigedo. Although the woman accompanies her husband to the battlefield, she does not participate in combat. Instead, the rebels assign her the role of nurse:

> Love, we are here now.
> Hand me my gun
> and prepare bandages
> for those that fall . . .
> See there someone wounded
> who awaits your help,
> look to aid him
> little white dove.[48]

Despite the fact that her stated goal is to fight for the same cause as her husband, the revolutionaries only allow her to be a nurse.[49] González Bayón, like other writers, did not consider women as combatants, and only by helping the wounded could they actively take part in the revolt. The poem celebrates the woman's valor and proclaims her a hero, but only within the accepted role of nurse. She was not given the chance to share in the glorious martyrdom afforded to the men who fought and died for the revolutionary cause. Later verses of "The Barricade" reinforce this theme. As the woman runs to help a wounded rebel, she names herself "proletarian mother" and declares that she has become "the mother of those that fight here."[50] She glorifies the male soldier's sacrifice by granting him the title "martyr" while at the same time becoming the living symbol of all that he fought for: mother, wife, daughter. The poem ends as the man, helped by the nurse, struggles to his feet and vows to return to avenge himself against his enemies. In the end it is only the male who achieves glory either through heroic actions or through death, while the woman's role is to assist and nurse him, to inspire him and to bear witness to his courage and masculinity. In this manner the interpretations of October emphasize the bravery and sacrifice of men alongside the aid and comfort of women.

For the most part, the commemorations of October described few cases of women becoming active fighters. The one important exception was a sixteen-year-old girl named Aida Lafuente who took up arms on behalf of the revolution, fought in Oviedo, and died at the church of San Pedro de los Arcos on the summit of a small hill called Mount Naranco. Although the specific details of her final hours vary widely depending on the source, all versions indicate that she worked in favor of the revolt in a variety of ways, including armed combat, and that she did not survive the insurrection. During the period following the revolt, images of Lafuente became a key element in the pro-revolutionary left's attempts to generate political unity. Instead of showing her as a revolutionary fighter, the commemorations of her actions present her both as a mother who ushered in a new age of social justice and as a virginal icon of political engagement and dedication. The imagery also served to neutralize the threat that female warriors posed to the existing gender norms.[51] Lafuente's combativeness suggested that her example might encourage other women to assert themselves outside of typical categories. In response to this challenge, many commentators resorted to depicting Lafuente through the use of conventional images of women in an attempt to counteract the unsettling ideal of a woman warrior. In doing so, the revolutionary commemorations transformed Lafuente from an authen-

tic woman warrior into a symbol of purity and motherhood. Despite Lafuente's radical actions in both a political and gendered sense, images of her
served ultimately to reinforce traditional notions of proper gender behavior.
By reiterating conventional gender roles, the pro-revolutionary forces committed themselves to the maintenance of the existing gendered order and
encouraged men to unify in order to defend that order.

Although Lafuente might not have been the only woman who fought,
she quickly became the most famous and most celebrated female combatant.[52] Biographical information regarding Lafuente is scarce and often contested.[53] Many sources list her birthplace as Oviedo, but others state that she
was born in the city of León in 1918 and later moved with her family to
Oviedo.[54] Lafuente was one of the youngest children in a large family; she
had two brothers and five sisters.[55] Her father, Gustavo Lafuente, painted
posters and backdrops for the Campoamor Theater in Oviedo, and although the family never had much wealth they had managed to live comfortably. According to some accounts, both Gustavo and his wife Jesusa
Penaos were extremely active in the local section of the PCE,[56] and others
even described Gustavo as one of the founding members of the party in
Asturias.[57] Meanwhile, the contemporary author Carlos Fernández Llaneza
declared that even though the father had been an ardent communist, the
mother's political involvement was limited to encouraging her daughters to
help the sick and those in need.[58] The children, however, became quite
involved in politics, and Lafuente was well known in radical circles as a
tireless worker.[59] The PCE propaganda written during the Civil War glorifies
her role in the party and credits her with founding the women's section of
the communist youth group, the Red Explorers, and being active in the
local section of International Red Aid (SRI).[60] According to Pilar Lafuente,
both Aida and their sister Maruja helped organize the youth section of the
Communist Party in Oviedo.[61] Maruja Lafuente even appeared on the list of
speakers at a communist meeting in August 1932.[62]

Pro-revolutionary writers used descriptions of Lafuente's activities during the revolt to promote and solidify unity among the forces of the political
left. Through the literary form of martyrology, the texts stressed her revolutionary spirit along with her extraordinary dedication and sacrifice for the
ideals of the insurrection. Lafuente was also held up as an example for
Spanish women to emulate, and she was featured as one aspect of the PCE's

campaign to attract new female members. The imagery describes her actions as those deemed acceptable for women in war, thereby helping to reinforce social stability by neutralizing the threat posed to traditional gender hierarchies by a woman warrior. Alejandro Valdés in his book *¡¡Asturias!! (Relato vívido de la insurrección de octubre)* [Asturias! (A Vivid Account of the October Insurrection)]claims that Lafuente led a group of women he calls the Revolutionary Red Cross. This "army of the rearguard" performed traditionally feminine tasks such as encouraging the troops with kind words or bringing food to the front lines so that the revolutionaries did not have to leave their posts. Among these women, Lafuente distinguished herself as an energetic worker and, according to Valdés, many believed that she had not slept during the entire revolt because they had seen her day and night in various places where fighting occurred. He omits the details of her death, stating simply that she was killed while fighting.[63] Later, Valdés refers to a speech given by the communist leader Dolores Ibárruri praising all the women who had participated in the revolution. Ibárruri celebrated Lafuente as a communist hero and claimed that, just like traditional Christian martyrs, she had had a premonition about her own death: "She [Lafuente] assumed she would meet her death, as a red heroine, at the foot of a machine gun. She assumed she would die like all the heroes of our cause die."[64]

Early in 1936, the communist newspaper *Mundo Obrero* published a long story on Lafuente under the headline "Our Heroes: Aida Lafuente Died at the Foot of a Machine Gun." The story briefly recounts her life and diligent work with communist youth group. It continues by declaring that Lafuente had been away from home during the first hours of the revolt and returned to find that the revolution had begun. In response, she immediately started helping the wounded and then spent the next few days bringing bread and milk to people on the outskirts of Oviedo and in neighboring villages. She also found time to care for the sick and look after children, as well as run tobacco, food, and drink to the troops on the barricades.[65] *Mundo Obrero* describes her activities prior to her death in ways typical of women in warfare; that is, she encouraged the men to fight while also providing logistical support in the form of food and nursing. Although Lafuente had no children of her own, the stories link her to motherhood by including her role as babysitter during the revolution. The story continues by reporting that Lafuente told her father she had to go to Mount Naranco because she felt something "abnormal" was going to happen there and she wanted to be with her comrades. Her mother entreated her to stay but Lafuente went anyway, stating: "It is the blood of the youth that marks the path of revolution."[66] This language echoes the familiar phrase that the blood of martyrs nourishes the seeds of the Church. The *Mundo Obrero* article describes how near the end of the fighting, soldiers advanced up Mount Naranco toward the church of San Pedro de los Arcos and surrounded the revolutionaries inside. The rebels decided to retreat, but twelve members of the group, including Lafuente, chose to stay behind in order to allow the others time to escape. At this point, the article changes voice to describe the testimony of Lafuente's sister, Maruja, who explains that after the battle an army officer came to her with a red handkerchief that she recognized as belonging to her sister. The soldier explained that despite the fact that Aida Lafuente had killed many of his men, he admired her bravery and he was keeping the handkerchief as a memory of her. The officer described how she continued fighting even after the soldiers had killed her remaining comrades. When gunfire critically wounded Lafuente, he reported that she still found the strength to yell: "I am a young communist. Long live the government of the workers and peasants!"[67]

The book *La rosa blindada* by the communist poet Raul González Tuñón commemorates the October revolt and includes verses dedicated to Lafuente. In his poem titled "La Libertaria," the young woman ceases to be a real person and instead becomes a mythic symbol. He invokes her memory for political effect by proclaiming her a national hero in whose death all parts of the country could unite in mourning:

> Come Catalan laborer to her burial,
> come Andalusian peasant to her burial,
> come to her burial Extremaduran plowman
> come to her burial Galician fisherman,
> come Vizcayan woodcutter to her burial,
> come Castillian laborer to her burial,
> do not leave the Asturian miner alone.[68]

As workers gathered together around her grave, so too could they unite around her memory.

During and after the electoral campaign of January 1936 commemora-

tions of Lafuente emerged as part of a broader campaign of political discourse championing the martyrs of October 1934.[69] A significant public
reminder of Lafuente's actions took place during a large multiparty rally
held in Madrid on 29 February 1936. A leftist newspaper report put the
attendance at close to 600,000.[70] The meeting was part of a general series of
postelectoral rallies held by the major political parties of the Popular Front
where ceremonies in homage of the heroes and prisoners of the October
revolution occupied a primary place.[71] The meeting of 29 February called
for an amnesty for jailed revolutionaries and featured representatives or
family members of the most celebrated martyrs, including Lafuente. Many
of the most powerful figures of the left, such as Francisco Largo Caballero,
Dolores Ibárruri, Eduardo Ortega y Gasset, and Rafael Alberti, spoke at the
meeting. In their speeches, both Ortega y Gasset and Alberti paid specific
homage to Lafuente, and Alberti even recited a poem titled "Libertaria
Lafuente" that he had written in honor of her memory.[72]

While many of the descriptions of Lafuente's activities came from communist sources, other pro-revolutionary writers did not hesitate to commemorate her actions. Following the rebellion, most leftists observed that it
was only in Asturias where the revolutionary movement was united, and it
was also there that the revolt was strongest. As part of a general movement
for greater cooperation among worker groups, many writers saw Lafuente
as a potential symbol of that unity.[73] In 1935 Narcís Molins i Fábrega, a
dissident communist and a member of the Izquierda Comunista (Communist Left, IC), composed a report on the events of 1934 titled *UHP: La
insurrección proletaria de Asturias* (UHP: The Proletarian Insurrection in Asturias). Although he was politically opposed to the PCE, Molins included in
the report a section dedicated to "Aida Lafuente, heroine of the insurrection."[74] In this section, Molins describes how the revolutionaries slowly
withdrew to defensive positions on Mount Naranco. Among the last of the
defenders were Lafuente and another young woman, both of whom inspired others with their bravery and determination. During the final assault
on the summit, the leader of the army troops expressed his admiration for
the rebels, especially the two young women. The officer wished to take
them alive but they answered his entreaties with shouts of resistance. As the
troops advanced with bayonets drawn, both young women called out,
"Long live the social revolution!"[75] Molins's account highlights the heroism

of the two young women, especially that of Lafuente. He stresses the cooperation and dedication that enabled the revolution to succeed as well as it
had. The author glorifies the memory of Lafuente in order to help galva-
nize resistance and encourage working-class cooperation. These sentiments
echoed the political line espoused by his party during 1935 when the IC was
in the process of joining together with the Bloc Obrer i Camperol (BOC) to
form a new revolutionary party called the Partido Obrero de Unificación
Marxista (Workers Party of Marxist Unification, POUM). Molins in fact,
served on the executive committee of the new combined organization.

The anarchist author Fernando Solano Palacio neglected to describe
Lafuente's actions in the text of his essay on the revolt; most likely he had no
wish to overly celebrate a communist hero. Nevertheless, the book contains
her photograph along with the following caption: "Aída Lafuente, 'La Libertaria,' heroic youth, died defending a barricade with a machine gun."[76]
The author also includes a picture of the church of San Pedro de los Arcos
and the wall nearby where, according to the caption, many revolutionaries
had been shot and subsequently buried. In the photo of the execution site
the author fails to mention Lafuente by name, but the reference probably
would have been clear to anyone familiar with the story of her actions
nearby.[77] Although many of the politically motivated commemorations
often included descriptions of her combative actions, they deemphasized
her role in the fighting while simultaneously promoting her image as a
victim of the government's suppression of the revolt. In many ways the
commemorations returned Lafuente to the proper gender roles of women
in war: nurse, supporter, and victim. This contrast reflects the organizations'
desire to mobilize and inspire women, albeit by channeling them into appropriate activities.

Journalists also reported on Lafuente's activities, and although they
claimed to offer objective accounts they generally sympathized with the
rebels.[78] These journalistic reports, which may have helped Lafuente become better known outside of the working-class organizations, generally
highlighted her active role in the fighting while remaining vague on the
circumstances of her death. To those interested primarily in selling stories of
the insurrection, the image of a woman warrior provided a deeply compelling and fascinating story line. One of the most dramatic versions was
written by the journalist Manuel Benavides in his *La revolución fué así.*[79]

Benavides was a well-known journalist and author; by 1936 his account of the October revolution was in its tenth printing. In a chapter titled "A Sixteen-Year-Old Heroine," he relates Lafuente's final hours. According to Benavides, Lafuente had seen action on all fronts during the insurrection. Dressed in a blue shirt with red tie, she was imbued with revolutionary consciousness, fighting hard to free the workers of the world and install a new society. In the last days of the revolt Lafuente faced inevitable defeat with grim determination; one young comrade described her as having "a corporal arrogance, a small figure and a head held high . . . like a Victory."[80] In the final days of battle, Benavides reports that Lafuente and fifty revolutionaries retreated to the church of San Pedro de los Arcos at the summit of Mount Naranco. As the soldiers advanced on their position, Lafuente had a premonition of her destiny. She then grabbed a machine gun and told her comrades to go, she would stay to cover their retreat. Benavides declares that Lafuente spoke in a voice of cool authority, and that under her hands the machine gun doubled its effectiveness. At first, her compatriots refused to leave her side, but finally they were gone and Lafuente continued firing until her ammunition ran out. As the troops advanced once again, the young woman drew a pistol and pledged that she would kill herself if they did not shoot her first. She fired upon them, forcing the soldiers to dive for cover, and when they finally rose and advanced they discovered Lafuente's corpse with a wound in the chest.[81] In compiling his story Benavides may have been aware of an account published in the journal *Estampa* shortly after the end of the insurrection. The article featured an interview with a soldier of the Foreign Legion who reportedly killed Lafuente. The Legionnaire claimed that as he advanced on Lafuente's position she knocked him to the ground with a steel rod and then drew a pistol and prepared to fire. The soldier reported, however, that he was quicker and before she could fire he shot her dead.[82]

The newspaper reporter and author José Canal also examined the events of Lafuente's death in his work *Octubre rojo en Asturias* (Red October in Asturias). In this text he calls her by what would become a common nickname, "La Libertaria," and describes her as the daughter of an anarchist. Dressed in red for combat, Lafuente and her comrades installed themselves on the top of Mount Naranco. She fired at the advancing troops with a rifle, while others operated a machine gun. Canal observes that she stood firm and that her bravery and courage were a cause of wonder among the enemy troops. His account omits the final details of her death, stating simply that "the following day the ambulances recovered her body and she was buried in a common grave. She was twenty years old and she was a communist."[83]

For the parties of the left and those sympathetic to their cause, the actions of Lafuente were something to be celebrated; but for the commentators of the right, they remained largely forgotten. Writers with a conservative point of view either deliberately chose not to relate the details of her struggle or simply did not know about them. Ignacio Núñez, in volume 1 of his study *La Revolución de Octubre de 1934,* characterizes her activities in the revolt as encouraging the rebels or caring for them as a nurse. He avoids giving any details surrounding her death by stating simply that she was killed by troops entering Oviedo. In another section describing the death of a priest killed during the revolt, Núñez writes that after revolutionaries had executed the cleric, "Nini Lafuente" was the only one with the good conscience to cover the slain man's body. He ends with what he calls a curious detail: "From the pockets of the dead man she took an image of the religious order that he belonged to, she kissed it and placed it inside her clothing."[84] Núñez continues by explaining the surprise of the undertaker when he later discovered the ornament among her possessions. The author expresses astonishment that the young woman whom he describes as running all over the city dressed in red, cheering the cause of the revolt, could also believe in God: "If she believed in the one! Why did she believe in the other?"[85] Núñez places Lafuente's actions within the boundaries of acceptable female behavior and ascribes to her the traditional characteristics of women in times of war. These themes coincide with the shocked incredulity with which he describes the participation of other women and children in the revolt. Women active in the revolt, Núñez claims, were among the most vicious and bloodthirsty of all revolutionaries as they seduced soldiers into joining the revolution, encouraged the murder of clerics, and supported attacks on the church. He relates incidents of crowds of women howling "Kill them! Kill them!" as revolutionaries led away groups of clerical prisoners. In another case, a band of knife-wielding women attacked a group of captives and stopped only when restrained by male revolutionary guards.[86]

Pro-revolutionary accounts celebrated Lafuente as a warrior and martyr, and she emerges as a powerful and positive symbol of revolutionary devotion. Nevertheless, writers and artists struggled to negotiate the complex interaction between her combative image and her gender. Many versions of her story, especially those appearing just before and during the Civil War, commemorate Lafuente's heroism by returning to familiar gender roles. Although they praise her willingness to fight, they subvert that message by recasting her deeds in terms of traditional gender stereotypes. Lafuente's violent actions represented a potential threat to the social status quo, and even if she herself never articulated feminist demands, her actions alone could motivate demands for change.[87]

In an attempt to promote a more traditional image of Lafuente's actions in war, as well as to encourage political unity, many accounts stress her youth and sexual purity. A young woman who had not yet assumed the cultural trappings associated with womanhood was not a paradigmatic woman and therefore might seem less threatening to the established gendered order. Since Lafuente had no husband or children, she could not be accused of shaming her spouse or abandoning her children—charges that frequently were leveled at proactive women. In addition, she had died a hero in a failed revolution, and this fact gave additional liberties to those who would represent her. Unlike the large-scale mobilizations of women during the early part of the Spanish Civil War, or in the Soviet Union before and during World War II, Lafuente could no longer demand uncomfortable changes in the position of women within the revolutionary society.[88] Because of her age and gender, commentators attributed to her a purity that had both moral and sexual connotations. The association of moral purity to virginity has roots not only in the Catholic tradition of the Virgin Mary but also in Marxist tradition. For many leftists, the decision to refrain from sexual activity suggested a strong and exclusive devotion to the revolutionary cause.[89] The chroniclers of Lafuente's actions drew upon both of these cultural streams to assemble a gendered image of her as a pure revolutionary hero.

In *El Valle Negro: Asturias 1934* (The Black Valley: Asturias 1934), Alfonso Camín goes to great lengths to defend Lafuente's feminine honor. The author reassures his audience that, although Lafuente had fought bravely in combat, she still embodied characteristics appropriate to her gender: "She did not have that virile aspect of bearded women who become discontented because of their doubtful sex and [because] Nature has made them ugly and as revenge they have formed the vanguard of all social malcontents from the good father Adam to our days."[90] He continues by declaring that such women often become writers or public agitators and usually dress in men's clothing. Camín then emphasizes Lafuente's heterosexuality and sexual innocence, proclaiming that she had flirted with "good bourgeois boys," and he ends by depicting her in virginal terms as having the "fresh aroma of new rosebushes."[91] Raul González Tuñón employs similar imagery in his poem "La Libertaria." He describes her in ways generally associated with young women; for example, she proves inspirational to male workers and he exhorted them to visit her grave

> Come, because she was the sweetheart of October, /
> Come, because she was the rose of October, /
> Come, because she was the sweetheart of Spain.[92]

Images of youth and purity also infuse Arturo Serrano Plaja's "Elegy" to Lafuente. The poem is filled with images of death and destruction, and the author presents Lafuente as a passive victim of that violence: "Eleven mortal fragments of furious lead / like black birds of insatiable metal / snatched you away."[93] Instead of taking a proactive role in the fighting, Lafuente becomes an absent figure, one who inspires future actions. The poet describes her memory in sacred terms, as only those with "pure hearts and privileged lips" can speak her name.[94] Serrano Plaja presents Lafuente's life as a noble sacrifice for the revolution, and he denies mention of her own combativeness. Another story of the actions of Lafuente is recounted by the writer and politician Matilde de la Torre as part of her series of newspaper articles titled "Scenes of Asturias." This account focuses on Lafuente's youth and innocence while remaining ambiguous about her role in combat. The story is filled with resurrection imagery and presents Lafuente as an innocent youth brutally cut down by soldiers. At one point the author addresses the dead woman by calling out, "Arise . . . demand justice for your death."[95] In her text de la Torre explains that the advancing government troops slowly surrounded Lafuente and her comrades at the church of San Pedro de los Arcos. The rebels began to withdraw, but Lafuente had been wounded and could not escape. Two young men offered to carry her, but as they bent to pick her up both were shot dead. Finally, as the enemy approached, she hid behind a wall before being discovered by the soldiers. Despite her wound, she struggled to her feet and faced them without fear. De la Torre states that like all great heroes Lafuente knew that the moment of her death had arrived.[96] As the troops raised their rifles to shoot, Lafuente screamed, "I am a Communist. Long live the social revolution!" and then died.[97] Later, de la Torre tells how she had traveled to Asturias and searched among the dead for the body of the young hero. Finding Lafuente's corpse, she looked upon her face and placed roses upon her head as a tribute. The author emphasizes Lafuente's youth by recalling her "innocent smile" and by observing that her clothing seemed to be that of a doll. The article ends by declaring her memory to be an inspiration for young people: "The Revolutionary Youth march into the city shouting . . . always shouting: Justice!"[98] When combined with de la Torre's article "Trinidad," published in the same newspaper, these accounts provide a powerful image of women demanding justice for the crimes committed during the repression. Lafuente and Alvarez represented all of those whose husbands, children, or fathers had been killed or imprisoned following the defeat of the uprising. Such imagery reinforced women's passive role as secondary victims of the repression, albeit ones whose duty it was to protect and demand justice for their loved ones.

In some cases, both pro- and anti-revolutionary writings on the events of October 1934 articulated physical threats to women through stories of sexual violence.[99] Despite the fact that reports and poems highlight her gender, no source claims that Lafuente had been sexually assaulted. Instead, the violence remained limited to a symbolic mutilation of her breasts that allowed for desecration but not violation; the heroic vision of Lafuente would not be tainted by the shame generally attached to rape. Narcis Molins i Fábrega reports in his account that both Lafuente and her young female comrade had been captured alive during the struggle on Mount Naranco. The author states that Lafuente soon died of wounds received during the fighting, but her companion did not. Instead, the unnamed victim "paid another more indignant tribute" to the vengeance of the government, as she was "stained in her agony by one of the assassins."[100] His version of the events simultaneously reveal the nature of the crimes committed against women while ensuring that the memory of Lafuente remains pure. If the memory of Lafuente came to symbolize visions of a revolutionary society she had to remain a virginal icon.

If Lafuente's youth allowed commentators to celebrate her as a pure revolutionary martyr, other accounts sought to commemorate her actions by placing her in the role of a symbolic mother who gave birth to a new age of social justice. In "Elegy to Aida Lafuente," Pascual Pla y Beltran described Lafuente's actions during the revolt as the typical functions of women in combat; that is, she inspired the troops both symbolically and physically:

> You were the wind present with your smile and your hand, I remember.
> You went, you came with water in your mouth, with encouragement in your
> [gaze. . . .
> You bandaged the wound, extinguished thirst, closed your
> [eyelids to death.[101]

In the poetic language of Pla y Beltran, Lafuente appears as a kind of benevolent and ephemeral figure that braved death to support the revolution. Her actions took on maternal characteristics as she passed throughout the city caring for and encouraging the rebels. The poet makes reference to her breasts, thereby emphasizing her womanhood and illustrating the terrible tragedy of her death. Finally he concludes by declaring that "the workers of Spain proclaim you our mother!"[102] In this poem Pla y Beltran praises her courage and commitment to the revolutionary cause, but he ignores the active violence of her actions and instead depicts her as a maternal figure.

At the public rally of 29 February 1936 Rafael Alberti read his poem dedicated to Aida Lafuente, titled simply "Libertaria Lafuente." By 1934, Alberti had begun writing poems with a decidedly political message. Through these "poem-slogans," Alberti hoped to create a cultural revolution by emphasizing the heroic nature of the working class.[103] His verses on Lafuente deliberately aimed to construct an epic story around the revolutionary martyrdom of the young communist. Significantly, the poet places in parentheses directly under the title the words "The Mother" and he also describes her "two cut breasts."[104] At one point, moreover, Alberti emphasizes how Lafuente's actions had become symbolic of the entire revolt:

> I want to unearth her.
> Wet your hand in her blood
> and on the walls, miner
> repeat this sign:
> Long live the Asturian October![105]

Alberti demands that her actions inspire others, and by transforming her into a symbolic representation of the uprising he neutralizes the revolutionary threat that her actions posed to social stability.[106] The poet's use of the term "mother," combined with the imagery of breast mutilation, intensifies the gendered content of her memory.

Some commentators cleansed Lafuente's action of its unsettling challenge to appropriate gender roles by emphasizing her youth and purity or by attempting to connect her symbolically with motherhood. Still other representations excused her actions by portraying her as having acted not as woman but rather as a masculine figure. An article in *Mundo Obrero* about Lafuente concludes with a small ode that celebrates her as a militant communist of the new generation. The article claims that women by nature shrank from violence and conflict due their delicate nature. The combative female communists became acceptable because they ceased to be women: "A communist woman is a militant communist before she is a woman" and when the times demand, she gathers her nerves "smothers her sensibilities and fights."[107]

Alfonso Camín declared that when the revolt started Lafuente and her sister stopped being normal schoolgirls and instead became totally committed to the revolutionary cause. According to the author, on 13 October the army advanced past the train station and approached the slopes of Mount Naranco. Inside the church of San Pedro de los Arcos, eighteen men and one woman remained behind. Camín declared that "Niní de la Fuente, 'La Libertaria,'" was among those who stayed to defend the church. The rebels fired on the advancing soldiers with rifles, machine guns, and other weapons. When one man fell, Lafuente took up his position at a machine gun and continued raining fire on the soldiers below. Soon the fighting became hand to hand within the walls of the church, and the soldiers quickly killed eight of the revolutionaries. The victorious troops ultimately captured the remaining survivors, including Lafuente. The soldiers wanted to execute the rebels in the street, but a lieutenant stopped them in order to interrogate the prisoners. Camín asserted that the officer took a special interest in Lafuente and wanted her stripped of her red clothing. She was questioned but refused to talk. The man offered to let her go into a vacant house to put on more clothing so that she would not be shot while dressed only in undergarments, but she refused this as well. Finally, the officer ordered the prisoners to stand against a wall, and Camín describes Lafuente's final moments: "The girl showed a great manliness [*varonía*]. She remained firm as a rod, cutting the leader of the force with eyes full of hard light. The picket was already prepared with arms in hand. The Lieutenant invited 'La Libertaria' to yell, 'Long live the Government.' She continued her silence, with a sarcastic rictus that made her chin tremble. . . . At the signal of 'Fire,' 'La Libertaria' tore open her bodice and clamored for the final time, with hands to her chest, barely covering her breasts: 'Shoot here, you miserable ones! Long live the Revolution!'"[108]

Even as Camín praises her for her actions he reinforces traditional gender roles. When acting as a revolutionary, Lafuente symbolically became male through the expression of her courage. Camín applaudes her for displaying masculine characteristics but he also emphasizes her womanhood by making explicit reference to her breasts. At the moment of her death she is transformed, despite her actions and her age, into an appropriately female icon: a mother. Joaquín Maurín, a prominent political figure and a future leader of the POUM, celebrates the heroism of Lafuente using similar imagery in his book *Revolución y contrarrevolución en España* (Revolution and Counterrevolution in Spain). Unlike others, however, he never once calls Lafuente by name; instead he refers to her only as a girl or a heroine. In his text he outlines how she fought off the soldiers until the ammunition ran out, and he follows by stating how she stood on the barricade, "tore off her brassiere, offered her breast to the bullets [and] yelled: 'Shoot you swine! Long live the revolution!,' leaving her blood as the red flag that covers that barricade."[109] Maurín's symbolism here has dual meanings, and both can be linked to commemorative representations of Lafuente. She was celebrated for her political radicalism and her actions on behalf of the revolt, and yet the traditional notions of proper gender roles remained central to depictions of her actions.

CONCLUSION

The decision to cast Lafuente's actions within the acceptable boundaries of female behavior reflected the increasing tensions of the Republic's final years, and it might also have been a reaction to the successful militarization of other young women. The poet González Tuñón recalled that after a reading of the poem dedicated to Lafuente, a young woman approached him and asked for a copy.[110] The growing participation of women within the PCE, and the formation of women's organizations such as the anarchist Mujeres Libres (Free Women) in 1936, might have also have played a role.[111] The need for proper adherence to gender roles continued following the outbreak of hostilities in 1936 as young women spontaneously joined militias despite the fact that there was no official program to recruit them. After the first few months of the war, however, the armed forces of the Republic slowly removed women already in combat positions and denied the opportunity to others who wished to volunteer. Instead, the government and political parties assigned women positions as "homefront heroines" relegated to traditionally feminine roles of support and encouragement.[112] The leftist propaganda continued to declare that women were combating tyranny, but now instead of fighting at the front they fought behind the lines, and rather than carrying guns and grenades they carried bandages and babies. The commemoration of Lafuente anticipated these trends, and even before the war had begun her commemorations had already taken on different meanings. Rosario Sánchez, for instance, related that when she went to Madrid in 1936 she enrolled in a sewing school sponsored by the Juventudes Socialistas Unificadas (Unified Socialist Youth, JSU) called the "Aida Lafuente Group."[113]

At the same time that the government was attempting to limit women's participation in combat, the commemorations of Lafuente stressed her image as a role model for women. During the Civil War the PCE held celebrations in honor of the second anniversary of the October insurrection. Under the headline "We are all Belligerents" the newspaper ran two portraits of fallen communist heroes: Lina Odena and Aida Lafuente. Odena was a young Catalan active in the JSU who was killed at the start of the Civil War and quickly became another celebrated communist martyr.[114] A brief caption under the photograph of Lafuente states that she had been "assassinated by fascist beasts" while defending the streets of Oviedo. The paper commented on the power of her example by stating, "The women who continue to sustain your presence and your combative force in our struggle will know that you fell for today's triumph."[115] Although the memory of her retains elements of her participation in the violent struggle, the newspaper portrays her as primarily a role model for women. Other invocations of Lafuente's actions include an item in the Asturian republican paper *La*

Prensa. Writing on the two-year anniversary of the beginning of the revolt
on 6 October, the edition memorializes the revolutionary actions of 1934 by
highlighting those who had sacrificed their lives for the revolution, including Aida Lafuente. The paper acknowledged the power of her story as
follows: "With the passage of time, the figure of Aida Lafuente grows and
has come to constitute a symbol; moreover, an example for the Spanish
woman who now, after some years, follows in the footsteps of the unforget-
table 'Libertaria,' striking out with the same heroism that was her charac-
teristic, in all the fronts where she fights against the reaction and fascism."[116]

    In these examples, Lafuente remains a hero, but the exact nature and
cause of her heroism begins to be forgotten or obscured. The article in *La
Prensa* relates in detail the heroic actions and deaths of the men whom it
celebrated alongside her, yet it relegated her to the status of a symbol and an
icon for women only and contains no mention of her own combative
actions. In another telling gesture, the article from the newspaper *P.O.U.M*
that celebrated the actions of revolutionary heroes included photographs of
all the men yet not one of Lafuente—instead there was a simple line drawing
of a woman.[117]

    The general depictions and imagery surrounding gender multiplied dur-
ing the Civil War, as both Republicans and Nationalists used the ideas and
forms developed in the aftermath of the October revolution to reinforce the
legitimacy of their political position and to undermine that of their opponents. In these ways the gendered interpretations of the uprising presaged
the forms that such relations would take during the years of the Civil War
and afterward. For the Republicans, images of masculinity and femininity
were momentarily in flux as the euphoria of revolution encouraged women
to join the militias and enter combat, thereby challenging their conventional place in wartime. This new role for women was quickly suppressed,
however, as the ideal of the "homefront heroine" increasingly replaced that
of the *miliciana* (militia woman).[118] For the rest of the war the Republican
imagery of women generally adhered to conventional depictions. As such
the gendered order remained fundamentally unchallenged, even while the
political and economic bases of Spanish society were being revolution-
ized. The Nationalist gender imagery remained fundamentally conservative
throughout the course of the war. Following the dominant themes emphasized in the wake of 1934, the traditional roles of men and women were

affirmed and reinforced by Franco's forces.[119] They identified women as wives, mothers, and Christians, while men became heroic defenders of home and nation. The conservative ideals of gender relations remained one of the central pillars of the Franco regime until well into the 1960s.[120]

Only with the transition to democracy following the death of Franco would a fundamental reshaping of roles occur, and Lafuente would soon become represented as an exemplar of such changes.

THE OCTOBER REVOLUTION IN DEMOCRATIC SPAIN

Should we erase the past so that its ghosts do not reappear?
—Eugenio de Rioja, *La Nueva España,* 8 July 1999

The commemorative imagery of the October 1934 revolution proved to be a key factor in triggering the outbreak of the Spanish Civil War in July 1936. The representations of martyrdom and gender had helped divide society and politics into two immutable blocs that viewed the contest for political power as a life-or-death struggle where defeat equaled nothing less than annihilation. The stories of gruesome atrocities and brutal sexual violence encouraged the belief that legal means could no longer protect society and that only violent action could preserve and protect the nation. The power of such representations can be demonstrated not only by their effects on the political process leading to the Civil War but also by their continued importance during the course of that conflict. The imagery of martyrdom quickly became a fundamental part of Nationalist propaganda.[1] Casimiro Cienfuegos, whose poetry helped join religious devotion to radical political action in the prewar period, published during the war a similar volume titled *Cancionario de la guerra*

(Anthology of War). This book, dedicated to Francisco Franco and General Antonio Aranda Mata, contains reprintings of several poems written following the October revolt, and as such reiterates many of the themes of that early work including the glorification of the military and the linking of the political and religious. Cienfuegos praises Aranda, who had managed to hold the city of Oviedo for the Nationalists during the initial stages of the Civil War, for "[making] the Martyr City into a second Covadonga."[2] The left also used commemorations of revolutionary martyrdom to promote unity of action during the Civil War, just as they had done in the aftermath of the October insurrection. A pamphlet encouraging cooperation between the Confederación Nacional de Trabajo and Unión General de Trabajadores, for example, invoked the lessons of 1934 to facilitate the merger of the two unions.[3] On the two-year anniversary of the October revolt, the newspaper *Milicia Popular* printed several stories on the government's actions during the repression of the uprising. As one headline declared: "The same Moors and Legionaires with the same results . . . but this time against a people strengthened and armed with a will to win!"[4] Representations promoting both the Nationalists and the Republicans as true exemplars of masculine virtue also continued to be produced. Perhaps the most ubiquitous imagery celebrated the soldier—either the dedicated Republican or determined Nationalist—as a strong, valiant hero.[5] This imagery sometimes referenced the events of October 1934; one Republican poster encouraged people to help refugees fleeing Asturias by depicting a heroic miner with dynamite in hand protectively standing in front of a woman holding a child.[6] Women, for the most part, continued to remain on the sidelines as symbols, caregivers, and mothers.[7]

As the poster and other materials show, in the short term the imagery surrounding the October revolt continued to have a powerful impact on political developments within Spain. With the passage of time, and as a result of the larger tragedy of Civil War, the events in Asturias gradually receded from public discourse.[8] The long dictatorship of Franco ensured that the insurrection never generated much public discussion.[9] With the process of democratization, which culminated in the new constitution of 1978, the events of October 1934 began slowly to reappear in social and political discourse. Images of the conflict had particular resonance in Asturias, and essentially it was only there that the revolt garnered intense public debate.[10] Memories of the insurrection continued to reverberate into the present (though with a curious combination of neglect and feeling), and became for the most part less polarizing and more open for discussion. Perhaps the most common and widespread reaction to the events of October 1934 was the attempt at its historicization. This meant that for many the revolt was a mistake of the past that should be studied with an aim toward learning from it so that the violent actions would never be repeated. In many ways this process of historicization was similar to what happened to the memories of the Civil War during the transition to democracy. Paloma Aguilar Fernández has argued that the Franco regime attempted to establish through the authoritarian apparatus of government a single collective memory of the Civil War. The government focused on a constant recitation of the horrors of the war and relied on a fear of repeating it to create a powerful collective memory against political strife. This process, what Aguilar Fernández calls "memory and forgetting," became a crucial element of the peaceful transition to democracy following the dictator's death. Aguilar Fernández also suggests that it was a generational change that enabled the process of forgetting to effectively neutralize the antagonisms that had led to conflict.[11] Not everyone, however, viewed the October rebellion in such a dispassionate manner, and some continued to see the representations of the events in strongly emotional terms. The conservatives retained emotional memories of the anticlerical violence that occurred during the insurrection, and many still accused the revolutionary parties who revolted in October 1934 of starting the Civil War, rather than the army who led the uprising in 1936. For many revolutionaries who had lived through or participated in the revolt, its goals and brutal defeat still retained a poignancy that was not shared by the general population. In addition to the leftists of old, many young radicals depicted October 1934 as an authentic rebellion against the domination of the state, and one untainted by the left's political factionalism during the Civil War.[12] Ultimately, the depictions of two key figures—the martyrs of Turón and Aida Lafuente—overshadowed other specific details of the revolt and continued to inspire debate and confrontation, though they also elicited a changing set of interpretations and meanings from the historical to the passionate.

HISTORICIZATION

The fiftieth anniversary of the uprising came just two years after the first free elections under Spain's new constitution. After so long, many people considered the events of October 1934 to be a thing of the past and something best left to history. Although the media coverage of the anniversary at a national level was generally sparse, the Asturian newspapers ran numerous stories that highlighted the process of historicization.[13] The commemorations of the fiftieth anniversary ranged from scholarly conferences to a nationally televised debate.[14] The host of the program, José Luis Balbín, acknowledged that the topic of the program had produced some controversy but deemed the amount slight compared to other subjects.[15] Another article in the same paper criticized the show for lacking a historical introduction to the events, stating bluntly that "the revolution of October is . . . little known in Asturias, and less so in the rest of Spain."[16] The study of the topic by academics was intense, however, and culminated in a conference held in Mieres during October 1984. The socialist Fundación José Barreiro and the Mieres city council sponsored a series of lectures by distinguished international historians of the revolt, including Adrian Shubert, David Ruiz, Paco Ignacio Taibo, and Santos Juliá. The tone of the lectures remained primarily academic and informative, with uncomplicated titles such as "The Participation of the Socialists in the October Revolution" and "The Participation of the Anarchists in the October Revolution." Eugenio Carbajal Martínez, the mayor of Mieres, stated that the goal of the proceedings was "to commemorate from a purely cultural focus, and above all to analyze from a rigorously scientific perspective this important historical event."[17] A book of teaching materials on the 1934 revolution reinforced the desire to examine the revolution critically with an unbiased eye. This text, titled *Revolución del 34 en Asturias: Materiales para el aula* (Revolution of '34 in Asturias: Materials for the Classroom), contains primary source excerpts, secondary sources, and a series of questions asking students to analyze the accompanying materials. The authors of the book stress that one of the main tasks of historians is interpreting the past in order to "give us an explanation of why things happened, how they happened and the lessons we can learn from history in order to live better today."[18] The aim of the text, as Roser Calaf Masachs makes clear in the prologue, is to "show that history is a

subjective material, that maybe [this book] will serve to shape, in the institution of the school, habits of tolerance necessary in a democratic society."[19]
Through the study of history, and more specifically through the teaching of
a controversial period of history, the educators hoped to instill ideas of
democracy. Such notions contrast with previous commemorations that encouraged hatred and ultimately helped to destroy democracy.

Ideas of peace and tolerance resonated with the general public as well. As
part of its coverage, *La Voz de Asturias* included in its edition of 4 October
1984 a commemorative poster designed by the thirty-eight-year-old artist
Miguel Angel Lombardía. In an accompanying story, the artist declared that
he hoped to create imagery that would "express hope and peace in contrast
to violence."[20] He claimed to view the events of the past without a political
agenda, and he expressed his desire to learn more about the insurrection so
as to prevent such events from happening again. Lombardía's view of the
rebellion as something from the past, from his grandparent's time, is reflected in his effort to represent a new perspective on the events through his
artwork: "I saw the event, fifty years after, at my age, with my artistic sense
and with my generation and I wanted to represent our Spain, our Asturias,
with hope and with brotherhood."[21] Other commentators echoed the desire to remember the events, but also hoped to consign them to the past.
One writer, after retelling his own childhood memories of the events,
summarized his feelings as follows: "The best thing that we Spaniards can do
is to strive to live in peace, to exercise tolerance, to respect one another and
to work to improve the nation. Peace to the dead and forgiveness to those
who have committed crimes, this is my slogan."[22]

To some, however, the process of historicization seemed to romanticize
or sanitize the true nature of the revolt. In a letter written to the editor of the
Asturian newspaper *La Nueva España,* published on 10 October 1984,
Tomás Recio stated that he had followed the newspaper's coverage of the
historical past with great interest. The stories relating to what he described
as "religious persecution" became particularly important to him. Recio
acknowledged that the incidents at Turón had received sufficient attention
yet many others had been forgotten, and his stated goal was to cite the
details of all crimes in order to make sure that each one of them was
remembered. He subsequently listed many incidents and briefly recounted
the details of each, describing the crimes in neutral terms and without

hyperbole. He disavowed any political motive, asserting that he wished to avoid unnecessarily arousing tensions over the events. Nevertheless, he clearly wondered about the nature of the memorialization of the revolution and asked how the events could be recalled as romantic and heroic gestures when such crimes were committed.[23] The letter showed that even if the ardent political use of the memories no longer remained, much of the sadness and bitterness continued. In an editorial from 1984 titled "A Reflection on '34," the assistant director of *La Voz de Asturias,* Lorenzo Cordero, argued against forgetting the true nature of the events. He called the insurrection of 1934 a genuine revolution bent on changing the entire structure of society and not simply aiming to replace the ruling class. He believed that many in the community hoped to obfuscate the radical goals of the insurrection. As he stated: "It is obvious that the intention is to analyze for clarity, for history, the causes of that Revolutionary Workers October in Asturias . . . to disperse them in symposiums, to reduce them to simple anecdotes in grand public acts with large audiences and finally, to control them—especially the institutions—by the intelligentsia of the party in power [i.e., the Partido Socialista Obrero Español]."[24] Cordero expressed disappointment with the general treatment of the revolt and called for accurate historical presentation. Like the poster artist, he claimed that he only wanted to shed light on the terrible events of the past in order to help prevent future conflicts. Nevertheless, he seemed to view the process of historization with some discomfort.

If Recio and Cordero represented those who claimed only a desire to accurately describe the events without political gloss, other groups and individuals attempted to employ the events directly for political gain. Despite the Civil War, some on both sides of the political spectrum continued to view the revolt in starkly political terms. To those on the right, the uprising retained the ideas of Marxist conspiracies designed to destroy the nation. These conservatives held up the example of October 1934 as proof of the fundamental danger posed by the Socialist Party, whether in the past or present. The continued participation of the Partido Socialista Obrero Español (PSOE) as one of the two dominant parties in contemporary Spanish politics led to a renewed scrutiny over the organization's role in the events of 1934.[25] In addition, conservative writers used the PSOE's interpretations of the insurrection as a tool for attacking contemporary socialist policies. In

José María García de Tuñón Aza's *El socialismo, contra la ley* (Socialism, Against the Law), the author places all blame for the October revolt on the socialist movement. At great length he responds to socialist publications and pronouncements on the revolution, especially in challenging the claims both recent and in the past that the revolution was in favor of democracy. The book is clearly intended to contest both historical interpretations of the revolt and the way that the insurrection had been employed in contemporary political discourse.[26] Similar accusations against the PSOE were lodged by the journalist Ángel Palomino in his work *1934: La Guerra civil empezó en Asturias* (1934: The Civil War Began in Asturias). In this book he contests previous historical accounts of the events, often by resurrecting the claims made by conservative critics in the months immediately following the defeat of the uprising. Palomino writes, for example, that Luis Sirval died following an "altercation" with various officials, when in fact the journalist had been murdered while in police custody.[27] By arguing that the Civil War began during the October insurrection Palomino absolves the military for sparking the larger conflict. The historian Pío Moa achieved popularity with several works that argued a similar case, although his books have not escaped criticism by other scholars.[28] In an editorial from the newspaper *El País,* the prominent historian Javier Tusell dismissed such publications as "revisionism." Tusell asserted that Moa "took part of the truth and put forth a completely offensive thesis that returns us to the 1940s."[29] Conservative interpretations of the October revolution continue to resonate among some segments of the population and have now been appropriated once again to attack the leadership of the PSOE. Nevertheless, such attacks are generally no longer linked to a call for violent reaction but instead are part of the discourse of opposition in a modern democratic state.[30]

The complexity of responses to the revolt can be illustrated by the events of 1994 in the towns of San Martín del Rey Aurelio and Laviana. The governments of these Asturian towns could not agree on an official commemoration, despite the fact that members of the conservative Partido Popular (Popular Party, PP) controlled both boards. In San Martín del Rey Aurelio, a PP spokesman denounced attempts to celebrate the revolt: "In this country common sense does not function when one seeks to institutionalize dates about which we should be ashamed."[31] He continued by criticizing the "historical ignorance" of those who wished to commemorate the events only to achieve political gain. The resistance of the PP to the commemoration provoked a strong reaction from a PSOE councilman. He accused conservatives of altering history and repeated the argument that the uprising had been a means of defending the Republic against an authoritarian government bent on overturning the constitution. The socialist deputy reacted strongly to the PP's assertion that the October revolution caused the Civil War: "To say that '34 provoked the Civil War is absurd. In 1936, it was not the people who rebelled but rather the army."[32] The conservative party in Laviana, however, saw the events differently and approved an official ceremony of remembrance. Rather than focusing on the death and destruction caused by the revolt, the councilors saw the sixtieth anniversary as an opportunity to commemorate "those men and women that risked their lives in defense of their ideals."[33] The differing responses to the events indicated not only how controversial the memories of October could be, but also how changes in Spanish society and political culture encouraged different interpretations of those memories even among political conservatives.

For both old and new leftists, the insurrection represented a genuine revolutionary event that could still be used to inspire radical changes in the current political system. Pilar Lafuente, sister of the young leftist hero Aida Lafuente, was one prominent veteran of October 1934 who retained a combative memory of the events. In a newspaper interview from 1998, she revealed that her opinion of the events had changed little in sixty-four years: "Madrid betrayed us, Barcelona betrayed us. Asturias was defeated and betrayed and left alone, completely alone."[34] At the dedication ceremony of a monument to her sister, she still spoke of fallen heroes and praised working-class unity, common elements of previous memories of the insurrection. The seventy-nine-year-old Lafuente also told of her sister's commitment to the revolutionary cause, declaring: "My sister gave her life for her communist ideas, and it was not in vain, now other, new generations are being educated with the same ideals."[35] Some elements of the new generations about which Lafuente spoke had been attempting to reintroduce the insurrection into active political debate. These organizations, however, had little concrete influence and remained marginal to the political process. One group, the Partido Obrero Revolucionario de España (Revolutionary Worker Party of Spain, PORE), published a collection of essays about the revolt, titled *La comuna de asturias, 1934–1984, en el 50 aniversario* (The Commune of Asturias, 1934–1984, on the Fiftieth Anniversary). The PORE was one of many Marxist-inspired groups that emerged in the waning years of the Franco regime and the first years of the transition to democracy. The authors of the pamphlet attack the staid nature of remembrance, arguing that "the general tone of the commemoration has been used to present [the factors] which initiated the socialist workers' revolution as something of the past that at best should be recorded for history but should never happen again."[36] Instead, the group argues that the time for change had again arrived and that only the formation of a new Alianza Obrera could ensure powerful action. The PORE charged that the mainstream Marxist parties, the Partido Comunista de España (PCE) and PSOE, had abandoned the workers and allied themselves with the bourgeoisie and the state. The commemoration of October 1934 was motivated by a desire to encourage political involvement: "The articles [contained within] do not treat the events strictly historically but rather discuss the events that occurred in order to draw political conclusions for the present fight."[37] Eventually the group changed its name to Partido Obrero Revolucionario and joined the Izquierda Unida (United Left, IU) in opposition to the mainstream leftist organizations, especially the PSOE.[38] The group clearly intended to recapture the revolutionary spirit of the October revolt, although without directly advocating armed insurrection.

The anarchist groups, who by now lacked the membership levels and influence of their previous organizations, also continued to interpret the events of the revolt in ways similar to the original accounts published between 1935 and 1939. A review article by José Luis Mulas Hernández in the journal *Orto* recounts the history of the revolt from an anarchist's perspective. He repeats the previous accusations that the socialists had supposedly withheld guns from anarchists in Gijón and thus contributed to the relatively quick defeat of the revolt in that city. The decision to include such an account probably reflected a desire to criticize the PSOE, which at the time of the article's publication was the nation's ruling party. In his piece Mulas Hernández retells stories of the alleged atrocities conducted by the Foreign Legion and Moroccan troops, claiming that they had stabbed women and children and suffered no penalties for these actions. Later he describes the last, desperate defense of Mount Naranco by one hundred men and two sixteen-year-old girls. As the troops advanced, the men were all killed,

leaving Aida Lafuente and her companion as the sole survivors. At the end
of the article Mulas Hernández recites the two young women's fates: "The
first was killed and the second raped beforehand."[39] Such accounts demonstrate that for some the revolution remained an active political issue that still
had the potential to ignite emotions and encourage political action.

THE MARTYRS OF TURÓN AND AIDA LAFUENTE

The martyrs of Turón and Aida Lafuente represent the two most remembered symbols from the October revolution. As symbols, both share common characteristics. During the Second Republic, each had become a particularly important rallying point for a variety of political groups that used
martyr imagery to create and perpetuate meaning: Following the transition
to democracy, these memories continued to retain importance and remained fully articulated within familiar cultural representations of martyrdom and gender. Those who perpetuated their memories no longer needed
to encourage others to fight violently for a cause, but instead hoped to use
them as examples of spiritual devotion in order to inspire action and commitment. The church, faced with declining membership and increased secularization, needed symbols of Catholic commitment to inspire and invigo-
rate Spanish youth. The martyrs of Turón thus became inspirational models
of religious commitment, especially to the principles of Catholic education.
Meanwhile, the political left, in order to combat declining voter support
and general apathy for progressive politics, cast Lafuente as a youthful idealist and a woman who defended democracy and equality.

In addition to providing an inspirational message for nationalist culture
during the Civil War, the martyrs of 1934 continued to have resonance fifty
years later. Recollections of the suffering, death, and destruction perpetrated against the church and its members revealed that the idea of martyrdom was one of the longest lasting and most powerful memories of the
October revolution. The case of the nine clerics killed at Turón continued
to be a central focus of commemorations, eventually outshining the other
religious figures killed in the revolt. The celebration of their memories
culminated in 1999 when Pope John Paul II canonized the martyrs of Turón
and entered them into the official list of saints of the Catholic Church.[40]
The process of beatification originally began in October 1944 on the tenth
anniversary of the revolution, and while the investigation was concluded by

1955 nothing more occurred in the case, primarily due to lack of interest on the part of the papacy. The martyrs' file was then reactivated after 1980 and the decision authorizing beatification received initial approval eight years later.[41] In September 1989, Pope John Paul II signed a decree recognizing "the martyrdom for the Christian faith of nine ecclesiastics in Turón, who died during the revolution of Asturias," and in April 1990 they were officially beatified.[42] The renewed attention given to the martyrs of Turón and their beatification triggered a revival of interest in the men and their stories and resulted in a spate of publications that described their lives and martyrdom.[43] For example, Pedro Chico González, himself a De La Salle Brother, wrote *Testigo de la escuela cristiana: Martíres de la revolución de Asturias* (Witness of the Christian School: Martyrs of the Asturian Revolution). The book describes the circumstances of the brothers' deaths and characterizes them as victims of the battle between good and evil. In this sense it echoes the language of the pre–Civil War accounts of their deaths, but unlike those texts the author does not dwell on the events of the revolt or characterize the killers as insane beasts. Instead, he emphasizes the positive impact of the martyrs on Christians today.[44] Calling them "torches [who] could illuminate paths" he stresses the lessons that can be learned from their lives: Christian education requires sacrifice, the work of God demands constant struggle, and the challenge of the Christian school is service to the faith of Christ.[45] Such sentiments echo the words that Pope John Paul II delivered to a group of Spaniards that came to Rome to venerate the newly beatified men in 1990.[46] The canonization of the martyrs also resonated beyond the borders of Spain; one of the clerics was the first saint born in Argentina, and then-president Carlos Memem attended the canonization mass in Rome.[47]

The deaths of the clerics continued to have the ability to invoke strong emotions, but by 1990 these feelings did not necessarily translate into direct political action. In October 1990, a local group called the Apostolado Social Católico celebrated a week of events in homage to the martyrs. The celebrants removed the most obvious political motives from the ceremony and no official representative of the Turón city government attended the service in Rome. A conservative council member did travel to the beatification events, but only as an individual citizen and not as a representative of any political party.[48] The change resulted, in part, from the evolving face of Spanish society, but also from changes within the church that helped prevent the memories from taking on a more partisan character. The overt de-politicization of the martyrs in Spain continued even as the pope announced the canonization of the nine men in July 1999. Newspaper accounts declared that the village of Turón received the pronouncement of canonization with great calm, "demonstrating that they want to heal grave and profound wounds that had been opened in a social context very distinct from today."[49] In an interview Miguel Ramos, director of the school where the clerics had taught, spoke of reconciliation: "The diocese is not interested in who killed them; they simply constitute an example of the people who were faithful to God and the Church until the end."[50] Ramos's words echoed those used by Catholic leaders when they began to distance themselves publicly from the Franco regime in the late 1960s. At that time, the church spoke of national reconciliation, harmony, dialogue, and public liberties.[51] Ramos's comments carried similar meaning as he tried to promote understanding and forgiveness.

Although both the newspaper and the director spoke of depoliticization, they also expressed concern over the potential effects of the canonization. Despite the changed social and political climate, memories of October still retained the ability to incite strong reactions. Contemporary accounts showed how individuals tried to "remember to forget" the potential power of memory. The fear expressed by Ramos and others of opening old wounds underlined how the previous use of these memories had generated strong reactions. The desire to avoid the politicization of memory evidenced a wish to avoid the consequences of that politicization—that is, democratic breakdown and Civil War. Ramos recognized this desire and stated explicitly that "there are people who want to agitate, while we only want to forget."[52] This process of forgetting echoed that of Civil War memory in general, as people chose to move beyond recriminatory accounts of the past in favor of conciliatory memories.[53] The direct acknowledgment of this dual process of remembering and forgetting represented an attempt to divorce the political use of memory from the memories themselves and thus marked a dramatic shift in the recollections of October 1934. The desire for depoliticization and "forgetting" nevertheless generated some resistance. Eugenio de Rioja, in a newspaper editorial, criticized Ramos by arguing that the Church and its representatives were not doing enough to celebrate the example of the murdered clerics. He asked if the Church and the people of Turón feared history: "Should we erase the past so that its ghosts do not reappear?"[54] The timid celebration of the martyrs as examples for contemporary Catholics, Rioja argued, demonstrated the inferiority of the present clergy compared to the precedent set by the dead clerics. The author challenged the assumption that celebrating the martyrs would stir antagonisms, suggesting instead that the canonization represented an acknowledgment of history. Rioja further charged that in Asturias the memories of the revolution favored the rebels, and he cited the case of Aida Lafuente who recently had a monument dedicated to her life and actions during the revolution. Rioja stated that Lafuente had become something of a lay saint, and that forces of the left were "still celebrating lost battles, as they celebrate the failed revolution fifty years after as a triumphant epic poem." The canonization of the martyrs of Turón, he argued, represented a way to restore neutrality to historical memory and create a more objective account of the past.[55] The exchanges over the proper way to commemorate the martyrs of Turón indicates that public contestation of the memories of October 1934 continued to the end of the century. Rioja charged members of the left of twisting the past to suit the needs of the present, and he argued that the reproduction of memory had overcome the objectivity of history. His essay simultaneously revealed how successful the leftist attempts had been at modifying contemporary memories of 1934 and represented an effort to recapture public memory. Finally, he showed how the memories of the martyrs of Turón and of Aida Lafuente had become the main symbolic representations of the revolution. For many conservatives and Catholics, the deaths of the clerics revealed the fundamental evil of the revolt and its excessive violence and anticlericalism. The leftists, meanwhile, viewed the actions of Lafuente as the true spirit of the revolt; as someone fighting and dying for her desire to improve socioeconomic conditions.

On 18 April 1998 a crowd of about three hundred people gathered at the park of San Pedro de los Arcos in the city of Oviedo to dedicate a newly erected memorial commemorating Aida Lafuente (see figure 4). The ceremony that took place more than six decades after her death was attended by a mixture of local political officials and the general public, and featured her sister Pilar Lafuente. The speeches that day emphasized Lafuente's dedication to an ideal, her heroism, and her willingness to fight for what she believed in.[56] Nearly absent was a specific acknowledgment of her participa-

Figure 4 Memorial for Aida Lafuente in the park of San Pedro de los Arcos, Oviedo.
PHOTO BY THE AUTHOR

tion in a revolutionary uprising against the democratically elected government of Spain. Instead she had become a symbol of heroism, idealism, and tolerance. The conversion of Lafuente from a revolutionary to an idealist allowed her to be seen as a metaphor for a changing society and an ideal personification of democracy. She had become a rebel who stood for progressive democratic politics, but not everyone shared this characterization of her. Those who recalled the polarization of 1934, like her sister, still remembered her more as a revolutionary hero than a political symbol.

Public celebration of Aida Lafuente had begun to reemerge during the 1970s, and two incidents during this time demonstrated that the memory and popularity of the young woman remained strong, even though decades had passed since her death. At a concert featuring the popular singers Ana Belén and Víctor Manuel in Oviedo's Palacio de Deportes early in 1978, a voice among the crowd demanded to hear the song "Aida." The following day, at a tribute to the poet Rafael Alberti, thousands of people insisted on a repetition of the tune dedicated to the young revolutionary.[57] Franco's victory in the Civil War and his decades in power had failed to erase the memory of the young revolutionary in at least some segments of the population. In addition, the fact that the singers could and did oblige the request by singing the "sentimental and romantic" song was further indication that Lafuente's memory remained strong.[58] Also in the 1970s, the band Nuberu recorded in honor of the young woman a popular song that exalted her beauty and her bravery,[59] while the group Xana produced a collection of songs about the revolution of 1934, including several dedicated to Lafuente.[60]

The interest in the actions and memories of Lafuente grew along with the general coverage of the fiftieth anniversary of revolt in 1984. Some newspapers contained long articles and multisegmented stories detailing the events of the revolt in Asturias, many of which naturally recounted the stories of her struggle and death at San Pedro de los Arcos.[61] At some point people began to gather near the church to honor her memory, and although it is unclear just when people began to publicly remember Lafuente, by the mid-1990s the ceremonies definitely had become larger. Newspaper accounts described the event as a traditional act of homage celebrated annually, although the regular coverage of the gatherings only began in 1992. That year's ceremonies included representatives of IU, the Asturian Communist Party, and two leftist Asturian nationalist groups, Lliberación and Griesca. One paper reported that Lafuente had fought alongside the miners and died in the repression that followed, and through her death she was "converted into the combative model of the working classes of Asturias, who continue always to maintain the tradition of fighting for their rights, for democracy and for social progress."[62] Lafuente was not the only leftist icon celebrated at the event; the gathering also featured a small homage to the Cuban revolutionary Che Guevara on the twenty-fifth anniversary of his death. The speakers that day made numerous references to current political issues, so that the celebration became a public forum for expressing grievances with the current administrations both local and national.[63] The ceremonies that took place in 1994 and 1995 again illustrated the use of the traditional homage as a political pulpit. Only approximately one hundred people attended the ceremony in 1994; among them were representatives of the same leftist groups from the years before. The words of one speaker demonstrated the changing meanings in the actions of Aida Lafuente, as he declared that her actions and the revolt itself spoke eloquently about the potential of the people to work together and to fight for liberty and the rights of all men and women.[64] During the 1995 ceremony the IU linked

Oviedo's current mayor to those in the past who had repressed the working class, calling his political ideology "neofascist" and accusing him of adopting methods of cruelty. Other speakers, such as the one from the Asturian Communist Youth, called for social justice in reference to contemporary issues including education, work, and gender equality.[65] The deliberate emphasis on women reflected changing attitudes toward gender issues, and Lafuente became increasingly celebrated not only as a woman who fought for her ideals but also specifically as a woman who struggled to create an equal society.

During the 1995 ceremony commemorating Lafuente the progressive political leaders broached for the first time the idea of building a permanent monument to the fallen hero. At the conclusion of that day's speeches, the local IU leader announced that donations were being collected to erect a monument in memory of the young woman, since the streets and plazas of the city represented a celebration of the winners of the Civil War and had few reminders of the losing side.[66] The organizers of the drive to build the monument stated that the goal was to "recover the historical memory of one of the most heroic women, and one respected by all democratic citizens of Oviedo."[67] According to supporters, the monument commemorated the fight for democracy and stood against intolerance. Rather than being recognized as an homage to a violent communist revolutionary, it became a monument to a society and culture that had come to terms with its past. Indeed, it was meant to display that both factions of the Civil War could and should be celebrated. Not only did the groups honor Lafuente as a leftist and representative of the losing side of a civil war she did not take part in, but also she was honored simply as a woman. The change in the form of her celebrations was complete; she had passed from a representative of the fighting spirit of the proletariat to become instead a symbol of democracy, tolerance, and womanhood in general.

Although the process to place a permanent memorial to Lafuente began in 1995, the monument itself was only officially inaugurated in 1998. In those three years the memory of Lafuente, and more generally the revolution itself, became further entangled in local political struggles. In addition, despite the fairly innocuous celebration of Lafuente as an icon of the left and not necessarily as a violent revolutionary, the decision to celebrate her actions publicly met with some resistance.[68] Following the initial call for donations, the organizers of the movement asked for help from the municipal governments of twenty local towns and cities. Only eight answered the request, with the city of Gijón agreeing to donate the largest single contribution of 100,000 pesetas. The municipal government of Oviedo itself, headed by members of the conservative PP, contributed nothing to construction of the monument.[69]

By fall 1997, the necessary funds had been collected and the monument itself was completed, but the conservative-led municipal government of Oviedo denied the request by representatives of the IU to erect the monument in the park surrounding San Pedro de los Arcos. The organizers of the campaign to create the memorial called this action "ideological discrimination" and complained that the city government "has a mouth full of terms like democracy and harmony, [but] it demonstrates scarce sensibility to a part of our history."[70] Less than a week later, another story appeared in *La Nueva España* reporting that requests to place the monument had already been denied multiple times.[71] Shortly afterward, the newspaper published an open letter to the mayor written by David Ruiz, a prominent historian and expert on the revolution of October 1934. Calling his effort a letter from "a resident" of Oviedo, Ruiz sarcastically berated the mayor for repeatedly turning down requests to place the monument. He wrote that the groups wished to pay homage to the young woman who died, so that "the people of the village would have lived better and also to avoid the destruction of the Republic by fascists."[72] He further stated that Lafuente could serve as an example to the youth of today; or, he asked rhetorically, would it have been better if she would have stayed home that day and not aided the workers? Ruiz also explained how the organizing committee had requested permission to erect the monument near San Pedro de los Arcos, and after waiting about six weeks they returned to city hall only to find that the request had been denied because the petition had to pass before the Parks and Gardens commission. A month later the committee visited city hall again, only to find that there was another problem; a further formality had to be attended to regarding the legal standing of the monument committee. Again the members of the committee waited, and after another month had passed they returned to the government offices for a third time. They were then informed that the functionary who had been handling the petition was ill and the mayor could take no action while the person familiar with the case was absent.

Ruiz's letter stated ironically that everyone knew that the case was obviously nothing more than an administrative problem, and that there were no political motivations behind what seemed to be a campaign of delay to forestall the monument. He gently reminded the mayor how quickly the city had placed a bust of Sabino Fernández Campo in a prominent park with much fanfare and with the mayor in attendance at the dedication (see figure 5). Fernández Campo, the Count of Latores, was a former lieutenant general and ex-chief general secretary of the royal household, and hence one of the closest advisors to King Juan Carlos himself. His list of honors is impressive, including the Grand Cross of Charles III, Grand Cross of Military Merit, Cross of Honor of Saint Raimundo de Peñafort, the crosses of Saint Hermenegildo and Cisneros, and many other awards both foreign and national.[73] The general played a key role in thwarting the failed coup attempt of 23 February 1981, and he even appeared on a list of "undesirable" military leaders assembled by the conspirators prior to the revolt.[74] Ruiz argued that the sculpture of Fernández Campo was a work supported by the respectable people of Oviedo and valued at something close to 15 million pesetas, while in contrast the monument to Lafuente was proposed and supported by leftists and funded through voluntary contributions with a final cost of around 350,000 pesetas. The section ended with withering sarcasm: "What the girl of the monolith had was the bad luck to be killed for helping others, but Mr. Sabino, as you know, has two important actions to his credit: one, when he was young he helped the government of Franco to triumph and the other, many years later, before he retired, to re-establish democracy helping Adolfo Suárez. As I said, no comparison is possible."[75] In the end Ruiz advised the mayor to authorize the placement of the monument, if only for two reasons: first, it would rid the mayor of more nuisances, and nobody of importance would ever see the monument anyway; and, second, it would demonstrate the mayor's sense of openness and tolerance.[76]

Ruiz's letter illustrates several issues regarding the changing meanings of Lafuente's memory. First, he advocated the monument not because Lafuente was a revolutionary hero but rather because she had been committed to helping people. Ruiz left aside the memory of her violent actions on behalf of the revolution in favor of a version that exalted her idealism and her desire to make people's lives better. Second, his letter symbolized the

Figure 5
Sculpture honoring
General Sabino Fernández
Campo, Oviedo. PHOTO BY
THE AUTHOR

belief among many that the polarized attitudes of the 1930s still reverberated in contemporary politics. Less than two weeks after the publication of Ruiz's letter, a notice appeared in the newspaper stating that the municipal government had approved the request to install the monument in the park at San Pedro de los Arcos. The conservative council members explained that the delay was due to the concern that it would reopen old wounds and cause pain to many families. The IU responded to this statement by declaring that the many streets, parks, and plazas named for the victors of the Civil War also caused pain to some families.[77]

Shortly after permission to erect the monument had been granted, a long article appeared in *La Nueva España* detailing the life and death of Aida Lafuente. It stated that three of her siblings were still living: two were in Mexico and the youngest, Pilar, was in the Ukraine. The article also offered, for the first time in print, the family's account of Lafuente's final hours. They believed that she fought in the church and fired a machine gun but was captured alive, and that after her capture she was executed, along with seven of her comrades, by Dimitri Iván Ivanoff—the same Legionnaire who killed Luis Sirval. Her clothing was recovered by her mother and another woman, and later it was exhibited at the family's home as a sign of her bravery. The *La Nueva España* article called her "the red rose of October 1934," and declared that although the monument committee had obtained permission, after a longer delay than usual, no date had yet been specified to inaugurate the memorial.[78] Later, a final date was chosen, which was timed to coincide with the celebrations revolving around the anniversary of the founding of the Second Republic. While this may have been done for other reasons, it is significant that the monument would celebrate an important date in the history of Spanish democracy and not the insurrection itself. The inauguration of the monument took place on Saturday, 19 April 1998, near the spot where Lafuente was killed on Mount Naranco. Representatives of the major leftist parties attended, along with a crowd estimated at three hundred, and Pilar Lafuente was designated the guest of honor. The ceremony began with a moment of silence in honor of those killed during the revolt, and then continued with a speech by Pilar, who stressed the dedication and commitment of her sister to the communist cause and expressed happiness that new generations continued to uphold these tenets. In an interview before the ceremony she was overcome with emotion as she thanked the people of Asturias for remembering her sister. As she declared: "To name Aida is to name a people known to defend its ideals, a people that was defeated and betrayed."[79] The members of the committee expressed satisfaction with the ceremony, stating that the monument would "help so that history is not written by only a few."[80] According to the coordinator of the Asturian IU, Francisco de Asís Fernández, the ceremony "has a popular and political character; it is not a nostalgic celebration or historicist and not of a funerary type."[81] The monument itself is a plain monolith of white marble incised with an outline of the province of Asturias and bearing the words "October Revolution 1934." Above the image of the province is a pentagon bearing a bronze plaque with a portrait of Aida. On the plaque below her portrait is the following inscription: "Aida de la Fuente, The Red Rose, 1918–1934, and your comrades."

The pronouncements surrounding the monument continued to demonstrate that the memory of Aida Lafuente had become one of heroism and commitment to ideals; a memory to be utilized as inspiration for a new

Figure 6
Monument to Aida
Lafuente, near the
church of San Pedro
de los Arcos in Oviedo.
PHOTO BY THE AUTHOR

generation of leftist politicians and their followers. As Asís Fernández's statement above makes clear, the politicians of today are less interested in history
than they are in memory. The history of Aida Lafuente and the things she
did in the revolution were submerged within the meanings drawn from her
memory, especially the construction of one that best suited the political
purposes of the leftist parties in the late 1990s. Such concerns included
generating political activism among the youth of Asturias; and by commemorating the heroism and dedication to progressive ideals of a teenager,
the political directors hoped to inspire a similar dedication among the youth
of today. Generating support was particularly important to the IU in the
period 1995–1997. The decline of the socialist government and the rise of
the conservative Popular Party culminated in the elections of 1996, when
José María Aznar defeated the long-reigning PSOE and was installed as the
first conservative president since the 1970s. The conservative turn in the
Spanish electorate reduced the support of the leftist parties, especially
the IU.[82] In many ways the IU used symbols of the left, including Aida

Figure 7
"Aida de la Fuente: The
Red Rose, 1918–1934.
And your comrades."
PHOTO BY THE AUTHOR

Lafuente and Che Guevara, as a deliberate strategy to energize supporters
and to gain support, particularly among the young.

In 1998, the municipal government of Oviedo was not the only city to
commemorate the young woman. In August of that year, the local government of Gijón announced that forty-nine streets would be receiving new
names. Although most of these streets had only recently been constructed,
seven were renamed in an effort to eliminate names with no link to the
history of the city. On 11 August 1998, the small street of Xovería in the
industrial zone of Tremañes was renamed after Aida Lafuente (see figure
8).[83] Despite the avowed purpose to choose names with some connection to
the city, Xovería was renamed for a young woman who had virtually no
direct connection to Gijón. One possible explanation for this is that many of
the new names had been chosen from suggestions made by citizens or
groups, and perhaps some group of residents from the largely working-class
section of the city submitted Lafuente's name. Indeed, the region did have
an active residents' association, which repeatedly protested the slow pace

Figure 8 Aida Lafuente Street, Gijón. PHOTO BY THE AUTHOR

with which the signs for the new streets were erected. In fact, members of the neighborhood accused city officials of discrimination by favoring improvements in other, more wealthy districts, since the streets in the working-class areas did not have markers until late March 1999.[84]

CONCLUSION

The continued persistence of the memories of October 1934 showed that the events still had enormous power, although the passage of time and the current social, political, and cultural factors have significantly modified interpretations. Many viewed the events as something largely irrelevant to their daily lives, but others continued to invoke the legacy of the insurrection. As shown in this chapter, two of the most popular and significant symbols are the martyrs of Turón and Aida Lafuente, and each shows no sign of diminishing in importance. Many individuals routinely pray to the martyrs of Turón, while others name their children after Aida Lafuente.[85] The martyrs and Lafuente are also now commemorated on a new medium for perpetuating memory—the Internet. Such connections, however, are often ephemeral. One such example is the Web site of the Colegio San Antonio in the city of Ciaño. Until recently the site included pages dedicated to a general history of the revolt; an account of the clerics' deaths and a general tribute to them; and detailed biographies of each of the nine ecclesiastics, including pictures.[86] A recent check of this Web site, however, shows that the material is no longer posted there. However, just as the previous commemorative sites disappear, new ones begin; Internet searches conducted every few months often turn up new references to the martyrs of Turón, Aida Lafuente, and the October revolt in general. Some recent finds include writings about the travels of a Passionist Brother, Victor Hoagland, who attended the canonization ceremony of the martyrs in 1999, and a story on the premiere of a short film about Aida Lafuente.[87] In spite of these efforts, while the martyrs and Lafuente are remembered for many reasons, they are generally not recalled for what ultimately might be their most important legacy: the role played by commemorations of them, and of the October revolt as a whole, in triggering the Spanish Civil War.

NOTES

INTRODUCTION

1. These include the anarchist's so-called *tres ochos* of 1933 and the military revolt led by General José Sanjurjo in 1932.
2. For a literary analysis of some of the material produced in the wake of the revolt, see Sanchez, *Fact and Fiction*.
3. Payne, *El colapso de la República*.
4. Graham, *The Spanish Republic at War*, 77.
5. Moa, *Los orígenes de la guerra civil española*, 9. See also, by the same author, *El derrumbre de la segunda república y la guerra civil*. For more on the public debate over Moa's books and others like them, see chapter 6 in this volume.
6. Moa, *El derrumbre de la segunda república y la guerra civil*, 9. See also Palomino, *1934: La guerra civil empezó en Asturias*. The belief is not, however, exclusive to conservative historians. Stanley Payne summarizes the views of prominent historians in *Spain's First Democracy*, 222–23.
7. This included postcards showing the destruction of buildings in Oviedo. Anonimo español, "Los sucesos revolucionarios de Asturias," 1 album, 8 cards. Archivo General de la Guerra Civil Española, PS-Madrid, Leg. 934.
8. Throughout the text I use the terms pro- and anti-revolutionary and leftist and conservative to refer broadly to those who either supported the rebels or opposed them. The two sides are not monolithic and each represents a diversity of political opinions, especially on the left where the groups ranged from conservative Republicans to anarchists. Not all of the groups I characterize as pro-revolutionary were in favor of a fundamental reshaping of society along the lines of that which briefly occurred in Asturias during the insurrection. Nonetheless, the organizations opposed the conservative administration's repression of the revolt and favored such measures as amnesty and the rehiring of workers fired in the wake of October's events. Most if not all of these groups eventually joined with the authentically revolutionary parties to form the Popular Front electoral coalition in 1936. The

choice of terminology also accurately reflects the polarization that emerged during 1935 with each side declaring the other to be either revolutionary or reactionary: there was no longer any middle ground.

9. Eksteins, *Rites of Spring.*
10. Avilés Farré, *La fe que vino de Rusia.*
11. Originally, work in the field of cultural memory focused on the role that memory played in developing and altering conceptions of national identity. See Nora, *Realms of Memory.* Perhaps only the study of Holocaust memorials and memories has generated more literature than that of the post–World War I period.
12. Halbwachs, *The Collective Memory* and *On Collective Memory.* Psychologists have also begun examining the social context of individual memory; see Rubin, *Remembering Our Past.*
13. Winter and Sivan, "Setting the Framework," 6, 9–10.
14. Sherman, "Art, Commerce, and the Production of Memory in France after World War I," 186.
15. Wertsch, *Voices of Collective Remembering,* 5–7. For similar arguments, see Kansteiner, "Finding Meaning in Memory," 180; Irwin-Zarecka, *Frames of Remembrance,* 4; and Radley, "Artefacts, Memory and a Sense of the Past," 46.
16. Kansteiner calls them "multimedia collages" ("Finding Meaning in Memory," 190).
17. Ibid., 188.
18. Wertsch, *Voices of Collective Remembering,* 27–28, 62–64.
19. Ibid.,13; and Kansteiner, "Finding Meaning in Memory," 183.
20. Wertsch, *Voices of Collective Remembering,* 60–62.
21. See Mosse, *Fallen Soldiers.*
22. On Europe in general, see Eksteins, *Rites of Spring*; for Germany, see Verhey, *The Spirit of 1914.*
23. Mosse, *Fallen Soldiers,* chapter 1.
24. Despite Spain's neutrality, the conflict did have a profound effect on the country; see Romero Salvadó, *Spain 1914–1918.*
25. See Álvarez Junco, "El nacionalismo español como mito movilizador."
26. On the martyrs themselves, see Coope, *The Martyrs of Córdoba*; and Wolf, *Christian Martyrs in Muslim Spain.*
27. On the nationalist significance of what is also known as the Peninsular War, see Álvarez Junco, "El nacionalismo español como mito movilizador." For a more detailed discussion on Spanish nationalism in the nineteenth century, see Álvarez Junco, *Mater Dolorosa.*
28. See Roberts, *Civilization without Sexes*; Kundrus, "Gender Wars"; and Thébaud, "The Great War and the Triumph of Sexual Division."
29. The fact that each side employed similar imagery also reveals a more fundamental point: the ubiquity of traditional notions of proper masculine and feminine behaviors. In many ways traditional standards of gendered conduct proved stronger and more lasting than any political ideology, whether conservative or revolutionary.

30. González Calleja, "The Symbolism of Violence during the Second Republic," 28.

31. Wertsch, in *Voices of Collective Remembering*, 151, relies on a series of questionnaires and surveys; and Kansteiner endorses a similar strategy in "Finding Meaning in Memory," 194–95.

32. See also González Calleja, "The Symbolism of Violence during the Second Republic."

33. I deal with such issues in chapter 6.

34. Wertsch, *Voices of Collective Remembering*, 121–22.

35. In determining reception Verhey discusses various materials and approaches before arguing that newspapers represent one of the only viable sources (*The Spirit of 1914*, 12–15). For events during the October revolt, see the local study of the press in Granada in Gutiérrez del Castillo, "El movimiento revolucionario de 1934."

36. For a good description of how conservatives viewed the trials, see Arrarás, *Historia de la Segunda República española*, vol. 3, 153–54. At the time of the trials Arrarás was a contributor to the conservative journal *Acción Española*. In the July 1935 edition he expressed his disappointment in the fact that those responsible for the murders at Turón would not be executed. See also Carretero, *1935: Un balance de vergüenzas políticas*.

37. Tusell, *La elecciones del Frente Popular en España*, vol. 1, 229–319. The campaign in Galicia generally focused more on regional rather than national concerns (319).

38. Benavides, *La revolución fué así*; Solano Palacio, *La Revolución de Octubre*.

39. López Ochoa, *Campaña militar de Asturias en octubre de 1934*. Accounts by revolutionaries include Manuel Grossi Mier, *La insurrección de Asturias*, and Solano Palacio, *La Revolución de Octubre*.

40. Villar wrote *La represión de octubre: Documentos para la historia de nuestra civilización* under the pseudonym Ignotus. The Bold Knight is the pen name of José María Carretero, whose works include *¡Viva la Revolución! Los malhechores de la politica*; *Traidores a la Patria (La verdad sobre Asturias y Cataluña)*; *1935: Un balance de vergüenzas políticas*; and *La Agonía de españa: Los culpables*.

41. Montseny wrote for Solano Palacio, while Oria contributed to Martínez, *Dos jesuitas martires en Asturias*. Oria was the brother of Ángel Herrera Oria, one of the most powerful conservatives in the country.

42. In the case of the communists, numbers from the Civil War show that the Spanish Communist Party often published pamphlets in large quantities. A list of forty publications dated 16 August 1938 shows that a total of 1,751,543 copies were produced, of which 1,105,117 had been distributed to that point. "Relación de las publicaciones del P.C.," Archivo General de la Guerra Civil Española, PS–Madrid 2102.

43. One official at an airport outside of Madrid reported firing two workers after he caught them in possession of such materials. See Souto Kustrín, *"Y ¿Madrid? ¿Qué hace Madrid?"* 378; see also chapter 3 in this volume.

44. See chapter 2 in this volume.

45. See the photographs in Arrarás, *Historia de la Segunda República Española,* vol. 4, 34, 53.

46. The date was 13 February 1936. Tusell, *La elecciones del Frente Popular en España*, vol. 1, 241–42, 254, 312.

47. The events were held in Medina del Campo and in Valencia. The leadership traveled between them by airplane (*New York Times,* 1 July 1935).

48. See Vincent, "The Martyrs and Saints."

49. Bowers, *My Mission to Spain,* 105. Another North American view can be found in Madero, *El Octubre español.* Although the author favors the left, the prologue expresses the sense of extremism that had been developing in the aftermath of the revolt.

50. Sir G. Graham, quoted in Ealham, *Class, Culture and Conflict in Barcelona,* 165.

51. Iglesias Somoza, *Episodios de la Revolución,* 11, 13–16, 164, 166.

52. Bergés, *Explicación de Octubre,* 19–20.

53. Ibid., 88–91. Later, during the Civil War, the socialist Antonio Ramos Oliveira claimed that the revolt had attracted the "sympathies of the middle classes and of a conservative minority" (*On the Eve of Civil War in Spain,* 21).

54. Bergés, *Explicación de Octubre,* 153, 199.

I. THE REVOLUTION OF OCTOBER 1934

1. Taibo, *Asturias 1934,* vol. 1, 123.

2. Adrian Shubert, in *The Road to Revolution in Spain,* 9–10, 16, explains why the revolt was most successful in Asturias. He argues that five developments between 1919 and 1934 proved decisive in leading Spain on the road to revolution: (1) a sustained crisis in the coal industry, (2) an inability of the miners' unions to alleviate the economic difficulties, (3) the failure of the Republican government to effect significant change in socioeconomic circumstances to improve living conditions, (4) the fear that conservative forces in the government would eliminate constitutional rule and implement an authoritarian regime, and (5) the creation of an Alianza Obrera that included all of the major working-class parties.

3. Many politicians and critics in the period 1934–1939 argued that the PSOE bore sole responsibility for the revolution, and conservative historians have echoed this claim. Recent examples include García de Tuñón Aza, *El Socialismo*; Moa, *El derrumbe de la segunda república y la Guerra Civil*; and De la Cierva, *La Revolución de Octubre.*

4. For a general survey of economic development, see Tortella, *The Development of Modern Spain.*

5. García Delgado, "Tensiones y problemas en la economía española de los primeros años trienta," 57–60.

6. *Boletín del Ministerio de Trabajo,* January 1935; quoted in Preston, *The Coming of the Spanish Civil War,* 219, n.2.

7. García Delgado, "Tensiones y problemas en la economía española de los primeros años trienta," 57–60.

8. Malefakis, *Agrarian Reform and Peasant Revolution in Spain,* 110.

9. Shubert, *The Road to Revolution in Spain,* 61.

10. Anes, "Early Industrialization in Asturias: Bounds and Constraints," 213–14.

11. Ojeda, "La crisis económica asturiana de los años 30," 67.

12. Vázquez García, "El contexto económico de octubre del '34 en Asturias," 77.

13. Ojeda, "La crisis económica asturiana de los años 30," 64, 67–70.

14. Vázquez García, "El contexto económico de octubre del '34 en Asturias," 79–80.

15. Juliá, *Historia del socialismo español,* 83.

16. For the results, see Payne, *Spain's First Democracy,* 180; and Irwin, *The 1933 Cortes Elections.*

17. Payne, *Spain's First Democracy,* 189.

18. Juliá, *Historia del socialismo español,* 85–87.

19. Heywood, *Marxism and the Failure of Organised Socialism in Spain,* 110–11.

20. Juliá, "Los socialistas y el escenario de la futura revolución," 116, 118.

21. Graham, *The Spanish Republic at War,* 46.

22. Although enthusiasm for a more radical plan was not unanimous within the socialist movement, the dissenters had grown increasingly weak by January 1934. On 27 January 1934, UGT representatives voted overwhelmingly—33 in favor, 2 against—to accept a more radical course. Rosal, *1934: Movimiento revolucionario de octubre,* 188–97; and Heywood, *Marxism and the Failure of Organised Socialism in Spain,* 136–38.

23. Payne, *Spain's First Democracy,* 193. For an insider's view of these changes within the leadership, see Rosal, *1934: Movimiento revolucionario de octubre,* esp. 151–205; and Vidarte, *El bienio negro y la insurrección de Asturias.*

24. Juliá, *Historia del socialismo español,* 93, 101–2. Largo Caballero's account of socialist preparations can be found in his *Escritos de la República,* 83–158.

25. Juliá, "Los socialistas y el escenario de la futura revolución," 124.

26. Founded in the early years of the twentieth century, the Radical Republican Party had become increasingly conservative over time. See Álvarez Junco, *El emperador del paralelo*; and Townson, *The Crisis of Democracy in Spain.*

27. Payne, *Spain's First Democracy,* 198.

28. Ibid.

29. Preston, "Spain's October Revolution and the Rightist Grasp for Power," 563.

30. Not all regulations had been repealed, and some, such as the system of labor negotiations, continued to return decisions favorable to workers. Payne, *Spain's First Democracy,* 197.

31. Payne, *A History of Fascism,* 255.

32. Preston, "Spain's October Revolution and the Rightist Grasp for Power," 556, 560.

33. Payne, *Spain's First Democracy,* 208.

34. See Boyd, "The Second Battle of Covadonga," 37–64; and chapter 2 in this volume.

35. *El Sol,* 11 September 1934, quoted in Taibo, *Asturias 1934,* vol. 1, 112.

36. Payne, *A History of Fascism,* 255. On the JAP, see Lowe, "The Juventud de Acción Popular and the 'Failure' of 'Fascism' in Spain."

37. Preston, "Spain's October Revolution and the Rightist Grasp for Power," 560–61.

38. Payne, *A History of Fascism*, 198.

39. See Heywood, *Marxism and the Failure of Organised Socialism in Spain*, 110–14.

40. Quoted in ibid., 129–30.

41. Heywood, *Marxism and the Failure of Organised Socialism in Spain*, 127; see also Souto Kustrín, *"Y ¿Madrid? ¿Qué hace Madrid?"* esp. 86–101.

42. Payne, *Spain's First Democracy*, 194; and Juliá, *Historia del socialismo español*, 103.

43. Serrano Poncela, "Crisis de confianza," *Renovación*, 18 April 1934, 134, quoted in Viñas, *La formación de la Juventudes Socialistas Unificadas* 12–13.

44. Viñas, *La formación de la Juventudes Socialistas Unificadas*, 13.

45. Thirteen people were killed in Madrid during this cycle of violence and another thirty-one were wounded. Of those killed eight had been affiliated with FE, five with the socialists, one with Acción Popular, and the remainder were without clear affiliation. Souto Kustrín, *"Y ¿Madrid? ¿Qué hace Madrid?"* 425.

46. Juliá, *Historia del socialismo español*, 105–6. A detailed description of the organizational process of the militias can be found in Rosal, *1934: Movimiento revolucionario de octubre*, 207–50.

47. See Payne, *Fascism in Spain*.

48. Juliá, *Historia del socialismo español*, 193–200.

49. Payne, *Spain's First Democracy*, 197–99.

50. Juliá, *Historia del socialismo español*, 122–23.

51. Preston, *The Coming of the Spanish Civil War*, 113–17.

52. Heywood, *Marxism and the Failure of Organised Socialism in Spain*, 143.

53. On Maurín, see Alba, *Dos revolucionarios Joaquín Maurín, Andreu Nin*; and Tyree, "Toward the Second Revolution."

54. Durgan, *BOC 1930–1936*, 22–171. On the *tres ochoas* of 1933, see Ealham, *Class, Culture and Conflict in Barcelona*, chapter 6; and Casanova, *De la calle al frente*, chapter 4.

55. Durgan, *BOC 1930–1936*, 186–91, 207–12, 240–47.

56. Juliá, *Historia del Socialismo español*, 4–115.

57. Bizcarrondo, "De las alianzas obreras al frente popular," 89–90, 106–14. See also, Payne, *The Spanish Civil War, the Soviet Union, and Communism*.

58. The Syndicates of Opposition, also known as *treintistas*, had split from the CNT in late 1931 and early 1932. Their moderate leaders opposed violent radicalism and stressed union cooperation and pragmatism. For details, see Ealham, *Class, Culture and Conflict in Barcelona*; Balcells, *Trabajo industrial y organización obrera en la Cataluña contemporánea*; and Kern, *Red Years / Black Years*.

59. Valeriano Orobón Fernández, quoted in Casanova, *De la calle al frente*, 133.

60. At the national meeting in February, other CNT regional affiliates who supported increased cooperation among worker groups included Galicia and Valladolid. See Casanova, *De la calle al frente*, 133.

61. Durgan, *BOC 1930–1936*, 248–49.

62. Barrio Alonso, *Anarquismo y anarcosindicalismo en Asturias,* 395–96.

63. The four main points of the pact stated: (1) the agreement was between the unions only and did not include the PSOE; (2) other worker groups would be accepted if they agreed to the principles of the alliance; (3) the ultimate goal was the formation of a federalist, socialist regime; and (4) the workers would be free to choose the form of social organizations after the successful conclusion of the revolution (Shubert, 157–58).

64. Barrio Alonso, *Anarquismo y anarcosindicalismo en Asturias,* 397–98.

65. Ibid., 399–400.

66. Bizcarrondo, *Octubre del 34,* 39.

67. Payne, *The Spanish Civil War, the Soviet Union, and Communism,* 50–52.

68. Bizcarrando, "De las alianzas al frente popular," 90.

69. General histories of the revolt include Taibo, *Asturias 1934;* Aguado Sánchez, *La revolución de octubre de 1934;* and Díaz Nosty, *La comuna asturiana.*

70. Payne, *Spain's First Democracy,* 214.

71. Preston, *The Coming of the Spanish Civil War,* 127.

72. Taibo, *Asturias 1934,* vol. 2, 48. See also Souto Kustrín, *"Y ¿Madrid? ¿Qué hace Madrid?"* chapter 3.

73. Payne, *Spain's First Democracy,* 216–17. On local events in Albacete, see Deogracias Carrión Iñiguez, *La insurrección de octubre de 1934 en la provincia de Albacete .*

74. Taibo, *Asturias 1934,* vol. 1, 120–21, 130.

75. Díaz Nosty, in *La comuna asturiana,* 169, judges that the first attacks took place in Llanera, a small town north of Oviedo.

76. Both Grossi and Solano Palacio later published accounts of the revolt.

77. Taibo, *Asturias 1934,* vol. 1, 134–39, 155–59.

78. Cardona, *El poder military en la España contemporánea hasta la guerra civil,* 205.

79. Many subsequent accounts of the revolution and the repression singled out these troops as the most violent and brutal. Writers often characterized the largely white troops of the Spanish Foreign Legion as criminals while referring to the African troops as "moors." Payne, in his account of the revolt, judged that these troops performed neither no more nor no less brutally than either the revolutionaries or the regular army. Payne, *Spain's First Democracy,* 430, n.65. See also chapter 4 in this volume.

80. Taibo, *Asturias 1934,* vol. 1, 194–207, 227–30, and vol. 2, 21–26.

81. Díaz Nosty, *La comuna asturiana,* 178–79.

82. Ibid., 184.

83. Llano Roza de Ampudia, *Pequeños anales de quince días,* 3–32, describes the first days of fighting.

84. Tabio, *Asturias 1934,* vol. 1, 242–44, 251.

85. Payne, *Spain's First Democracy,* 220.

86. Llano Roza de Ampudia, *Pequeños anales de quince días,* 116–24.

87. Taibo, *Asturias 1934,* vol. 2, 87–95.

88. *La Revolución de octubre en España: La rebelión del Gobierno de la Generalidad (octubre 1934),* 40.

89. Taibo, in *Asturias 1934,* vol. 2, 243, lists the famous buildings damaged or destroyed in Oviedo. He further states that most of the destruction occurred in the course of the conflict and that the buildings were not deliberately harmed by either side. In the wake of the governmental repression, however, the conservative press placed the blame solely on the revolutionaries.

90. *La Revolución de octubre en España,* 36, 40.

91. Llano Roza de Ampudia, *Pequeños anales de quince días,* 207.

92. Taibo, *Asturias 1934,* vol. 2, 243; and Payne, *Spain's First Democracy,* 220. Taibo states that one reason why the government casualties are underreported is the lack of statistics regarding the African troops.

2. SACRED BLOOD

1. The account is based on *Los mártires de Turón: Notas biográficas y reseña del martiro de los religiosos bárbaramente asesinados por los revolucionarios en Turón (Asturias), el 9 de octubre de 1934,* 57–72. The official name of the order is the Institue of the Brothers of the Christian Schools but they are commonly called De La Salle Brothers.

2. In one town the JCE was accused of being fascist because its members were seen wearing blue uniforms during a soccer match in June 1932. According to the same author, they only had blue shirts because they were the cheapest type available. See Noral Suárez, *Langreo Rojo,* 149–50. On the JCE, see Watanabe, *Confesionalidad católica y militancia política.*

3. The account of the death of Father Inocencio given in *Episodios de la revolución en Asturias 1934: Los Pasionistas de Mieres (Asturias) y la Revolución de Octubre de 1934: Episodios narrados por los mismos protagonistas* claims that the prisoners knew this to be hypocrisy and that they would soon be killed by the rebels (55).

4. *Los mártires de Turón,* 67–68.

5. Ibid., 72.

6. Shots of the funerals appear in ibid., 107, 109, 111, 113, 115, 117–21.

7. In many fascist regimes the state becomes the religion. For example, see Gentile, *The Sacralization of Politics in Fascist Italy.*

8. See Ullman, *The Tragic Week.*

9. For details, see Cárcel Ortí, *La persecución religiosa en España ndurante la Segunda República,* 107–15; and Callahan, *The Catholic Church in Spain,* 282–86, esp. n.33.

10. Ullman, *The Tragic Week,* 285.

11. See Lannon, "Modern Spain."

12. The rhetoric of foreign invaders often included varying degrees of anti-Semitism. I discuss this issue further at the end of this chapter.

13. Vincent, *Catholicism in the Second Republic,* 154.

14. Callahan, *The Catholic Church in Spain,* 311.

15. On anticlericalism in October 1934, see Álvarez Junco, "El anticlericalismo en el movimiento Obrero." General treatments of the theme can be found in Caro Baroja, *Introducción a una historia contemporánea del anticlericalismo español*; and in Sanabria, "Anticlerical Politics."

16. Quoted in Ordovas, *Historia de la Asociacíon Católica Nacional de Propagandistas*, 177.

17. Other conservative parties with Catholic identities include Derecha Liberal Republicana (Liberal Republican Right, DLR) and the monarchist Unión Monárquica Nacional (National Monarchist Union). See Robinson, *The Origins of Franco's Spain*, chapter 1.

18. The ACNP was founded in 1909 by a Jesuit priest named Ángel Ayala. During the Second Republic its official membership never exceeded four hundred, but it did include highly important and influential figures such as Herrera and José María Gil Robles—future leader of the CEDA. See Ordovas, *Historia de la Asociacíon Católica Nacional de Propagandistas*, 68–69, 181.

19. Vincent, *Catholicism in the Second Republic*, chapter 5.

20. Ordvas, *Historia de la Asociacíon Católica Nacional de Propagandistas*, 188–91.

21. Blasco, *Paradojas de la ortodoxia*, 232.

22. AN's original leadership council of ten included seven Propagandists. Later ACNP regulations declared that those in the organization's leadership positions should not be directly affiliated with any political party. As a result Gil Robles replaced Herrera as AN's president in October 1931. See Ordovas, *Historia de la Asociacíon Católica Nacional de Propagandistas*, 188–91, 221.

23. Callahan, *The Catholic Church in Spain*, 313–14.

24. Vincent, *Catholicism in the Second Republic*, 142.

25. Blasco, *Paradojas de la ortodoxia*, 230.

26. The election also revealed the relatively feeble support for Alcalá-Zamora's DLR, which managed to obtain only twenty-seven seats. Payne, *Spain's First Democracy*, 51.

27. Payne, *Spain's First Democracy*, 167–69. See also Montero, *La CEDA*. The debate over the true nature and intentions of the CEDA remains intense. Some (e.g., Payne and Robinson) view the CEDA as essentially legalist while still hoping for radical revisions of the Republican system. Others (e.g., Preston, *The Coming of the Spanish Civil War*; and Graham, *The Spanish Republic at War*) view the CEDA as more or less determined from the beginning to destroy the Republican system and seize power.

28. Despite their differences, the forces of the right often maintained cordial personal relationships and continued by and large to work together in the Cortes.

29. On Alfonsine monarchists, see Gil Pecharromán, *Conservadores subversivos*; and for Carlists, see Blinkhorn, *Carlism and Crisis in Spain*. The smallest and perhaps least influential party on the right of the political spectrum was the Falange Española (Spanish Phalanx, FE). Founded in 1933 the FE largely remained outside of the political mainstream. Its greatest impact prior to the Civil War came during spring 1936 when fascists engaged in running battles with socialist militias. Stanley Payne remains the leading scholar of Spanish fascism and his classic study is *Falange: A*

History of Spanish Fascism, and an updated account is Payne's *Fascism in Spain, 1923–1977.* The Spanish version is *Franco y José Antonio: El extraño caso del fascismo español.* For comparisons with other fascist movements, see Payne's *A History of Fascism, 1914–1945.*

30. Gil Pecharromán, *Conservadores subversivos,*188.

31. One of the most famous examples in Spanish history is that of the martyrs of Cordoba. Many of those killed seemingly went out of their way to be martyred as a response to the increasing attraction of the Islamic culture and religion that threatened the continued existence of the Christian community. See Collins, *Early Medieval Spain,* 213–19.

32. Lannon, "The Church's Crusade against the Republic," 48–51. See also Mary Vincent, *Catholicism in the Second Republic: Religion and Politics in Salamanca, 1930–1936,* chapter 1.

33. Payne, *Spain's First Democracy,* 81–86.

34. Blasco, *Paradojas de la ortodoxia,* 222.

35. Quoted in Boyd, *Historia Patria,* 227–28.

36. *Los mártires de Turón,* 19, 53, 63.

37. Lannon, "Modern Spain," 571, 577.

38. Asociación Católica de Propagandistas de Oviedo, *Asturias roja,* 5–9.

39. Martínez, *Dos jesuitas mártires en Asturias,* 11–21.

40. Ibid., 68–70.

41. *Los mártires de Turón,* 18.

42. Ibid., 25, 32.

43. The six devotees of Mary were Brothers Ancieto-Adolfo, Augusto-Andrés, Benjamín-Julian, Victoriano-Pío, Marciano-José, and Father Inocencio de la Inmaculada (*Los mártires de Turón,* 11–56).

44. *Los mártires de Turón,* 25, 48–49.

45. *Los mártires de Turón* quoted Brother Benjamin-Julian as saying he would go wherever the order sent him "even to Peking" (32, 56).

46. Rucabado, *Los mártires de Asturias,* 18.

47. Ibid., 14.

48. Although not a martyrology per se, the actions of members of the Catholic Miners Syndicate of Moreda who fought the revolutionaries were celebrated in a first-person account in Madera's *El Sindicato Católico de Moreda y la revolución de octubre.* Sarah Sanchez, in *Fact and Fiction* (chapters 4 and 5), offers a literary analysis of this text as well as the ones by Jenaro G. Geijo and Ignacio Núñez cited below.

49. Geijo, *Episodios de la revolución,* 3.

50. Ibid., 3.

51. Nuño del Robleda, *¿Por qué Oviedo se convirtió en ciudad mártir?* 32.

52. Ibid., 25–27. The phrasing echoes one of the most persistent explanations of the anticlericalism of the revolt, which argued that the rebels committed the crimes due to their hatred of religion.

53. Nuño del Robleda, *¿Por qué Oviedo se convirtió en Ciudad Mártir?* 35, 50.

54. Ibid., 121.

55. During the Civil War, as the Nationalist forces captured Asturias some leftists began referring to the province as a martyr. See Solano Palacio, *La tragedia del norte.*

56. Similarly, *Episodios de la revolución en Asturias 1934*, viii, compared the sufferings of the Passionist community during the revolt to that of Jesus at the crucifixion.

57. Cienfuegos, *Elegía de Asturias y otros poemas del dolor trágico de España*, 40–41. Pelayo was the legendary king of Asturias who began the reconquest of Spain after defeating Islamic forces at the Battle of Covadonga. Auseva is the mountain where Pelayo and his followers fled to a cave. The authors of *Octubre Rojo: Ocho dias que conmovieron a España* called General López Ochoa a new Pelayo (116).

58. Boyd, "The Second Battle of Covadonga," 41–56.

59. Ibid., 56.

60. Rieber and Kelly, "Substance and Shadow: Images of the Enemy," 7. A classic study of this process is Dower, *War without Mercy.*

61. Corbin, "Truth and Myth in History," 622.

62. Geijo, *Episodios de la revolución*, 155, 201–6.

63. Ibid., 125, 200, 287.

64. *Episodios de la revolución en Asturias 1934*, v, vii.

65. Ibid., 6–10, 27–28.

66. Ibid., 34–39, 244–47. The text also includes a slightly different version of the death of Father Inocencio, who was killed in Turón (53–60).

67. *Los mártires de Turón*, 73. The photograph of the hammer appears on page 74.

68. Acción Popular, *Terror*, 4. I address the issue of the young women more fully in chapter 5.

69. Asociación Católica de Propagandistas de Oviedo, *Asturias Roja*, 30–31, 17.

70. Cienfuegos, *Elegía de Asturias y otros poemas del dolor trágico de España*, 7, 55–58.

71. The Marqués served as a witness at Franco's marriage in 1923. See Preston, *Franco*, 41, 89.

72. Montero, *La CEDA*, vol. 1, 479; Gil Pecharromán, *Conservadores subversivos*, 236, 237.

73. Preston, "Alfonsist Monarchism and the Coming of the Spanish Civil War," 94.

74. Cienfuegos, *Elegía de Asturias y otros poemas del dolor trágico de España*, 47.

75. Montero, *La CEDA*, vol. 1, 262, 265, 269, 374; vol. 2, 348, 430–31. Arboeya also favored the creation of Catholic unions independent of both the church hierarchy and wealthy businessmen and land owners. See Benavides Gómez, *El fracaso social del catolicismo español*, and "Maximiliano Arboleya y su interpretación de la revolución de octubre," 253–67. On the rightist unions, see Winston, *Workers and the Right in Spain.*

76. Montero, *La CEDA*, vol. 1, 620; vol. 2, 430.

77. While extremely limited, the leftist organizations were not completely suppressed. See chapter 3 in this volume.

78. Arrarás, *Historia de la Segunda República Española*, vol. 2, 647.

79. Ibid., vol. 3, 129 and note 1. Arrarás reports that a total of 9,722,300 pesetas were given to the army. He records the following distributions (although they do not total the entire amount): 137,000 to the families of 137 officials and soldiers killed; 520,000 to 260 seriously wounded; 232,000 to 310 lightly wounded; 4,525,250 to 18,310 troops who took part in combat, and 3,074,550 to the 16,491 who served during the repression.

80. For example, see Carretero, *1935: Un balance de vergüenzas políticas*; and the issues of *Acción Español* for March, April, and July 1935.

81. An additional nine men received sentences of ten to twelve years in prison. The death sentences were never carried out. See Arrarás, *Historia de la Segunda República Española*, vol. 3, 153.

82. The trials were held in military courts, except the proceedings against Azaña that took place in parliament and those against Largo Caballero that were held in the Supreme Court. See Arrarás, *Historia de la Segunda República Española*, vol. 3: for González Peña, 73–79; for Azaña, 94–100, 167–68; for Bueno, 191; and for Largo Caballero, 253–56. Javier Bueno edited the Socialist newspaper *Avance* and was one of the leaders of the October revolt. A famous photograph of him was often cited as evidence of torture, Taibo, *Asturias 1934*, vol. 2, 14–16.

83. Gil Pecharromán, *Conservadores subversivos*, 190.

84. Blinkhorn, *Carlism and Crisis in Spain*, 188.

85. Gil Pecharromán, *Conservadores subversivos*, 191.

86. Blinkhorn, *Carlism and Crisis in Spain*, 192–97.

87. Gil Pecharromán, *Conservadores subversivos*, 192; and González Calleja, "La violencia y la política," 212–13.

88. For a detailed discussion of José Antonio's attitudes toward violence, see Payne, *Franco y José Antonio*, chapters 4 and 5.

89. Manuel Mateo, speech delivered at the Cine Madrid, 19 May 1935. The text of the speech was reprinted in *Arriba*, 23 May 1935 (*Arriba: Reproducción facsimil del Semanario de la Falange*, 2–3).

90. Payne, *Franco y José Antonio*, 275–81.

91. "La situación política," *Arriba*, 30 January 1936; reproduced in Río Cisneros and Conde Gargollo, *Obras completas de José Antonio Primo de Rivera*, 1032.

92. In chapter 3, I address the use of October by the left.

93. Montero, *La CEDA*, vol. 2, 111, 114–15.

94. Ibid., 317–21.

95. Reproduced in *Imágenes en guerra: Memoria estampada en la españa de los años 30*, 74.

96. Tusell, *La elecciones del Frente Popular en España* , vol. 1, 200, 203.

97. Castro Albarrán, *El derecho a la rebeldía*, 441.

98. Ibid., 423, 425–28. The play was written around 1619 by Lope de Vega. The plot involves a corrupt lord who abuses local peasant girls while conspiring to commit treason against the ruling monarchs, Ferdinand and Isabel. In response to these crimes the villagers of Fuenteovejuna murdered their tormentor. During the royal

investigation that followed, the villagers refused to reveal the individuals responsible for the killing and instead stated that the true author of the murder was "Fuente-ovejuna." During the Republic the play was reinterpreted by liberals as a tool for constructing a culturally educated population dedicated to democratic values. See Holquín, *Creating Spaniards*, esp. chapter 3.

99. Castro Albarrán, *El derecho a la rebeldía*, 437–38.

100. Carretero, *Traidores a la Patria*. *¡Los Responsables!* appeared in 1935, the others in 1936.

101. Carretero, *La Agonía de españa*, 92.

102. Ibid., 12–13.

103. Ibid., 81.

104. Ibid.

105. This later became a fundamental theme of both sides during the Civil War. See Núñez Seixas, "Nations in Arms Against the Invader."

106. Carretero, *La Agonía de España*, 34; *Traidores*, 107–8; and *1935: Un balance de ver-güenzas políticas*, 47.

107. The alleged historic crimes ranged from Judas's betrayal of Jesus to allegations related to the invasion of Islamic armies in 711 CE. See Blinkhorn, *Carlism and Crisis in Spain*, 179–80.

108. Pyrene, *Antiespañolismo*, 161. The index of the Comín Colomer collection in Madrid's National Library identifies Pyrene as the pseudonym of Victoriano Navarro González.

109. Ibid., 174.

110. Núñez, *La revolución de octubre de 1934*, vol. 1, 9.

111. Karl, *Asesinos de España*, 154. The original quotation reads: "Only knowledge of Judaism provides the key to understanding the true proposals of social democracy."

112. Those named by Karl included the socialist Ramón González Peña and the anarchist Eleuterio Quintanilla. See Karl, *Asesinos de España*, 20–21, 163, 247, 388–89.

113. Karl, *Asesinos de España*, 19, 335.

114. Vélez, *La revolución y la contrarevolución en españa*, 3, 65.

115. Blinkhorn, *Carlism and Crisis in Spain*, 204.

116. *El Pensamiento Navarro*, 2 February 1936; quoted in Tusell, *La elecciones del frente popular en España*, vol. 1, 286.

117. The parties of the Popular Front won 263 seats compared with just 133 for all rightist groups combined. Later maneuvering would increase the Popular Front's advantage. See Tusell, *La elecciones del frente popular en España*, vol. 2, 82–83; see also Payne, *Spain's First Democracy*, 271–77.

118. Gil Pecharromán, *Conservadores subversivos*, 249–50, 255, 271. The author states that the letters help explain the "climate of bellicose exaltation" that existed among conservatives during this period (276, n. 46). Lisardo Doval, the Civil Guard officer who governed Asturias in the immediate aftermath of the revolt, also received such letters. One note was signed "A Friend of Authority" while another provided

details on the alleged hiding place of a member of Oviedo's revolutionary committee. Sometimes the letters described crimes, including one from Vicente Peláez
Alonso who listed things taken from his house, including ten bottles of champagne,
nine hams, and two cans of anchovies. See Archivo General de la Guerra Civil
Española, PS-Gijon Serie j, Legajo 50, Expediente 1.

119. Blinkhorn, *Carlism and Crisis in Spain*, 219, 237–39, 243–50; and González Calleja,
"Hacia una nueva 'guerra carlista,'" 114.

3. "YOUR COMRADES WILL NOT FORGET!"

1. The Popular Front was an electoral alliance negotiated among various parties of the
left and center-left to contest the elections set for February 1936. For details on the
formation of the Popular Front, see Juliá, *Orígenes del frente popular en España*; and
Alexander and Graham, *The French and Spanish Popular Fronts.*

2. Pepe (José) Diaz at the Monumental Cinema [*sic*], Madrid. 2 June 1935. A tran-
script can be found at Fundación Pablo Iglesias (hereafter cited as FPI), AASM-517–7.

3. Benavides, *La revolución fué así.* 477. See also Sanchez, *Fact and Fiction*, chapter 7.

4. Carral, *Por qué mataron a Luis de Sirval,* 12. Casas Viejas was a small village where an
anarchist revolt in January 1933 triggered a brutal reaction by members of the
government's security forces. In the end twenty-two civilians were killed, with at
least twelve executed in cold blood. The incident caused a scandal within the
Republican-socialist government and helped speed the downfall of the coalition.
See, Payne, *Spain's First Democracy,* 129–34.

5. González Tuñón, *La rosa blindada,* 7.

6. "El pequeño cementerio fusilado," González Tuñón, *La rosa blindada,* 23.

7. Francisco Largo Caballero at the Cine Europa, Madrid, 12 January 1936; quoted in
Tusell, *La elecciones del frente popular en España,* vol. 1, 197.

8. During the Civil War some victims of the revolt petitioned the Republican government for compensation for injuries or deaths that occurred during the fighting.
Some examples of the cases handled by the Junta Provincial de Socorros e Indem-
nizaciones Pro-victimas de Octubre de 1934 include a father who wanted payment
because his fifteen-year-old daughter had been wounded by a bomb and subsequently had her arm amputated, and a widow with a two-year-old child whose
father had been killed in the fighting. Archivo General de la Guerra Civil Española
(hereafter cited as AGGC), PS-Gijón, serie H, carpeta 1, expedientes 11 and 2.

9. The most common number given during the time, as well as in subsequent histories, is 30,000. The historian Manuel Tuñón de Lara argues that the number
included all of those arrested following the insurrection as well as those previously
jailed for various political or common crimes. He estimates that the total number of
new prisoners was around 21,000, and that some of them were released at various
points during 1935 (Tuñón de Lara, *La II República*, vol. 2, 108). Pío Moa, on the
other hand, asserts that the total number arrested was around 15,000 and that most

of these were released within a few months (Moa, *El derrumbe de la Segunda República y la guerra civil*, 88). On the local level, Sandra Souto Kustrín reports that 2,000 people were jailed in Madrid following the defeat of the revolt there (Souto Kustrín, *"Y ¿Madrid?¿Qué hace Madrid?"* 282–83).

10. The report is reproduced in Gordón Ordás, *Mi Política en España*, vol. 2, 260–95. See also *What I Saw in Spain* by Leah Manning, who as a member of the British Labour Party visited Spain shortly after the revolt.

11. Details on the death of Vázquez can be found in Taibo, *Asturias 1934*, vol. 2, 161–62. In the same volume the author also describes the repression in great detail (97–145). For a conservative treatment of Vázquez's story, see Romero Cuesta, *El Sargento Vázquez*.

12. Díaz Nosty, *La comuna asturiana: Revolución de octubre de 1934*, 340.

13. Payne, *Spain's First Democracy*, 222.

14. For conservative examples, see chapter 2 in this volume.

15. Salazar, *El presidiario número 317*, 8.

16. Ibid., 31–128, 130–31. For information on the split in the Spanish socialist movement, see chapter 1 in this volume. The abbreviation UHP was a revolutionary slogan that, despite Salazar's account, generally stood for *Uníos, Hermanos Proletarios* (Unite, Proletarian Brothers) or *Union de Hermanos Proletarios* (Union of Proletarian Brothers).

17. Alvarez Portal, *Sirval*, 3–4.

18. Carral, *Por qué mataron a Luis de Sirval*, 22–30.

19. The published reports are reproduced in ibid., 39–64.

20. Alvarez Portal, *Sirval*, 30–53.

21. "To Luis de Sirval," by Angel Lazaro, *La Libertad*, 11 January 1936, 3.

22. Carral, *Por qué mataron a Luis de Sirval*, 12.

23. Ibid., 13–14.

24. The paintings celebrated the Spanish resistance to Napoleon. The first image depicts the fighting in the Puerto del Sol of Madrid that triggered the uprising. The second canvas shows French soldiers executing a long line of Spanish prisoners.

25. Solano Palacio, *La Revolución de Octubre* [1994], 176–78.

26. Martínez, *Dos jesuitas mártires en Asturias*, 55.

27. Vincent, *Catholicism in the Second Republic*, 96, 110.

28. Conservatives vehemently denied that the phrase had any political significance. See Vincent, *Catholicism in the Second Republic*, 231.

29. Solano Palacio, *La Revolución de Octubre* [1936], 49.

30. José María Martínez, an influential leader of the Asturian section of the CNT, was killed during the revolutionary events of October and not in the repression that followed. See Solano Palacio, *La Revolución de Octubre* [1936], 30, 43. The photos of the soldiers appear on 49–50, the martyrs of the revolt are on 64. Martínez is eulogized on 97 and 125. The memory of José María Martínez as a heroic martyr was perpetuated into the Civil War. A drawing of his image appeared for the month

of October on a calendar printed by an anarchist publishing house in 1937. Underneath the drawing was a brief biographical sketch that described him as one of the greatest and most active combatants of the October revolution. The work portrayed Martínez as "a true apostle of the social and revolutionary unity of action of the two fraternal syndicates" (Molne, *Calendario 1938*). Here Martínez's belief in union cooperation, often vilified before 1936, became the centerpiece of homage in reaction to developments during the Civil War that encouraged more active cooperation between the CNT and UGT.

31. Ignotus (Manuel Villar), *La represión de octubre,* 129.

32. Ibid., 5, 7.

33. Genesis 2:23 reads, "And the man said: This one at last is bone of my bones and flesh of my flesh! She is to be called Woman, because she was taken from Man" (*The New Jerusalem Bible*).

34. Ideological debates raged within the anarchist movement regarding political participation, including the act of voting itself. Even while Villar published the account that seemed to condone unity of action, he edited *Solidaridad Obrera* (the main CNT paper in Barcelona). The position of the newspaper was unambiguously against voting; in the issue of 11 January 1936 it declared: "The Socialists say: elections. We say: October. Elections? Deputies, politics? October! Asturias!" (quoted in Tusell, *La elecciones del frente popular en España*, vol. 1, 222). In general the "official" line remained firmly dedicated to apoliticism, but suggestions like Villar's were quite common. On the response of the anarchists to the 1934 revolt, see Ignotus, *El anarquismo en la insurrección de Asturias*; and Lopez, *La unidad de la CNT y su trayectoria*. For a cogent discussion of these debates, see Getman Eraso, "Rethinking the Revolution"; and Ealham, *Class, Culture and Conflict in Barcelona*, esp. 166–69.

35. Propaganda directed at anarchists both by the left, favoring voting, and by the right, favoring abstentionism, was particularly intense in Andalucia. See Tusell, *La elecciones del frente popular en España*, vol. 1, 229–47.

36. Sección Española del Socorro Rojo Internacional, *Los crímenes de la reacción española,* 69, 77.

37. Ibid., 23.

38. The book specifically lists five charges against General López Ochoa: first, that he provided gasoline to the legionnaires in order to burn workers alive; second, that the he paid each soldier ten pesetas for every person killed, requiring evidence in the form of victim's hand; third, that the legionnaires under his command buried workers alive; fourth, that his soldiers blew open the safe of the Bank of Asturias and stole its contents; fifth, that he gave his soldiers liquor and encouraged them to machine gun women and children. Sección Española del Socorro Rojo Internacional, *Los crímenes de la reacción española* 30–37, 43–44.

39. Reporte Sindicalista, *La represión en Asturias*, 8.

40. Ibid., 14.

41. Sanchez argues a similar point in *Fact and Fiction*; see, for example, 120–33.

42. See Ignotus (Manuel Villar), *La repression de octubre*; detailed accounts of the incidents are on 11, 22, 26, 118, 170–88. Photos of the bodies appear on 25, 31, 55, 61, 113. Regular army troops are shown on 43, 75, 109; the African soldiers can be seen on 97–103.

43. Sección Española del Socorro Rojo Internacional, *Los crímenes de la reacción española*, 5. The reference to the investigation by an ex-minister is the work of Gordón Ordás mentioned above.

44. Ibid., 10, 16.

45. Benavides, *La revolución fué así*, 400.

46. Ibid., 236, 356–58, 369, 403, 410–12.

47. The stories of atrocities can be found almost daily in the pages of *La Libertad* during January and February 1936.

48. Ruiz del Toro, *Octubre*, 173–74, 184–85, 189.

49. Signatories of the Popular Front electoral alliance include IR, UR, PSOE, UGT, JSU, PCE, Partido Sindicalista, and the POUM. The official electoral program is reproduced in Juliá, *Orígnes del frente popular en España*, 216–23.

50. Reporte Sindicalista, *La represión en Asturias*, 29. Similar ideas were expressed in Jaume, *La insurrección de octubre*, 67, 254. Yusti, *Octubre marxismo práctica,* advocates unity but only under the leadership of the Socialist Party, 81–83.

51. González Bayón, *El romancero de octubre*, 7–8.

52. Ibid., 16.

53. Los Presos de Asturias, *¡Acusamos!*, 3–4.

54. Ibid., 6. See also the Comité Central del Bloque Obrero y Campesino–Federación Comunista Ibérica, "Las lecciones de la insurrección de octubre."

55. Mont-Font (Joaquín Maurín), *Alianza Obrera,* 22. When the book was published, the BOC had recently merged with other small revolutionary groups to form the POUM. Maurín expressed similar ideas in *Revolución y contrarrevolución en España.*

56. Sección Española del Socorro Rojo Internacional, *Los crímenes de la reacción española*, 99. The shift in PCE strategy corresponded to the changing policies of the Soviet Union regarding cooperation with other leftist organizations. See Bizcarrondo, "De las Alianzas Obreras al Frente Popular."

57. Alvarez Suarez, *Sangre de octubre*, 55, 223.

58. Toucet, *El pueblo esta preso*, 20–30.

59. Ibid., 9–12.

60. The proposal was forwarded to the national offices and discussed at the executive committee meeting of 19 September 1935. *Actas de la UGT-CE 1935*. FPI, UGT-CE AARD-XX.

61. The representatives included Julio Alvarez del Vayo, Enrique de Francisco (Agrupación Socialista Madrileña), Juan Simon Vidarte (PSOE), Esteban Vega (SRI), Fernando Cazorla (JSU), Dolores Ibárruri (PCE), Manuel Lois (UGT), Belarmino Tomás, Juan José Manso (Representing Asturian workers), and Ramón Navarro (Partido Sindicalista). AGGC, PS-Madrid, legajo 2128. The document itself is undated, except for

the day of the scheduled rally (August 30), but the year is 1936. On 6 July 1936 the Provincial Committee of the Alianza Obrera of Vizcaya sent a letter to the National Committee of Homage to Asturias [*sic*]. The local committee asked for a clarification of the scheduled events and questioned why they had chosen the week of 30 August and not the anniversary dates of October. See FPI, PCE-CC/Correspondencia Alianza Obrera-Vizcaya AASM-517–10.

62. AGGC, PS-Madrid, legajo 2128.

63. See the proposal sent to the UGT and subsequently dealt with at the executive committee meeting of 26 March 1936. *Actas de la CE de UGT 1936*. FPI, UGT-CE AARD-XXI.

64. AGGC, PS-Madrid, legajo 2128. I could find no evidence that the events described ever took place. In all likelihood the event was canceled after the outbreak of Civil War in July, especially since Oviedo was quickly seized by the military. Despite the war, however, celebrations did take place on the anniversary of the revolt. See, for instance, *La Batalla*, 7 October 1936 (Barcelona), and *El Socialista*, 6 October 1936 (Málaga). Several decades later a monument dedicated to Aida Lafuente would be erected nearby (see chapter 6 in this volume).

65. The executive committee of the UGT received the proposal and ultimately declined to support the project, declaring that they were already committed to a previous one. Meeting of 26 March 1936, *Actas de la CE de UGT 1936*, FPI, UGT-CE AARD-XXI.

66. *El Socialista*, 15 April 1936.

67. Comité Central de Ayuda a los Presos y sus Familiares, *El pleno nacional resoluciones y acuerdos adoptados por las asamblea*, 3–5, 18, 23. For an example of PCE propaganda promoting unity, see Partido Comunista de España, "Los combates de octubre." A detailed discussion of PCE tactics can be found in Payne, *The Spanish Civil War, the Soviet Union, and Communism*, chapters 3 and 4.

68. For information on the organizational difficulties faced by the revolutionary organizations in Madrid following the defeat of the revolt, see Souto Kustrín, "*Y ¿Madrid? ¿Qué hace Madrid?*" chapter 4.

69. Executive committee of the UGT, meeting of 23 May 1935, *Actas de la UGT-CE 1935*, FPI, UGT-CE, AARD-XX.

70. Investigations during the Civil War by Franco's Servicio Nacional de Seguridad concluded that large sums of money had been sent to Spain through groups like SRI. A report from 31 October 1938 claimed that in 1935 SRI received 1,400,000 pesetas from the Soviet Union (Servicio Nacional de Seguridad, *Boletín de Información Antimarxista*, 14. AGGC Hemeroteca B126). The figures given by the Nationalists during the war may have been influenced by the enormous amounts of aid provided to the Republic by the Soviet Union. On such aid, see Kowalsky, *Stalin and the Spanish Civil War*. There was also a group called Comite Nacional de Ayuda a las Víctimas that operated out of Paris and was funded by the Comintern with an initial budget of 3 million francs; see Payne, *The Spanish Civil War, the Soviet Union, and Communism*, 65–66.

71. Elorza and Bizcarrondo, *Queridos camaradas*, 229–31.

72. PSOE, Comisón Ejecutiva, *Actas: 3 de enero de 1934—10 de diciembre de 1935,* FPI, AH-20–3, meetings of 6 November and 9 November 1934.

73. Ibid., meeting of 17 December 1934.

74. Souto Kustrín, "Taking the Street," 145–50.

75. For information on the process and results of labor unification, see Graham, "The Eclipse of the Socialist Left"; and Julía, *Historia del socialismo español*. On the youth groups, see Julía, *Historia del Socialismo Español*; and Viñas, *La formación de las Juventudes Socialistas Unificadas (1934–1936)*.

76. PSOE, Comisón Ejecutiva, *Actas: 3 de enero de 1934—10 de diciembre de 1935,* FPI, AH-20–3, meeting of 20 March 1935.

77. UGT, Comisón Ejectiva, *Actas 1935,* FPI, AARD-XX, meetings of the dates indicated.

78. The letter was read at the meeting of 25 April 1935, UGT, Comisón Ejectiva, *Actas 1935,* FPI, AARD-XX.

79. PSOE, Comisón Ejecutiva, *Actas: 3 de enero de 1934—10 de diciembre de 1935,* FPI, AH-20–3, meeting of 17 September 1935.

80. *Boletín de la Agrupación Socialista Madrileña,* no. extraordinario, May 1936.

81. "Manifesto electoral de Izquierda," reproduced in Julía, *Orígenes del frente popular en España,* 217.

82. A pamphlet published on the eve of elections stated that the drive for amnesty helped create the Popular Front. See Lopez Olivella, *¿Qué es el "Frente Popular"?* 15.

83. One was held in Madrid on 12 January and another in the nearby suburb of Getafe on 13 February. See Souto Kustrín, *"Y ¿Madrid? ¿Qué hace Madrid?"* 388.

84. Shubert, "A Reinterpretation of the Spanish Popular Front," 219, 220–21.

85. Ealham, *Class, Culture and Conflict in Barcelona,* 167. This is precisely what the organization did during spring 1936. See Getman Eraso, "Rethinking the Revolution."

86. Shubert, "A Reinterpretation of the Spanish Popular Front," 219, 220–21.

87. The first notice appears in *El Liberal,* 20 October 1934, and examples of benefit announcements can be seen in the issues for 27–29 March 1935.

88. PSOE, Comisón Ejecutiva, *Actas: 3 de enero de 1934—10 de diciembre de 1935,* FPI, AH-20–3, meeting of 14 August 1935.

89. UGT, Comisón Ejectiva, *Actas 1935,* FPI, AARD-XX, meeting of 12 September 1935.

90. See, for example, Ramos Oliveira, *La revolución española de octubre.*

91. Aznar Soler, *II Congreso Internacional de Escritores Antifascistas,* vol. 2, 69–71, 83. For information on the *Misiones Pedagógicas,* see Holguín, *Creating Spaniards.*

92. Quoted in Aznar Soler, "La revolución asturiana de octubre de 1934 y la literatura española," 87, 89.

93. "Nota de los Partidos Republicanos," reproduced in Julía, *Orígenes del frente popular en España,* 190–91.

94. Bergés, *Explicación de Octubre,* 173, 203.

95. Alvarez Portal, *Sirval,* 60.

96. López-Rey y Arrojo, *Un delito de asesinato.*

97. *El Socialista,* 28 February and 1 March 1936. Word of other ceremonies of homage can be found in *El Socialista,* 18 December 1935 and 10 March 1936.

98. Alvarez Portal, *Sirval,* 28.

99. Ibid., 29. It is unclear why Sirval's alleged notes used the name "Daida Peña." The story undoubtedly refers to Aida Lafuente, and Alvarez Portal himself later claimed that Sirval had already written an article that described how three legionaries murdered Aida Lafuente. In his account of Sirval's killing, Iganacio Carral reports that Sirval's notes included information on the shooting of "Aida Peña, known as La Libertaria" by Ivanoff (*Por qué mataron a Luis de Sirval,* 130). For more on Lafuente, see chapter 5 in this volume.

100. Alvarez Portal, *Sirval,* 36.

101. Ramos Oliveira, *La revolución española de octubre,* 54–55, 251.

102. "Guion para los oradores del Partido en los Mitines," 10 May 1935, and "Lo que enseña la experiencia" (n.d.), AGGC, PS-Madrid, Legajo 2128.

103. Agrupación de Abogados Defensores de los Encartados por los Sucesos de Octubre, *Boletín,* enero 1936, AGGC PS-Madrid, Legajo 1716.

104. Souto Kustrín, "*Y ¿Madrid? ¿Qué hace Madrid?*" 373.

105. Ibárruri, *¡A la carcel los verdugos de octubre!,* 7, 16.

106. Ibid., 8.

107. Payne, *Spain's First Democracy,* 318.

4. GRANDSONS OF THE CID: MASCULINITY, SEXUAL VIOLENCE, AND THE DESTRUCTION OF THE FAMILY

1. The imagery also clearly defines the woman's role as both mother and victim.

2. Hagemann, "German Heroes: The Cult of Death for the Fatherland in Nineteenth-Century Germany"; Bloom, Hagemann, and Hall, *Gendered Nations*; and Hoganson, *Fighting for American Manhood,* 8–9.

3. See Tosh, "Hegemonic Masculinity and the History of Gender."

4. Horne, "Masculinity in Politics and War in the Age of Nation-States and World Wars," 35. Stearns calls this the "breadwinner role" in *Be a Man,* 72.

5. See, for example, the collections of poems by Rafael Alberti and González Bayón.

6. Hagemann, "German Heroes," 129.

7. Vincent, "The Martyrs and Saints," 82–83.

8. Mosse, *Nationalism and Sexuality,* 10, 13, 154. Recent scholarship has acknowledged the power of this imagery while also arguing that it is not hegemonic. See Kundrus, "Gender Wars"; and Funck, "Ready for War?"

9. Balfour, *Deadly Embrace,* 172, 173, 174. El Tercio was a term for the military units commonly used during Spain's golden age of empire when the nation's military superiority was virtually unchallenged.

10. Hagemann in "German Heroes" argues that a similar process occurred in Germany over the course of the nineteenth century.

11. Karl, *Asesinos de España*, 20.

12. Ibid., 158.

13. Ibid., 391.

14. Ibid., 388–89.

15. Balfour, *Deadly Embrace*, 259.

16. Carretero (El Caballero Audaz), *Traidores a la Patria*, 50, 52.

17. Carretero (El Caballero Audaz), *La agonía de España*, 223.

18. Carretero (El Caballero Audaz), *Traidores a la Patria*, 88.

19. Ibid., 109.

20. Quoted in Alpert, "The Spanish Army and the Popular Front," 56.

21. Carretero (El Caballero Audaz), *La agonía de España*, 121.

22. On the development of "military nationalism" and the role of Millán-Astray, see Jensen, *Irrational Triumph*, esp. chapter 7. On the Foreign Legion, see Álvarez, *The Betrothed of Death*. A detailed discussion of the pre-Republican period can also be found in Boyd, *Praetorian Politics in Liberal Spain*.

23. Jensen, *Irrational Triumph*, 153.

24. Quoted in ibid., 166. Later, during the Civil War, Millán-Astray emphasized the similarities between Jesuits and soldiers, 167–68.

25. Ideologically the UME represented a diversity of conservative opinion ranging from fascist to Carlist, see Balfour, *Deadly Embrace*, 250.

26. Balfour, *Deadly Embrace*, 248.

27. See chapter 3 in this volume.

28. Camín, *El valle negro*, 80.

29. Solano Palacio, *La Revolución de Octubre* [1936], 43, 83.

30. Solano Palacio, *La Revolución de Octubre* [1994], 50–51.

31. Acción Popular, *Terror*, 4.

32. Prada, *Caminos de sangre*, 29. For more information on the formal aspects of the book, see Sanchez, *Fact and Fiction*, chapter 5.

33. González Bayón, *El romancero de octubre*, 69.

34. Ibid., 44.

35. Reporteros Reunidos, *Octubre rojo*, 109.

36. Nye, *The Origins of Crowd Psychology*.

37. Falasca-Zamponi, *Fascist Spectacle*, 24. See also Spackman, *Fascist Virilities*.

38. Coupled with the contestation of public space through meetings, the political rivals also violently fought for control of the streets. The fights, shootings, and other attacks were primarily conducted by young people, but the larger organizations showed little inclination or ability to end them.

39. Gutiérrez del Castillo, "El movimiento revolucionario de 1934," 228.

40. On the JAP, see Báez y Pérez de Tudela, "El ruido y la nueces"; and Lowe, "The Juventud de Acción Popular and the 'Failure' of 'Fascism' in Spain." The official history of AP covers the JAP, see Monge y Bernal, *Acción Popular*; as does Gil Robles, *No fue posible la paz*, chapter 10.

41. Carretero (El Caballero Audaz), *La agonía de España*, 19.

42. Some of the locations included Santiago de Compostela, the Escorial, and Uclés. See Báez y Pérez de Tudela, "El ruido y la nueces," 137–38; and Lowe, "The Juventud de Acción Popular and the 'Failure' of 'Fascism' in Spain," 37, n.113.

43. Arrarás, *Historia de la Segunda República Española*, vol. 1, 3, 91.

44. The manifesto appeared on 7 April 1935 and is quoted in ibid., vol. 3, 108–9.

45. The broadsheets are reproduced in Tusell, *La elecciones del Frente Popular en España*, vol. 2, 381, 383, 386. A satire of these political posters and Gil Robles's image appeared in *La Libertad*, 11 January 1936. One poster by *Acción Popular* displayed a woman's hands holding aloft a baby while the text urged women to protect their children by voting for AP. The newspaper's image, in contrast, showed a pair of hands holding a smallish figure resembling Gil Robles. The caption, "For the love of God! A rope, or we'll all be in the shit!" poked fun at the hysterical language frequently employed by election propaganda.

46. Arrarás, *Historia de la Segunda República Española*, vol. 3, 155, 178.

47. Ibid., 111.

48. Ibid., 133–34.

49. González Calleja, "Hacia una nueva 'guerra carlista,'" 113; and Arrarás, *Historia de la Segunda República Española*, vol. 3, 135.

50. Blinkhorn, *Carlism and Crisis in Spain*, 189, 210–14. The militarization of the Carlist paramilitary group *Requeté* accelerated throughout 1935, and by early 1936 they had organized and trained 25,000 volunteers who could be ready and armed to fight in twenty-four hours. See González Calleja, "La violencia y la política," 211–12.

51. Arrarás, *Historia de la Segunda República Española*, vol. 3, 240.

52. Ibid., 137–42.

53. On the role of the FE and other youth groups in fomenting violence, see González Calleja, "The Symbolism of Violence during the Second Republic," 38–42.

54. Arrarás, *Historia de la Segunda República Española*, vol. 3, 130–32; *New York Times*, 16 June 1935.

55. Souto Kustrín, *"Y ¿Madrid? ¿Qué hace Madrid?"* 373. Arrarás, *Historia de la Segunda República Española*, vol. 3, 146, puts the date at 5 June, adding that the government banned meetings by socialists and monarchists.

56. Gil Robles, *No fue possible la paz*, 284. See also Arrarás, *Historia de la Segunda República Española*, vol. 3, 156–59, which declares that the rightist meetings in Valencia were "a response to the parade of revolutionaries in Mestalla" (156).

57. Arrarás, *Historia de la Segunda República Española*, vol. 3, 159.

58. Azaña, *Obras completas*, vol. 3, 183.

59. *El Socialista*, 1 March 1936; and *Mundo Obrero*, 2 March 1936.

60. González Calleja, "The Symbolism of Violence during the Second Republic," 35.

61. Payne, *El colapso de la República*, 536, estimates the total number of political killings during the Republic at 2,225, with the following breakdown by years: 1931, 76;

1932, 102; 1933, 205; 1934, 1,527; 1935, 45; 1936, 300. See also Payne, "Political Violence during the Spanish Second Republic," 284.

62. Prada, *Caminos de sangre*, 8.

63. Nuño del Robleda, *¿Por qué Oviedo se convirtió en Ciudad Mártir?* 56.

64. Ibid., 87, 95, 159.

65. Prada, *Caminos de sangre*, 70–74.

66. On the importance of purity in Catholic youth culture, see Vincent, "Gender and Morals in Spanish Catholic Youth Culture" and "The Martyrs and the Saints," esp. 84–88.

67. Ruffinelli, *El vino y el pan de hombre,* n.p.

68. Solano Palacio, *La tragedia del norte,* 11.

69. Prada, *Caminos de sangre*, 83.

70. Vincent, "Gender and Morals," 283–84.

71. Acción Popular, *Terror,* 4.

72. *La Libertad,* 18 January 1936, 3. The photograph and statement appeared on 19 January 1936.

73. Taibo, *Asturias 1934,* vol. 2, 155–60.

74. Grayzel, *Women's Identities at War,* 85.

75. Seifert, "War and Rape," 59.

76. Copelon, "Surfacing Gender," 65–66, 76.

77. Karl, *Asesinos de España,* 391.

78. Nuño del Robleda, *¿Por qué Oviedo se convirtió en ciudad mártir?* 39–44.

79. Such imagery is common in commemorations of the revolt; see chapter 5 in this volume.

80. *Estampa,* 20 October 1934, 3.

81. On the changing roles of women during the period, see chapter 5 in this volume.

82. Glick, "Sexual Reform, Psychoanalysis, and the Politics of Divorce in Spain in the 1920s and 1930s," 68. Glick includes a listing of prominent figures (93–96). The public debate also included the formation in 1932 of a Spanish section of the World League for Sexual Reform. See Sinclair, "The World League for Sexual Reform in Spain."

83. Cleminson, "Beyond Tradition and 'Modernity,' " 116, 118.

84. Ibid., 121. See also Cleminson, " 'Science and Sympathy' or 'Sexual Subversion on a Human Basis'?" Despite such ideals the anarchist movement generally proved unable to escape from established notions of sexual behavior and identity so that the despised "bourgeois" notions of "respectability, 'manliness,' and 'femininity,' . . . were still exalted as the norm" (123).

85. Benavides, *La revolución fué así,* 41, 47.

86. Hoganson, *Fighting for American Manhood,* 49–50; Harris, "The 'Child of the Barbarian,' " 170–207; and Gullace, "Sexual Violence and Family Honor."

87. Seifert, "The Second Front," 39.

88. When the socialist leader Belarmino Tomás negotiated the surrender of revolution-

ary forces with General Lopez Ochoa he demanded that the African troops and the Foreign Legion not be allowed to enter Oviedo in the vanguard, supposedly because of the crimes they had committed. For details on the negotiations, see Taibo, *Asturias 1934*, vol. 2, 87–96. A sympathetic treatment of Tomás is offered in Menéndez García, *Belarmino Tomás.* Stories on the alleged crimes of Moroccan troops were even reported in the *New York Times*, 29 October 1934.

89. González Tuñón, *La rosa blindada*, 26.

90. Ibid., 27.

91. The emphasis is mine. González Tuñón, *La rosa blindada*, 26, 27. The poet's choice of words contained some interesting double meanings. The word *arena*, which I have translated as "sand," could also be read as "battlefield," while the reference to the priest's coffer alludes to the biblical Ark of the Covenant.

92. Solano Palacio, *La Revolución de Octubre* [1936], 172.

93. Grayzel, *Women's Identities at War*, 65.

94. Manning, *What I Saw in Spain*, 147. Other incidents of torture and abuse appear throughout chapter 6.

95. González Tuñón, *La rosa blindada*, 33.

96. The historical reality of this notion is debated. Militarily the Islamic forces had little difficulty in raiding the territory and even occupying Gijón for a time in the early eighth century. Due to internal disputes, especially between the Arabs and the Berbers, the forces that might have settled in Asturias and nearby Galicia were withdrawn and never became reestablished. In addition, the geography and climate of both regions probably made them less attractive to Muslim settlers. It is certain that the first independent Christian kingdom to emerge on the peninsula after 711 was established in Asturias.

97. On the discourse of sexuality between different religious communities in the Middle Ages, see Glick, *Islamic and Christian Spain in the Early Middle Ages*; and Nirenberg, *Communities of Violence.*

98. Ramos Oliveira, *La Revolución española de octubre*, 190. Interestingly he declared that the brutalities of the October repression would be seen by colonized peoples, presumably in Africa, thus making it more difficult to maintain authority in those regions.

99. Ignotus (Manuel Villar), *La represión de octubre*, 103. Another photo of an African sergeant appears on 97.

100. Reproduced in Tusell, *La elecciones del Frente Popular en España*, vol. 2, 392.

101. Spanish commanders of Moroccan troops sanctioned the continuation of such activities during the colonial wars. See Balfour, *Deadly Embrace*, 196; see also Madariaga, "Imagen del moro en la memoria colectiva del pueblo español y retorno del moro en la guerra civil de 1936."

102. On the interactions between racism and sexuality, see Mosse, *Nationalism and Sexuality*, chapter 7.

103. Solano Palacio, *La Revolución de Octubre* [1994], 179.

104. Taibo, *Asturias 1934*, vol. 1, 255–56.

105. Balfour, *Deadly Embrace*, 250.

106. Madariaga, "Imagen del moro en la memoria colectiva del pueblo español y re-torno del moro en la guerra civil de 1936," 587–88.

107. Such notions re-appeared during the Civil War, see ibid., 595.

108. Jensen, *Irrational Triumph*, 153.

109. Ibid., 155.

110. Balfour, *Deadly Embrace*, 256. On the development of the idea of a "messianic mission" within the Army of Africa, see 171. For the role played by the Army of Africa and its leading officers in the coup of 1936, see chapters 9 and 10.

111. For example, Geijo, *Episodios de la revolución*, 125, 200, includes photographs of the wives and children of officials who had been killed during the insurrection.

112. Vincent, "The Martyrs and the Saints," 70.

113. Acción Popular, *Terror*, 13.

114. Ibid., 7–8.

115. Biblioteca Nacional de España, Servicio de Dibujos y Grabados, 178.

116. Ibid., 406.

117. Ibid., 364.

118. *La Libertad*, 25 January 1936, 3.

119. Sección Española del Socorro Rojo Internacional, *Los crímenes de la reacción española*; the details of the shootings and the photos of children appear on 33–34 and the appeal is on 97.

120. González Bayón, *El Romancero de octubre*, 38.

121. Ibid., 38.

122. See Vincent, "The Martyrs and Saints," and Llorente Hernández, *Arte e ideología en el franquismo*.

5. HYENAS, HARPIES, AND PROLETARIAN MOTHERS

1. See, for example, Bingham, *Gender, Modernity, and the Popular Press in Inter-war Britain*; Roberts, *Civilization without Sexes*; Søland, *Becoming Modern*; and De Grazia, *How Fascism Ruled Women*.

2. Kent, *Making Peace*, 99, 107.

3. Many Americans believed that imperialism and war degraded the character of both women and the nation. See Hoganson, *Fighting for American Manhood*, chapter 8.

4. Vincent, "Gender and Morals in Spanish Catholic Youth Culture."

5. Nash, "Identidades, representación cultural y discurso de género en la españa con-temporánea," 196.

6. Nash, "Un/Contested Identities," 26.

7. Ibid., 27–35.

8. Shubert, *A Social History of Modern Spain*, 32–38.

9. Folguera Crespo, "La II República," 494–95. See also Cleminson, "Beyond Tradition and 'Modernity.'"

10. Núñez Perez, *Trabajadoras en la segunda república*, 49–59.

11. Ibid., 151, 156.

12. The figures on school enrollment increased from 5,557 to 37,642. Folguera Crespo, "Revolución y restauración," 466, 469–70.

13. Munson, "Walking on the Periphery," 63–75.

14. See Bussy Genevois, "El retorno de la hija pródiga."

15. Victoria Kent was appointed director of prisons in 1931. See Keene, " 'Into the Clear Air of the Plaza,' " 334.

16. Blasco, *Paradojas de la ortodoxia*, 18–19.

17. Quoted in Ibid., 225.

18. Ibid., 27.

19. Graham, "Women and Social Change," 105.

20. Blasco, *Paradojas de la ortodoxia*, 242.

21. Ibid., 245, 247, 265. The most notable departure was that of Juana Salas who resigned from her position on the governing council of Acción Popular to become president of the CMCE.

22. The annual figures for the Republican years were: 1931, 22,506; 1932, 28,301; 1933, 33,000; 1934, 48,229; 1935, 57,321; and 1936, 70,000 (Blasco, *Paradojas de la ortodoxia*, 258, 259).

23. Nash, "Identidades, representación cultural y discurso de género en la españa contemporánea," 201.

24. Graham, "Women and Social Change," 102.

25. Nash, " 'Ideals of Redemption,' " 349–50.

26. Total membership rose from 4,600 to 20,000. See Erice Sebares, "Mujeres comunistas," 319–21, 325.

27. The outbreak of Civil War triggered a renewed attempt to mobilize women. See Nash, *Defying Male Civilization*, chapter 3.

28. Erice Sebares, "Mujeres comunistas," 322.

29. Nuño del Robleda, *¿Por qué Oviedo se convirtió en ciudad mártir?* 14.

30. Nash, "Un/Contested Identities," 27–35.

31. Blasco, *Paradojas de la ortodoxia*, 205–6, 210–11.

32. Xavier, *Sangre jesuita*, 36.

33. Geijo, *Episodios de la revolución*, 158.

34. Acción Popular, *Terror*, 7–8.

35. Matilde de la Torre, "Estampas de Asturias: Trinidad," *El Socialista*, 7 April 1936.

36. Ibid.

37. Prada, *Caminos de sangre*, 59.

38. Ibid., 58.

39. Los Presos de Asturias, *¡Acusamos!*, 5.

40. It should be noted that the women described in both incidents preyed on the old, sick, or wounded. In keeping with my analysis in chapter 4, both pro- and anti-revolutionary forces wished to depict themselves as virile men who vigorously defended themselves and their families.

41. *Estampa,* 20 October 1934, 9. No evidence ever emerged to verify such accounts.

42. Martínez, *Dos jesuitas mártires en Asturias,* 50.

43. Solano Palacio, *La Revolución de Octubre,* [1994], 180.

44. The *mono* is the set of overalls traditionally worn by workers; see Solano Palacio, *La Revolución de Octubre* [1994], 81. Later images of female fighters during the Civil War nearly always show women wearing the mono.

45. In 1936 after the communist leader Dolores Ibárruri gave a speech in the Cortes, one Republican deputy stated, "Pasionaria spoke like a man. Like the only man that spoke this afternoon in the Chamber" (quoted in Ibárruri, *¡A la carcel los verdugos de octubre!* 16).

46. See De Pauw, *Battle Cries and Lullabies,* esp. 17–18.

47. González Bayón, *El romancero de octubre,* 70.

48. Ibid., 71.

49. Earlier in the poem the woman declares that if he is killed her life will be a disgrace. He tells her that if that happened she would take up arms against the "bourgeoisie." In this way he gives her leave to fight only after her life has ceased to be respectable, which places her outside of traditional gender categories.

50. González Bayón, *El romancero de octubre,* 72.

51. The confusion of sexual categories that such transgressions represented posed a serious threat to both public and private order. See Mosse, *Nationalism and Sexuality,* 16–17.

52. The precise number of female combatants is impossible to determine. Contemporary accounts of the revolt often mentioned that women fought, but they provided few details. Manuel Grossi Mier, for instance, declared that from the beginning women had "decided with great enthusiasm to include themselves in the fight" (*La insurrección de Asturias,* 36), and the Mexican journalist Luis Octavio Madero reported that many women and children participated in combat (*El Octobre español,* 42). Leah Manning also reported on the various activities of women (*What I Saw in Spain,* chapter 6). The historian Bernardo Díaz Nosty offered virtually no discussion of the role of women in the revolt, declaring simply "Many of the chronicles speak of a feminine presence in the areas of the most intense fighting," and he ends by stating that many women ran field kitchens in the combat zones (*La comuna asturiana,* 264–65). In 1935, the newspaper of the POUM published a photograph of Teresa Vives, who according to the caption died in the fighting of 6 October in Barcelona (*La Batalla,* 11 October 1935).

53. Confusion regarding the hero begins with her name; she was interchangeably called Aida de la Fuente, Aida de Lafuente, and Aida Lafuente. Rarely, her first name was spelled with an accent ("Aída"). She had two common nicknames: "La Libertaria" and, less often, Niní or Nina. The former was a common nickname for female revolutionary heroes, while the latter was a diminutive of the name Aida. For the sake of consistency, I will refer to her in this chapter as Aida Lafuente.

54. A recent source listing her birthplace as Oviedo is *Apéndice de la Gran Enciclopedia Asturiana,* vol. 16, 280. In a letter to the editor of *La Nueva España* on 22 November

1997 (p. 63), Ernesto Abad Barrientos named her birthplace as León. He, in turn, quoted from a series published in the newspaper *Diario de León* titled "Nuestros Mujeres." The official newspaper of the PCE, *Mundo Obrero,* also gave her birthplace as León (11 January 1936, 1).

55. In an interview for the short film *De la fuente* (dir. Ramón Lluís Bande, Gijón: Vera Robert, 2004, DVD), Pilar Lafuente provides more information about the family and the sisters' political activities.

56. *La Nueva España,* 1 December 1997, 4.

57. *Apéndice de la Gran Enciclopedia Asturiana*, vol. 16, 280; and Taibo, *Asturias 1934*, vol. 2, 57.

58. Fernández Llaneza, *San Pedro de los Arcos,* 112. This book may represent a more conservative interpretation of her life and background. Unlike any other source, he lists Penaos's occupation as midwife and gives evidence of her stress on the importance of traditional feminine actions like caring for the sick.

59. *La Nueva España,* 1 December 1997, 4. Fernández Llaneza states that she sold PCE materials, yet he describes her membership in the party as "uncertain" (112).

60. *Mundo Obrero,* 11 January 1936, 1. See also Erice Sebares, "Mujeres comunistas," esp. 321–22.

61. *La Nueva España,* 19 April 1998, 4.

62. Erice Sebares, "Mujeres comunistas," 320.

63. Valdés, *¡¡Asturias!!* 182. See also Sanchez, *Fact and Fiction*, chapter 7.

64. Dolores Ibárruri, speech at the Monumental Cinema in Madrid, June 1935; quoted in Valdés, *¡¡Asturias!!* 183.

65. *Mundo Obrero,* 11 January 1936, 1.

66. Ibid., 1, 2.

67. Ibid., 2. The story also appears in Carnelli, *U.H.P. Mineros de Asturias,* 149.

68. González Tuñón, *La rosa blindada,* 20. González Tuñón was a member of the PCE. See Bonet, *Diccionario de las vanguardias en españa,* 309–10.

69. See chapter 3 in this volume.

70. *Mundo Obrero,* 2 March 1936. An announcement and description of the ceremony is in *El Socialista,* 28 February 1936. A review of the event appears in *El Socialista,* 1 March 1936.

71. The PSOE meeting in Madrid took place on 27 February 1936 (*El Socialista,* 28 February 1936). The PCE met on 28 February 1936 (*Mundo Obrero,* 2 March 1936).

72. *El Socialista,* 1 March 1936, 3. The same story, virtually word for word, appears in *Mundo Obrero,* 2 March 1936. The lineup of speakers and invited guests comes from *El Socialista,* 28 February 1936. The left Republican newspaper *La Libertad* reported the attendance at 100,000 (1 March 1936), 4. Alberti's poem is discussed in detail below.

73. Texts advocating greater collaboration include Federación Nacional de Juventudes Socialista, *Octubre segunda etapa*; Lopez, *La unidad de la CNT y su trayectoria*; and Mont-Font, *Alianza Obrera*.

74. Molins i Fábrega, *UHP*, 186–87. Molins had actively participated in the rebellion. A literary analysis of the text can be found in Sanchez, *Fact and Fiction*, chapter 4.

75. Molins i Fábrega, *UHP*, 187, 205.

76. Solano Palacio, *La Revolución de Octubre* [1936], 97.

77. Ibid., 160.

78. Luis Sirval apparently concluded that Lafuente had been shot by members of the Foreign Legion, but his story never made it to press. For more on Sirval, see chapter 3 in this volume.

79. According to Sanchez, Benavides was a member of the Socialist Party. She calls his account of the revolt a "non-fictional novel" (*Fact and Fiction*, 245–58, 284, n.22).

80. Benavides, *La revolución fué así*, 338.

81. Ibid., 338–40.

82. The original report is in *Estampa*, 3 November 1934. The story is reproduced in *La Libertad*, 18 January 1936, and also in Taibo, *Asturias 1934*, vol. 2, 58.

83. Canal, *Octubre rojo en Asturias,* 191. José Canal is the pseudonym of José Díaz Fernández, an influential author and journalist associated with Manuel Azaña's *Izquierda Republicana*. He was elected to the Cortes in 1931 and later served in the Popular Front government. See Sanchez, *Fact and Fiction*, 304.

84. Núñez, *La Revolución de Octubre de 1934,* vol. 1, 103–4.

85. Ibid., 104.

86. Ibid., vol. 2, 105, 117, 119.

87. In different contexts, other young women who stepped outside common gender stereotypes have, inadvertently or not, challenged the existing social order. See Maria Fraddosio, "The Fallen Hero," 101.

88. See Nash, *Defying Male Civilization*; and Conze and Fiesler, "Soviet Women as Comrades-in-Arms," esp. 224–29.

89. For Catholic culture, see Vincent, "Gender and Morals in Spanish Catholic Youth Culture"; for Marxist culture, see Maynes, "Adolescent Sexuality and Social Identity in French and German Lower-Class Autobiography," 406–10.

90. Camín, *El Valle Negro*, 213. See also Sanchez, *Fact and Fiction*, chapter 6.

91. Camín, *El Valle Negro,* 213–14.

92. González Tuñón, *La rosa blindada*, 21. The rose has long symbolized martyrdom, and it is often associated with the Virgin Mary.

93. Serrano Plaja, *Versos de guerra y paz,* 19. Serrano Plaja was a member of the PCE. See Bonet, *Diccionario de las vanguardias en España*, 570.

94. Serrano Plaja, *Versos de guerra y paz*, 18.

95. *El Socialista,* 13 March 1936, 3.

96. The martyrs of Turón had similar intuitions; see chapter 2 in this volume.

97. *El Socialista,* 13 March 1936, 3. The notion that Lafuente was executed rather than killed in combat was repeated by the communist leader Juan Ambou in 1977. He claimed that Lafuente, along with twelve others, were lined up and shot beside the

walls of San Pedro de los Arcos. Ambou's account is reproduced in Taibo, *Asturias 1934*, vol. 2, 57–58.

98. *El Socialista,* 13 March 1936, 3.

99. For an extended discussion of this imagery, see chapter 4 in this volume.

100. Molins i Fábrega, *UHP,* 187.

101. Pla y Beltran, *Antologia Poetica,* 161. Pla y Beltran was a member of the PCE and had spent time in the Soviet Union. See Bonet, *Diccionario de las vanguardias en España,* 486–87.

102. Pla y Beltran, *Antologia Poetica,* 161.

103. Millan Jimenez, *La poesía de Rafael Alberti,* 97–102.

104. Alberti, *Poesía,* 314.

105. Ibid., 315.

106. See Mosse, *Nationalism and Sexuality,* 90–93, for a similar transformation in depictions of Marianne in France.

107. *Mundo Obrero,* 11 January 1936, 2.

108. Camín, *El Valle Negro,* 215.

109. Maurín, *Revolución y contrarrevolución en España,* 163.

110. González Tuñón, *La rosa blindada,* 10.

111. Debates over women's role in the anarchist movement had been going on throughout 1935 and early 1936. See Ackelsberg, *Free Women of Spain,* 97.

112. Nash, *Defying Male Civilization,* esp. 101–39.

113. Mangini González, *Memories of Resistance,* 82. Sánchez, later called Rosie the Dynamiter, became a famous warrior in her own right. See Nash, *Defying Male Civilization,* 50, 82, 105, 110, 120.

114. *Lina Odena, Heroína del pueblo.* A few months before her death, Odena had been in Oviedo to participate in a ceremony honoring Lafuente. See Erice Saberes, "Mujeres comunistas," 323.

115. *Mundo Obrero,* 5 October 1936, 1.

116. *La Prensa,* 6 October 1936, reproduced in *Guerra Civil en Asturias,* vol. 2, 9.

117. *P.O.U.M.,* 14 October 1936, 5.

118. Nash, "*Milicianas* and Homefront Heroines," 235–44; Nash also explores the question in her *Defying Male Civilization.*

119. See Vincent, "The Martyrs and the Saints."

120. See Roca i Girona, *De la pureza a la maternidad;* and Gomez, *True Catholic Womanhood.*

6. THE OCTOBER REVOLUTION IN DEMOCRATIC SPAIN

1. See Vincent, "The Martyrs and Saints" and Cruz, "Old Symbols, New Meanings."

2. Cienfuegos, *Cancionario de la guerra,* 6. The revolt also conditioned the regime's attitude toward the province in the years after the Civil War. The government paid

special attention to Asturias in order to prevent any kind of uprising; if Spain had entered World War II on the side of Germany the region might be a natural place for an allied invasion. See David Ruiz's introduction to Camus, *Rebelión en Asturias,* 33–34.

3. Union General de Trabajadores—Guipuzcoa, *Memoria y Orden del dia del IV congreso provincial.*
4. *Milicia Popular,* 7 October 1936. The paper also reproduced Raul González Tuñon's poem about Aida Lafuente. Ramón González Peña also invoked the October revolt to encourage fighting during the battle for Asturias in 1936 (*El Socialista,* 22 October 1936).
5. Navarro Navarro, "La imagen en la propaganda politica durante la Guerra civil española," 25. See also Vincent, "The Martyrs and the Saints."
6. The image is reproduced in Carulla and Carulla, *La guerra civil en 2000 carteles,* vol. 2, 37. Solano Palacio, in *La tragedia del norte,* also tried to use the events of 1934 to help motivate action during the Civil War.
7. Navarro Navarro, "La imagen en la propaganda politica durante la guerra civil española," 34–36. See also Grimau, *El cartel republicano en la guerra civil,* chapter 4; Julian González, *El cartel republicano en la guerra civil española*; and Carabias Álvaro, "Las madonnas se visten de rojo."
8. In many ways the process has continued to the present day. During my dissertation research I often had to explain to Spaniards that the October revolution was a separate event from the Civil War.
9. A magazine published in 1947 celebrated the Nationalist victory in Asturias during the Civil War. The publication listed the important events from Spanish history that had taken place in October, including the birth of Cervantes, the battle of Lepanto, and the voyage of Columbus. The October 1934 revolution was mentioned only in reference to the destruction of buildings in Oviedo. See *Octubre 1936-1947-1937,* 1, 14. The leftists in exile continued to invoke the memory of October 1934, primarily on the annual anniversary of the rising: see *Asturias* 2, no. 3 (5 October 1943), published in Mexico; and Saborit, *Asturias y sus hombres,* published in France. A series of strikes during the 1960s prompted some discussion, especially after the leftists accused the authorities of mistreating strikers. See Ruiz Ayucar, "Los 'intelectuales' y Asturias," for a defense of the Civil Guard and the government.
10. In 2001 the newspaper *El Comercio Digital* held a public vote to name the twenty greatest Asturians of the twentieth century. Alongside the politicians, scientists, and writers so designated, Belarmino Tomás, one of the leading figures of the October revolt, appeared along with General Sabino Fernández Campo (discussed below). See *El Comercio Digital,* 25 April 2001. The complete list of nominees is at http://canales.elcomerciodigital.com/extras/asturiano/c1_10.htm.
11. Aguilar Fernández, *Memoria y olvido de la guerra civil española;* the English translation was published as *Memory and Amnesia: The Role of the Spanish Civil War in the Transition to Democracy.*

12. See Graham, *The Spanish Republic at War.*

13. For example, *El País,* one of Spain's most important daily newspapers, contained little coverage of the events during the fiftieth anniversary. During the same period the national magazine *Interviú* advertised, alongside nude photos of Sofia Loren, a special section dedicated to the October uprising.

14. *La Nueva España* and *La Voz de Asturias,* for example, both featured extensive coverage of the revolution over the course of several days in October.

15. Interview with José Luis Balbín in *La Nueva España,* 7 October 1984, 24.

16. *La Nueva España,* 7 October 1984, 5, 24.

17. Fundación José Barreiro, *La revolución de octubre 50 años despues,* 3.

18. Calaf Masachs, *Revolución del 34 en Asturias,* 3.

19. Ibid., 9.

20. *La Voz de Asturias,* 4 October 1984, 40.

21. Ibid.

22. *La Nueva España,* 20 October 1984, 16.

23. "La Revolución de Octubre en Asturias y la persecución religiosa," letter to the editor by Tomás Recio in *La Nueva España,* 10 October 1984, 27.

24. *La Voz de Asturias,* 10 October 1984.

25. In 1994 the Asturian section of the PSOE stated during its annual conference: "We value the immense effort and the many sacrifices made by our predecessors during more than a century and we are proud of the work of the organization toward democracy and justice in our country, toward liberty and the well being of our citizens" (PSOE-Federación Socialista Asturiana, *26 Congreso Oviedo, 22–23–24 April 1994.*

26. García de Tuñón Aza, *El Socialismo,* 22–23, 30–31. The text is filled with photographs of the destruction of Oviedo caused by the rebellion, 37–38, 113–14, 127–28.

27. Palomino, *1934,* 10, 175.

28. See Moa's series of books on the Civil War: *Los orígenes de la guerra civil española, Los personajes de la República vistos por ellos mismos, El derrumbe de la segunda república y la guerra civil,* and *Los mitos de la guerra civil.*

29. Javier Tusell, "El revisionismo histórico español," *El País,* 8 July 2004.

30. While concluding research for this book in summer 2004 I encountered a man on the Madrid Metro who was railing loudly against both the historic and contemporary PSOE. Among the "crimes" he listed was the revolution of October 1934.

31. *La Nueva España,* 22 October 1994.

32. Ibid.

33. Ibid.

34. *La Nueva España,* 19 April 1998.

35. *La Voz de Asturias,* 19 April 1998.

36. Partido Obrero Revolucionario de España, *La comuna de Asturias 1934–1984 en el 50 aniversario,* 3.

37. Ibid.

38. See the group's Web site at http://www.netpor.org/esp/.

39. Mulas Hernández, "Octubre de 1934," 38. The account is undoubtedly based on that given in Molins i Fábrega, *UHP: La insurrección proletaria de Asturias.*

40. The process of canonization is a long and arduous one. For details, see Woodward, *Making Saints.* The decision of Pope John Paul II to celebrate the men after years of inactivity was probably a result of his strong anticommunist views.

41. Chico González, *Testigos de la escuela cristiana* [1989], 453–57.

42. *La Nueva España,* 15 October 1990.

43. See Chico González, *Testigos de la escuela cristiana* [1999]; Valdizán, *Mártires de Turón escritos;* Mazariegos, *Juntos como un solo hombre;* Lopez Lopez and Reyes Lopez, *El nuevo beato de la diócesis Hermano Marciano-José;* and Luke Salm, *The Martyrs of Turón and Tarragona.* On the Passionist clerics killed at the same time, see González, *San Inocencio Canoura Arnau.*

44. In his homily during the mass celebrating the beatification of the martyrs, Pope John Paul II stressed the cooperation shown between the clergy and the religious orders. The homily is reproduced in González, *San Inocencio Canoura Arnau,* 146.

45. Chico González, *Testigos de la escuela cristiana* [1989], 10, 475.

46. The remarks are reproduced in González, *San Inocencio Canoura Arnau,* 151–52.

47. *La Gaceta Online,* 4 July 1999.

48. *La Nueva España,* 15 October 1990.

49. *La Nueva España,* 4 July 1999.

50. Ibid.

51. Pérez Díaz, *The Return of Civil Society,* 168.

52. *La Nueva España,* 4 July 1999.

53. See Aguilar Fernández, *Memoria y olvido de la Guerra Civil española.*

54. Eugenio de Rioja, "Los mártires de Turón no tienen quien les cante," *La Nueva España,* 8 July 1999.

55. Ibid.

56. *La Nueva España,* 19 April 1998, 4.

57. *La Voz de Asturias,* 8 January 1978, 14.

58. Ibid.

59. Fernández Llaneza, *San Pedro de los Arcos,* 115–16. The group credits the lyrics as "traditional," and they are written in Asturian, the local language of the region. The poet González Tuñón, in *La rosa blindada,* 10, also mentions a popular song titled "La Libertaria" and speculated that the author is anonymous.

60. *La Nueva España,* 1 December 1998, 4.

61. General coverage of the fiftieth anniversary of the revolt can be seen throughout the month of October in both *La Voz de Asturias* and *La Nueva España.* The actions of Aida Lafuente are briefly recounted in *La Nueva España,* 13 October 1984.

62. *La Voz de Asturias,* 18 October 1992, 14.

63. Ibid.

64. *La Voz de Asturias*, 23 October 1994, 18.

65. *La Voz de Asturias*, 22 October 1995, 14; and *La Nueva España*, 22 October 1995, 5.

66. *La Voz de Asturias*, 22 October 1995, 14.

67. *La Nueva España*, 4 November 1997, 9.

68. *La Voz de Asturias*, 22 October 1995, 14. Monument building is intricately con-
nected to both local and international politics as well as historical memory. The
literature on this issue is quite extensive, but for representative studies see Young,
The Texture of Memory; Gillis, *Commemorations*; and Koshar, *From Monuments to
Traces*.

69. *La Voz de Asturias*, 25 October 1997, 32; and *La Nueva España*, 10 November 1997,
79.

70. *La Voz de Asturias*, 25 October 1997, 32. The artist who sculpted the memorial,
Félix Alonso Arenas, is a former professor at the School of Fine Arts in Oviedo. See
La Nueva España, 10 November 1997, 79.

71. *La Nueva España*, 4 November 1997, 9.

72. *La Nueva España*, 10 November 1997, 79.

73. See the entry on Fernández Campo in *Quien es quien en España*.

74. For information on the failed coup, see Preston, *The Triumph of Democracy in Spain*, especially chapter seven. The list of "undesirables" is reproduced in *El País*, 6 June 1999, 8.

75. *La Nueva España*, 10 November 1997, 79. Suárez was one of the leading figures of the
transition to democracy. See Preston, *The Triumph of Democracy in Spain*.

76. *La Nueva España*, 10 November 1997, 79

77. *La Nueva España*, 21 November 1997, 3. In a personal interview on 5 May 1998,
David Ruiz offered to me one version of how the final authorization came about.
Every year the heir to the throne of Spain, the Prince of Asturias, presents a series of
major awards similar to the Nobel Prize in such fields as literature, art, and science.
In October and November 1997, when the polemic regarding the monument was
reaching its peak, the ceremony for these awards was being planned, and the ceremony itself was to be held in Oviedo. The occasion brought in many illustrious
people, from important cultural figures to royalty. Among them was Sabino Fernández Campo, the same man whom Ruiz mentioned in his open letter to the
mayor. Ruiz claimed that Fernández Campo had read his open letter to the mayor
and decided that, in the interest of tolerance, the monument should be allowed to go
forward. Accordingly, Fernández Campo telephoned the mayor, and shortly afterward permission was granted.

78. *La Nueva España*, 1 December 1997, 4. The decision to refer to Lafuente as the Red
Rose of October brings together several interesting and contrasting symbols. Since
the Middle Ages, Mary the mother of Jesus has often been referred to as the Rose of
Spain. In addition, Rosa Luxemburg was celebrated in a similar way following her
death. The symbolism is appropriate since within Christian iconography the rose has
long been linked to martyrdom. See O'Callaghan, *Alfonso X and the Cantigas de Santa
Maria*.

79. *La Nueva España*, 18 April 1998, 5.

80. *La Voz de Asturias*, 19 April 1998, 12.

81. *La Nueva España*, 18 April 1998, 5.

82. The percentage of votes for the PSOE has declined in every election, from a high of 48.4 percent in 1982 to 37.7 percent in 1996. The IU's totals improved slightly between 1989 and 1996, increasing from 9.1 percent to 10.6 percent. See Edles, *Symbol and Ritual in the New Spain*, 146.

83. *El Comercio*, 8 August 1998; and *El Comercio Digital*, 24 March 1999, http://www .elcomercio-sa.es/pg990324/suscr./gijon18.htm.

84. *El Comercio Digital*, 24 March 1999. This was not the first street in Gijón to be named for Lafuente. During the Civil War the street that had been called Melquiades Alvarez was renamed in honor of the young hero; however, it reverted to its former name after the conflict. In contrast to the peripheral location of the present Aida Lafuente Street, Melquiades Alvarez is located near the historic center of the city.

85. Special prayers can be found on the Christian Brothers' Web site, http://db .cbconf.org/shareware.nsf/pages/turon.htm. During summer 1999 a newspaper supplement for children called "My History" featured ten-year-old Aida García Fresno, who lived in the city of Gijón. Young Aida stated that her father took her name from a local song, one that likely commemorated Aida Lafuente (*La Nueva España*, 10 July 1999).

86. Formally at http://www.geocities.com/Athens/Ithica/5544/martires.htm, http:// www.geocities.com/Athens/Ithica/5544/revolucion.htm, http://www.geocities .com/Athens/Ithica/5544/martirio.htm, http://www.geocities.com/Athens /Ithica/5544/unoauno.htm.

87. "Travels with Fr. Victor Hoagland C.P.," http://www.cptryon.org/hoagland/ travels/. The story on the film appeared in *El Commerico Digital*, 21 November 2003, http://www.elcomerciodigital.com. The film is titled *La rosa roja*.

GLOSSARY OF ORGANIZATIONS

AC   Acción Católica (Catholic Action). A nonpolitical group organized by the Catholic Church.

ACM   Acción Católica de Mujeres (Women's Catholic Action). The women's section of *Acción Católica* was founded in 1919.

ACNP   Asociación Católica Nacional de Propagandistas (National Association of Catholic Propagandists). An elitist and highly influential Catholic lay group that was closely linked with the formation of AP and the CEDA.

AN   Acción Nacional (National Action). The first conservative political organization formed after the creation of the Republic in 1931. It later became Acción Popular.

AP   Acción Popular (Popular Action). A Catholic party that formed the core of the CEDA.

BOC   Bloc Obrer i Camperol (Worker and Peasant Bloc). A Marxist organization, headed by Joaquín Maurín, opposed to the official Communist Party. In 1935, the BOC fused with the IC to form the POUM.

CEDA   Confederación Española de Derechas Autónomas (Spanish Confederation of Autonomous Rightist Groups). A coalition of Catholic organizations headed by José María Gil Robles. The CEDA emerged as the largest conservative political party.

CMCE   Confederación de Mujeres Católicas de España (Confederation of Spanish Catholic Women). A new organization created in 1934 after the fusion of two older women's groups, including the *Acción Católica de Mujeres*. It was designed to mobilize and channel women's public action into charitable, rather than political activities.

CNT   Confederación Nacional de Trabajo (National Confederation of Labor). The anarchosyndicalist trade union.

CT   Comunión Tradicional (Traditionalist Communion). The monarchist group that supported a pretender to throne; more commonly known as the Carlists.

DLR   Derecha Liberal Republicana (Liberal Republican Right). A small conservative and Catholic party that supported the Republic.

FE   Falange Española (Spanish Phalanx). The Spanish fascist party led by José Antonio Primo de Rivera. It later merged with the JONS.

FJS   Federación de Juventudes Socialistas (Federation of Socialist Youths). The socialist youth organization.

FNTT   Federación Nacional de Trabajadores de la Tierra (National Federation of Agricultural Workers). The largest single section of the socialist UGT.

IC   Izquierda Comunista (Communist Left). A Marxist organization opposed to the official Communist Party. Joined with the BOC to form the POUM.

IR   Izquierda Republicana (Republican Left). A moderate Republican party led by Manuel Azaña.

IU   Izquierda Unida (United Left). A coalition of leftist political groups founded in 1986 and led by the Communist Party.

JAP   Juventud de Acción Popular (Youth of Popular Action). The youth section of the CEDA.

JCE   Juventud Católica Española (Spanish Catholic Youth). The Catholic youth group for young men founded in 1923. The organization was closely linked to the ACNP.

JCF   Juventud Católica Femenina (Young Catholic Women). The Catholic youth group for young women.

JONS   Juntas de Ofensiva Nacional Sindicalista (Groups of National Syndicalist Action). A fascist party that later joined with the FE.

JSU   Juventudes Socialistas Unificadas (Unified Socialist Youth). The youth organization formed by the merger of the FJS and the Communist Party's youth group.

PCE   Partido Comunista de España (Spanish Communist Party). The orthodox Communist Party officially sanctioned by the Soviet Union.

PORE   Partido Obrero Revolucionario de España (Revolutionary Workers Party of Spain). A Trotskyist party founded in the 1960s and affiliated with the IU.

POUM   Partido Obrero de Unificación Marxista (Workers Party of Marxist Unification). The unification of the BOC and IC created this revolutionary party in the wake of the October revolution.

PP   Partido Popular (Popular Party). The largest and most successful conservative party in postdictatorship Spain.

PSOE   Partido Socialista Obrero Español (Spanish Socialist Workers Party). The socialist political party.

SMA   Sindicato Minero Asturiano (Asturian Miners Syndicate). A miners' union of Asturias affiliated with the UGT.

SRI   Socorro Rojo Internacional (International Red Aid). A Comintern organization providing assistance to leftist prisoners and their families.

Radicals   Partido Republicano Radical (Radical Republican Party). A conservative Republican party. Under the leadership of Alejandro Lerroux, the group formed part of the conservative coalition that governed Spain between 1933–1936.

RE   Renovación Española (Spanish Renovation). The Alfonsine monarchist party led by José Calvo Sotelo.

UGT   Unión General de Trabajadores (General Union of Workers). The socialist trade union; it eventually merged with the communist union in 1935.

BIBLIOGRAPHY

ARCHIVAL SOURCES

Archivo Histórico Nacional, Madrid
Archivo General de la Guerra Civil Española (AGGC), Salamanca
Biblioteca de Asturias, Oviedo
Biblioteca Nacional de España, Madrid
Fundación Pablo Iglesias (FPI), Madrid
Pabellón de la República, Barcelona

PRIMARY SOURCES: BOOKS, PAMPHLETS, AND OTHER MATERIALS

Acción Popular. *Terror: El Marxismo en España: Revolución de Octubre de 1934.* [Madrid?]:
   F. P. Palomeque, n.d. [ca. 1936].
Agire y Lekube, José Antonio de. *Entre la libertad y la revolución 1930–1935: La verdad de un
   lustro en el País Vasco.* Bilbao: E. Verdes Achirica, 1935.
Alberti, Rafael. *Poesía: 1924–1937.* Madrid: Signo, 1938.
Alianza de Sindicatos Portuarios de España. *Actas de la segunda conferencia de sindicatos
   portuarios de España, 1935.*
Alvarez, Ramon. *José María Martínez: Símbolo ejemplar del obrerismo militante.* Gijón:
   Artegraf, 1990.
Alvarez Portal, M. *Sirval.* Barcelona: Ediciones Adelante, 1936.
Alvarez Suarez, Maximiliano. *Sangre de Octubre U.H.P.* 2nd ed. Madrid: Editorial Cenit,
   1936.
Araquistain, Luis et al. *La revolución española de octubre: Documentos sensacionales ineditos.*
   Santiago: Editorial Occidente, 1935.
Arriba: Reproducción facsimil del semanario de la Falange. Madrid: Ediciones Fe, 1939.
Asociación Católica de Propagandistas de Oviedo. *Asturias roja: Sacerdotes y religiosos
   perseguidos y martirizados.* Oviedo: Moderna Imprenta Trufero, 1935.

Azaña, Manuel. *Obras completas.* Vol. 3. Mexico D.F.: Ediciones Oasis, 1967.

Balius, Jaime. *De Jaca a octubre.* Barcelona: Editorial Renacer, n.d. [ca. 1935].

Baráibar, Carlos de. *Las falsas "posiciones socialistas" de Indalecio Prieto.* Madrid: Ediciones Yunque, 1935.

Benavides, Manuel D. *Curas y mendigos. Prólogo de la guerra civil.* Barcelona: Imprenta Industrial, 1936.

——. *La revolución fué así: Octubre rojo y negro.* Barcelona: Imprenta Industrial, 1935.

Bergés, Consuelo. *Explicación de Octubre: Historia comprimida de cuatro años de República en España.* Madrid: Imprenta Garcigoy, 1935.

Bloque Obrero y Campesino–Federación Comunista Ibérica. *La lecciones de la insurrección de Octubre.* Barcelona: Imp. Cervantes, 1935.

Bowers, Claude G. *My Mission to Spain: Watching the Dress Rehearsal for World War II.* New York: Simon and Schuster, 1954.

Brones, A. *¡Conquistemos las masas! La acentuación de la crisis revolucionaria en España y las tareas del Partido Comunista.* Madrid: Ediciones Mundo Obrero, n.d. [ca. 1934].

Cabezas, Juan Antonio. *Morir en Oviedo.* Madrid: Editorial San Martin, 1982.

Calaf Masachs, Roser. *Revolución del 34 en Asturias: Materiales para el aula.* Oviedo: Fundación José Barreiro, 1984.

Camín, Alfonso. *El valle negro: Asturias 1934.* Mexico D.F. Editorial Norte, 1938.

Canal, José. (José Díaz Fernández). *Octubre rojo en Asturias.* Madrid: Agencia General de Libreria y Artes Gráficas, 1935.

Canals, Salvador. *El bienio estéril. Errores de la derecha. Extravíos en el centro. Despreocupación a la izquierda. Perspectivas electorales.* Madrid: Tipografia Artistica, 1936.

Carnelli, Maria Luisa. *U.H.P. Mineros de Asturias.* Buenos Aires: A. J. Weiss, 1936.

Carral, Ignacio. *Por qué mataron a Luis de Sirval.* Madrid: Imp. Sáez Hermanos, 1934.

Carretero, José María (El Caballero Audaz). *Frente rojo contra España.* Madrid: Ediciones Caballero Audaz, 1946.

——. *Gracias a España . . . (2´ parte de Rusia . . . ¡Jamas!).* Madrid: Ediciones Caballero Audaz, 1946.

——. *Horas del Madrid rojo.* 2nd ed. Madrid: Ediciones Caballero Audaz, 1941.

——. *La agonía de españa: Los culpables.* Madrid: Ediciones Caballero Audaz, 1936.

——. *1935: Un balance de vergüenzas políticas.* Madrid: Ediciones Caballero Audaz, 1936.

——. *Traidores a la Patria. (La verdad sobre Asturias y Cataluña): ¡Los Responsables!* Madrid: Ediciones Caballero Audaz, 1935.

——. *¡Viva la revolución! Los malhechores de la política.* Madrid: Ediciones Caballero Audaz, 1934.

Castrillo Santos, Juan. *Cuatro años de experiencia republicana.* Madrid: Gráfica Administrativa, 1935.

Castro Albarrán, A. de. *El derecho a la rebeldía.* Madrid: Gráfica Universal, 1934.

Cienfuegos, Casimiro. *Cancinaro de la guerra.* San Sebastian: Editorial Española, 1939.

——. *Elegía de Asturias y otros poemas del dolor trágico de España.* N.p.: Editorial Ibérica, 1935.

Claramunt, Jaime. *El peor enemigo de la República.* 2nd ed. Barcelona: Talleres Graficos Esparza, 1934.

Comité Central de Ayuda a los Presos y sus Familiares. *El pleno nacional resoluciones y acuerdos adoptados por las asamblea.* Madrid: Gráfica Tabaquera, 1936.

Comité Central del Bloque Obrero y Campesino–Federación Comunista Ibérica. "Las lecciones de la insurrección de octubre." In *Octubre del 34: Reflexiones sobre una revolución,* edited by Marta Bizcarrondo. Madrid: Ayuso, 1977.

Confederación Nacional de Trabajo. *Convocatoria para la conferencia nacional que se celebrará el . . . de octubre de 1934.* Madrid: Graficus Aurora, 1934.

——. *El Congreso Confereral de Zaragoza 1936.* Madrid: Zero, 1978.

——. *Hacia la unidad de acción de la clase de obrera: Discrsos pronunciados por Baráibar, Guillén, Vázquez, Rubiera, Montseny, y Peiró en el historico acto celebrado en Valencia el 1° de mayo de 1937.* Valencia: Ediciones de la C.N.T., 1937.

——. *Ponencia sobre la construción de los comités de defensa,* 1934. N.p., n.d. [ca. 1935].

Confederación Regional del Trabajo de Cataluña. *Memorias de la conferencia regional extraordinaria.* Barcelona, 1936.

Cossío, Francisco de. *Hacia una nueva España, de la Revolución de Octubre a la revolución de julio, 1934–1936.* Valladolid: Editorial Castilla, 1936.

Díaz Fernández, José. *Octubre rojo en Asturias.* Gijón: Silverio Cañada, 1984 [1935].

Documentos de la revolución. San Antonio, Tex.: FIAT, 1935.

Episodios de la revolución en Asturias 1934: Los Pasionistas de Mieres (Asturias) y la Revolución de Octubre de 1934: Episodios narrados por los mismos protagonistas. Santander: El Pasionario, 1935.

Federación Nacional de Juventudes Socialista. *Octubre segunda etapa.* Madrid: Editorial Renovacion, n.d. [ca.1935].

Fersen, L. *¿A dónde va el partido socialista? (¿Rectificación o reincidencia?).* Madrid: Ediciones Comunismo, 1934.

——. *Antecedentes del triunfo del frente popular. De octubre a febrero 1936.* Castellón: T. Colectivo S.T., 1937.

Fundación José Barreiro. *La revolución de octubre 50 años después (Mieres 5–30 octubre 1984).* Mieres: Ayuntamiento de Mieres, 1984.

Geijo, Jenaro G. *Episodios de la revolución.* Santander: Librería Moderna, 1935.

Gil Robles, José María. *No fue possible la paz.* Esplugues de Llobregat: Ediciones Ariel, 1968.

González Bayón, J. *El romancero de octubre: Poesías de la revolución española.* Buenos Aires: Editorial Claridad, 1935.

González Tuñón, Raul. *La rosa blindada.* Buenos Aires: Ediciones Horizonte, 1962 [1936].

Gordón Ordás, Félix. *Mi Política en España.* 3 vols. Mexico D.F.: Imprenta Figaro, 1961–1963.

Grossi Mier, Manuel. *La insurrección de Asturias.* Madrid: Ediciones Júcar, 1978 [1935].

Guerra civil en Asturias: Periódicos de los bandos. 6 vols. Salinas, Santander: Ayalga, 1980.

Hernández Zancajo, Carlos. *Tercera etapa de octubre.* Valencia: Editorial Meabe, 1937.

Ibárruri, Dolores. *¡A la carcel los verdugos de octubre! Discurso pronuncido el día 16 de junio de 1936.* Madrid: Prensa Obrera, 1936.

Iglesias Somoza, Eraclio. *Episodios de la revolución: Asesio y defensa de la cárcel de Oviedo.* Vitoria: Tipografía de J. Marquínez, 1935.

Ignotus (Manuel Villar). *El anarquismo en la insurrección de Asturias: La C.N.T. y la F.A.I. en octubre de 1934.* Valencia: Ediciones Tierra y Libertad, 1935.

——. *El peligro comunista: Sus causas y su remedio.* Madrid: Imp. Regina, n.d.

——. *La represión de octubre: Documentos para la historia de nuestra civilización.* 2nd ed. Barcelona: Ediciones Tierra y Libertad, 1936.

Izcaray, Jesus, and Nicolas Escanilla. *El socialismo español después de octubre (posición de lidres y masas).* Madrid: Ediciones Reportajes, 1935.

Jaume, Alejandro. *La insurrección de Octubre: Cataluña Asturias Baleares.* Felanity: Tipografía Felanigense, 1935.

Karl, Mauricio [M. Carlavilla de la Vega]. *Asesinos de España: Marxismo anarquismo masonería.* Madrid: Ediciones Bergua, 1935.

La Revolución de Octubre en España: La rebelión del gobierno de la generalidad (octubre 1934). Madrid: Bolaños y Aguilar, 1935.

Largo Caballero, Francisco. *Escritos de la República: Notas historicas de la Guerra en España (1917–1940),* edited by Santos Juliá. Madrid: Editorial Pablo Iglesias, 1985.

La transformación de la revolución democrático-burguesia en revolución socialista: Los problemas de la revolución española. Barcelona: Publicaciones Edeya, n.d.

Lina Odena: Heroína del pueblo. Madrid: Ediciones Europa America, 1936.

Llano Roza de Ampudia, Aurelio. *Pequeños anales de quince días: La revolucón en Asturias octubre 1934.* Oviedo: Talleres Tipograficos, 1935.

Lopez, Juan. *La unidad de la CNT y su trayectoria.* Valencia: Impresos Cosmos, 1936.

López Ochoa, Eduardo. *Campaña militar de Asturias en octubre de 1934.* Madrid: Ediciones Yunque, 1936.

Lopez Olivella, L. *¿Qué es el "Frente Popular"?* Barcelona: Ediciones A.A., 1936.

Lopez-Rey y Arrojo, Manuel. *Un delito de asesinato (El caso Sirval).* Madrid: Imprenta Helénica, 1936.

Los mártires de Turón: Notas biográficas y reseña del martirio de los religiosos bárbaramente asesinados por los revolucionarios en Turón (Asturias), el 9 de octubre de 1934. Madrid: Ediciones La Instrucción Popular, 1935.

Los Presos de Asturias. *¡Acusamos!* . . . . N.p., 1935.

Madera, Vicente. *El sindicato Católico de Moreda y la Revolución de Octubre.* Madrid: Sáez Hermanos, 1935.

Madero, Luis Octavio. *El Octubre español.* Mexico D.F.: Talleres Gráficos de la Nacion, 1935.

Manning, Leah. *What I Saw in Spain.* London: Victor Gollancz, 1935.

Martínez Aguilar, Manuel. *¿A dónde va el Estado español? Rebelión socialista y separatista de 1934.* Madrid: Editorial e la Revista Las Finanzas, 1935.

Martínez, Francisco. *Dos jesuitas mártires en Asturias.* Burgos: Imprenta Aldecoa, 1936.

Maurín, Joaquín. *Revolución y contrarrevolución en España.* Paris: Ruedo ibérico, 1966 [1935].

Molins i Fábrega, N. *UHP: La insurrección proletaria de Asturias.* Madrid: Ediciones Júcar, 1977 [1935].

Molne. *Calendario 1938.* Barcelona: Ediciones Tierra y Libertad, 1937.

Mont-Font [Joaquín Maurín]. *Alianza Obrera.* Barcelona: Imprenta Cervantes, 1935.

Morón, Gabriel. *El fracaso de un revolución.* Madrid: Gráfica Socialista, 1935.

Mulas Hernández, José Luis. "Octubre de 1934: Revolución en Asturias." *Orto: Revista cultural de ideas ácratas* 14, no. 83 (1994): 35–38.

Nelken, Margarita. *Por qué hicimos la revolución.* Barcelona: Ediciones Sociales Internacionales, 1936.

Noral Suárez, Senén. *Langreo Rojo: Historia del martirio y persecución de los sacerdotes en al arciprestazgo de Langreo, durante las suceso revolucionarios del año 1934.* La Felguera: La Torre, 1935.

Núñez, Ignacio. *La Revolución de Octubre de 1934.* 2 vols. Barcelona: Editorial José Vilamala, 1935.

Nuño del Robleda, Gil. *¿Por qué Oviedo se convirtió en ciudad mártir?* Oviedo: Talleres Tipográficos F. de la Prensa, 1935.

Oliveros, Antonio L. *Asturias en el resurgimiento español.* Madrid: Imp. Juan Bravo, 1935.

Orbón, Julián. *Avilés en el movimiento revolucionario de Asturias (octubre de 1934).* Gijón: Tipográficos La Fe, 1934.

——. *Patriotismo y ciudadanía (en el palenque periodístico).* Gijón: Tipográficos La Fe, 1935.

Partido Comunista de España. "Los combates de octubre." In *Octubre del 34: Reflexiones sobre una revolución,* edited by Marta Bizcarrondo. Madrid: Ayuso, 1977.

——. *Pleno amplificado del C.C. del Partido Comunista de España.* Valencia: Ediciones del PCE, 1937.

——. "Proposicion del Partido Comunista al Partido Socialista y a Las Alianzas Obreras y Campesinos para las elecciones municipales." [*El Debate* ?], (n.d. [ca. 1934])

Partido Obrero Revolucionario de España. *La comuna de Asturias, 1934–1984, en el 50 aniversario.* Barcelona: Ediciones Aurora, 1984.

Partido Socialista Obrero Español–Federación Socialista Asturiana. *Resoluciones: 26 Congreso Oviedo, 22–24 April 1994.*

Pla y Beltran, Pascual. *Antología Poética (1930–1961).* Valencia: Ayuntamiento de Valencia, 1985.

Prada, Francisco. *Caminos de sangre: Asturias la desventurada.* Madrid: Editorial Castro, 1934.

Pyrene [Victoriano Navarro González]. *Antiespañolismo: Marxistas y seperatistas contra españa.* Zaragoza: Heraldo de Aragon, 1935.

Ramos Oliveira, Antonio. *La revolución española de octubre: Ensayo político.* Madrid: Editorial España, 1935.

——. *On the Eve of Civil War in Spain.* London: Friends of Spain, 1937.

Reporteros Reunidos. *Octubre rojo: Ocho días que conmovieron a España*. Madrid: Imp. Vallinas, n.d.

Reporte Sindicalista. *La represión en Asturias*. N.p., n.d.

Revolución en Asturias: Relato de la última guerra civil por un testigo imparcial. Madrid: Editorial Castro, 1934.

Río Cisneros, Agustín del, and Enrique Conde Gargollo, eds. *Obras completas de José Antonio Primo de Rivera*. Madrid: Editora Nacional, 1942.

Romero Cuesta, José. *El Sargento Vázquez*. Madrid: Gráficas Aglaya, 1936.

Rosal, Amaro del. *Problemas sindicales y de unidad (después de octubre)*. Madrid: Rehyma, 1936.

Rucabado, Ramón. *Los mártires de Asturias: La escuela mártir de Turón*. Barcelona: Catalunya Social, 1935.

Ruffinelli, Federico Gerard. *El vino y el pan de hombre*. Montevideo: Editorial Libertad, 1936.

Ruiz del Toro, José. *Octubre (etapas de un periodo revolucionario en España)*. Buenos Aires: Editorial Araujo, 1935.

Saborit, Andrés. *Asturias y sus hombres*. Toulouse: Imprimerie Dulaurier, 1964.

Salazar, Victor. *El presidiario número 317: Ramón González Peña*. Madrid: Publicaciones Indice, 1936.

Salazar Alonso, Rafael. *Bajo el signo de la revolución*. Madrid: R. de San Martín, 1935.

Seccion Española del Socorro Rojo Internacional. *Los crímenes de la reacción española*. Madrid: Ediciones de Seccion Española del Socorro Rojo Internacional, 1935.

Serrano Plaja, Arturo. *Versos de guerra y paz*. Buenos Aires: Editorial Nova, 1945.

Serrano Poncela, Segundo. *El partido socialista y la conquista del poder*. Barcelona: Ediciones L'Hora, 1935.

Solano Palacio, Fernando. *La Revolución de Octubre: Quince días de comunismo libertario en Asturias*. Madrid: Fundación de Estudios Libertarios Anselmo Lorenzo, 1994.

——. *La tragedia del norte (Asturias mártir)*. 2nd ed. Barcelona: Ediciones Tierra y Libertad, 1938.

——. *La Revolución de Octubre: Quince días de comunismo libertario en Asturias*. Barcelona: Ediciones El Luchador, 1936.

S.T.V., Alianza Sindical U.G.T.–C.N.T. *Mensaje a los trabajadores,* Toulouse, 1963.

Toucet, Pablo. *El pueblo está preso: Teatro revolucionario octubre 1934—febrero de 1936*. Santander, 1936.

Trigueros Engelmo, F. *Asturias por la libertad*. Teatro del Pueblo no. 4, Aug. 1936. Barcelona: Ediciones Boreal, 1936.

Unión General de Trabajadores—Guipuzcoa, *Memoria y Orden del dia del IV congreso provincial*. San Sebastian: Tipográficos República, 1936.

Valdés, Alejandro. *¡¡Asturias!! (Relato vívido de la insurrección de octubre)*. Valencia: Ediciones Verdad, n.d. [ca. 1935].

Valdivielso, José Simon. *Farsa y tragedia de España en el 1934*. Oviedo: Talleres Tipográficos F. De la Prensa, 1935.

Vélez, P. M. *La revolución y la contrarevolución en España: Antes y después de la batalla electoral.* Madrid: El Siglo Futuro, 1936.

Villar, Manuel. *El anarquismo en la insurrección de Asturias: La C.N.T. y la F.A.I. en octubre de 1934.* Madrid: Fundación de Estudios Libertarios Anselmo Lorenzo, 1994 [1935].

Xavier, Adro [Alejandro Rey-Stolle]. *Sangre jesuita: Asturias 1934.* Bilbao: El Mensajero del Corazon de Jesus, 1938.

Yusti, Pablo Maria. *Octubre marxismo práctico.* Madrid: Marsiega, 1936.

PRIMARY SOURCES: SELECTED NEWSPAPERS AND PERIODICALS

Acción Española 1934–1936

Combat 1937

El Comunista 1936

El País 1984, 2004

El Socialista 1934–1936

Emancipación 1937

Estampa 1931–1936

Estudios 1934–1937

La Antorcha 1936

La Batalla 1934–1937

La Libertad 1936

La Nueva España 1984–1999

La Voz de Asturias 1978–1999

L'espurna 1937

Milicia Popular 1936

Mundo Obrero 1934–1937, 1984

P.O.U.M. 1936

New York Times 1935–1936 (selected issues)

SECONDARY SOURCES

Ackelsberg, Martha A. *Free Women of Spain: Anarchism and the Struggle for the Emancipation of Women.* Bloomington: Indiana University Press, 1991.

Aguado Sánchez, Francisco. *La Revolución de Octubre de 1934:* Madrid: Librería Editorial San Martín, 1972.

Aguilar Fernández, Paloma. "Aproximaciones teóricas y analíticas al concepto de memoria histórica: La memoria histórica de la guerra civil española (1936–1939)." Instituto Universitario Ortega y Gasset, Madrid, 1995.

———. *La memoria histórica de la guerra civil española (1936–1939): Un proceso de aprendizaje político.* Madrid: Centro de Estudios Avanzados en Ciencias Sociales, 1995.

———. *Memoria y olvido de la guerra civil española.* Madrid: Alianza Editorial, 1996.

——. *Memory and Amnesia: The Role of the Spanish Civil War in the Transition to Democracy.* New York: Berghahn Books, 2002.

Alba, Víctor. *The Communist Party in Spain*, translated by Vincent G. Smith. New Brunswick, N.J.: Transaction, 1983.

——. *Dos revolucionarios Joaquín Maurín, Andreu Nin.* Madrid: Seminarios y Ediciones, 1975.

Alexander, Martin S., and Helen Graham., eds. *The French and Spanish Popular Fronts: Comparative perspectives.* Cambridge: Cambridge University Press, 1989.

Alpert, Michael. "The Spanish Army and the Popular Front." In *The French and Spanish Popular Fronts: Comparative Perspectives,* edited by Martin S. Alexander and Helen Graham. Cambridge: Cambridge University Press, 1989.

Álvarez, José E. *The Betrothed of Death: The Spanish Foreign Legion during the Rif Rebellion, 1920–1927.* Westport, Conn.: Greenwood Press, 2001.

Álvarez Junco, José. "El anticlericalismo en el movimiento obrero." In *Octubre 1934: Cincuenta años para la reflexión,* edited by Gabriel Jackson. Madrid: Siglo Veintiuno Editores, 1984.

——. *El emperador del paralelo: Lerroux y la demagogia populista.* Madrid: Alianza Editorial, 1990.

——. "El nacionalismo español como mito movilizador: Cuatro guerras." In *Cultura y movilización en la españa contemporánea,* edited by Manuel Pérez Ledesma. Madrid: Alianza Editorial, 1997.

——. *La comuna en España.* Madrid: Siglo Veintiuno de España Editores, 1971.

——. *Mater Dolorosa: La idea de España en el siglo XIX.* Madrid: Taurus Editorial, 2001.

Anes, Rafael. "Early Industrialization in Asturias: Bounds and Constraints." In *The Economic Modernization of Spain, 1810–1930,* edited by Nicolás Sánchez Albornoz. New York: University of New York Press, 1987.

Apéndice de la Gran Enciclopedia Asturiana. Vol. 16. Gijón: Gran Enciclopedia Asturiana, 1981.

Aróstegui, Julio, Jordi Canal, and Eduardo González Calleja. *El Carlismo y la guerras carlistas: Hechos, hombres e ideas.* Madrid: La Esfera de los Libros, 2003.

Arpaia, Bruno. *Tiempo perdido.* Barcelona: Ediciones B, 1999.

Arrarás, Joaquin. *Historia de la Segunda República Española.* 4 vols. Madrid: Editorial Nacional, 1956–1968.

Avilés Farré, Juan. *La fe que vino de Rusia: La revolución bolchevique y los españoles (1917–1931).* Madrid: Biblioteca Nueva, 1999.

Aznar Soler, Manuel. *II Congreso Internacional de Escritores Antifascistas (1937).* 2 vols. Barcelona: Editorial Laia, 1978.

——. "La revolución asturiana de octubre de 1934 y la literatura española." *Los Cuadernos de Asturias,* no. 26 (1984): 86–104.

Báez y Pérez de Tudela, José Maria. "El ruido y la nueces: La Juventud de Acción Popular y la movilización 'cívica' Católica durante la Segunda República" *Ayer,* 59, no. 3 (2005): 123–45.

Balcells, Albert. *Trabajo industrial y organización obrera en la Cataluña contemporánea, 1900–1936.* Barcelona: Editorial Laia, 1974.

Balfour, Sebastian. *Deadly Embrace: Morocco and the Road to the Spanish Civil War.* Oxford: Oxford University Press, 2002.

Barrio Alonso, Angeles. *Anarquismo y anarcosindicalismo en Asturias (1890–1936).* Madrid: Siglo veintiuno editores de españa, 1988.

Benavides Gómez, Domingo. *El fracaso social del catolicismo español: Arboleya-Martínez, 1871–1951.* Barcelona: Editorial Nova Terra, 1973.

———. "Maximiliano Arboleya y su interpretación de la revolución de octubre." In *Octubre 1934: Cincuenta años para la reflexión,* edited by Gabriel Jackson. Madrid: Siglo Veintiuno Editores, 1985.

Bingham, Adrian. *Gender, Modernity, and the Popular Press in Inter-war Britain.* Oxford: Oxford University Press, 2004.

Bizcarrondo, Marta. "De las Alianzas Obreras al Frente Popular." *Estudios de Historia Social* 16–17 (January–June 1981): 83–116.

———. "Democracia y revolución en las estregia socialista de la II República." *Estudios de Historia Social* 16–17 (January–June 1981): 227–459.

———. *Octubre del 34: Reflexiones sobre una revolución.* Madrid: Ayuso, 1977.

Blasco, Inmaculada. *Paradojas de la ortodoxia: Política de masas y militancia Católica femenina en España (1919–1939).* Zaragoza: Prensas Universitarias de Zaragoza, 2003.

Blas Guerrero, Andrés de. *El socialismo radical en la II República.* Madrid: Tulcar Ediciones, 1978.

Blinkhorn, Martin. *Carlism and Crisis in Spain, 1931–1939.* Cambridge: Cambridge University Press, 1975.

———, ed. *Spain in Conflict, 1931–1939: Democracy and Its Enemies.* London: Sage, 1986.

Bloom, Ida, Karen Hagemann, and Catherine Hall, eds. *Gendered Nations: Nationalisms and Gender Order in the Long Nineteenth Century.* Oxford: Berg, 2000.

Bonet, Juan Manuel. *Diccionario de las vanguardias en España (1907–1936).* Madrid: Alianza Editorial, 1995.

Borkenau, Franz. *The Spanish Cockpit.* Ann Arbor: University of Michigan Press, 1963.

Boyd, Carolyn P. *Historia Patria: Politics, History, and National Identity in Spain, 1875–1975.* Princeton, N.J.: Princeton University Press, 1997.

———. *Praetorian Politics in Liberal Spain.* Chapel Hill: University of North Carolina Press, 1979.

———. "The Second Battle of Covadonga: The Politics of Commemoration in Modern Spain." *History and Memory* 14, nos. 1–2 (2002): 37–64.

Broué, Pierre, and Emile Témine. *The Revolution and the Civil War in Spain.* Cambridge, Mass.: MIT Press, 1970.

Brugos, Valentín, and Francisco Erice Sebares, eds. *Los comunistas en Asturias, 1920–1982.* Gijón: Ediciones Trea, 1996.

Bussy Genevois, Danièle. "El retorno de la hija pródiga: Mujeres entre lo peublico y lo privado (1931–1936)." In *Otras visiones de España,* edited by Pilar Folguera. Madrid: Editorial Pablo Iglesias, 1993.

Callahan, William. *The Catholic Church in Spain, 1875–1998.* Washington, D.C.: Catholic University Press, 2000.

Camus, Albert. *Rebelion en Asturias.* Oviedo: Ayalgal Ediciones, 1978.

Carabias Álvaro, Mónica. "Las madonnas se visten de rojo: Imágenes de paganismo y religiosidad en la guerra civil española." In *Las mujeres y las guerras,* edited by Mary Nash and Susana Tavera. Barcelona: Icaria Editorial, 2003.

Cárcel Ortí, Vicente. *La persecución religiosa en España durante la Segunda República (1931–1939).* Madrid: Ediciones Rialp, 1990.

Cardona, Gabriel. *El poder militar en la España contemporánea hasta la guerra civil.* Madrid: Siglo Veintiuno de España Editores, 1983.

Caro Baroja, Julio. *Introducción a una historia contemporánea del anticlericalismo español.* Madrid: Istmo, 1980.

Carrión Iñiguez, José Deogracias. *La insurrección de octubre de 1934 en la provincia de Albacete.* Albacete: Instituto de Estudios Albacetenses de la Excma, Diputación de Albacete, 1990.

Carulla, Jordi, and Arnau Carulla. *La guerra civil en 2000 carteles: República-guerra civil-posguerra.* 2 vols. Barcelona: Postermil, 1997.

Casanova, Julián. *De la calle al frente: El anarcosindicalismo en España (1931–1939).* Barcelona: Crítica, 1997.

Chico González, Pedro. *Testigos de la escuela cristiana: Martires de la revolución de Asturias.* Valladolid: Hermanos de las escuelas cristianas, 1989.

——. *Testigos de la escuela cristiana (símbolo para tiempos nuevos).* Valladolid: Hermanos de las Escuelas Cristianas, 1999.

Cierva, Ricardo de la. *La Revolución de Octubre: El PSOE contra la República.* Madrid: Arc, 1997.

Cleminson, Richard. "Beyond Tradition and 'Modernity': The Cultural and Sexual Politics of Spanish Anarchism." In *Spanish Cultural Studies: An Introduction,* edited by Helen Graham and Jo Labanyi. Oxford: Oxford University Press, 1995.

——. " 'Science and Sympathy' or 'Sexual Subversion on a Human Basis'? Anarchists in Spain and the World League for Sexual Reform." *Journal of the History of Sexuality* 12, no. 1 (January 2003): 110–21.

Collins, Roger. *Early Medieval Spain: Unity in Diversity, 400–1000.* New York: St. Martin's Press, 1983.

Confino, Alon. "Collective Memory and Cultural History: Problems of Method." *American Historical Review* 102, no. 5 (December 1997): 1386–1403.

——. *The Nation as a Local Metaphor: Württemberg, Imperial Germany, and National Memory, 1871–1918.* Chapel Hill: University of North Carolina Press, 1997.

Connerton, Paul. *How Societies Remember.* Cambridge: Cambridge University Press, 1989.

Conze, Susanne, and Beate Fiesler. "Soviet Women as Comrades-in-Arms: A Blind Spot in the History of the War." In *The People's War: Responses to World War II in the Soviet Union,* edited by Robert W. Thurston and Bernd Bonwetsch. Urbana: University of Illinois Press, 2000.

Coope, Jessica A. *The Martyrs of Córdoba: Community and Family Conflict in an Age of Mass Conversion*. Lincoln: University of Nebraska Press, 1995.

Copelon, Rhonda. "Surfacing Gender: Reconceptualizing Crimes against Women in Time of War." In *The Women and War Reader,* edited by Lois Ann Lorenten and Jennifer Turpin. New York: New York University Press, 1999.

Corbin, John. "Truth and Myth in History: An Example from the Spanish Civil War." *Journal of Interdisciplinary History*, 25, no. 4 (Spring 1995): 609–25.

Crane, Susan. "Writing the Individual Back into Collective Memory." *American Historical Review* 102, no. 5 (December 1997): 1372–85.

Cruz, Rafael. "Old Symbols, New Meanings: Mobilising the Rebellion in the Summer of 1936." *The Splintering of Spain: Cultural History and the Spanish Civil War*, edited by Chris Ealham and Michael Richards, Cambridge: Cambridge University Press, 2005.

Delgado Ruiz, Manuel. *Las palabras de otro hombre: Anticlericalismo y misoginia*. Barcelona: Muchnik Editores, 1993.

Deogracias Carrión Iñiguez, José. *La insurrección de octubre de 1934 en la provincia de Albacete*. Albacete: Instituto de Estudios Albacetenses de la Excma, Diputación de Albacete, 1990.

De Grazia, Victoria. *How Fascism Ruled Women: Italy, 1922–1945*. Berkeley: University of California Press, 1992.

De Pauw, Linda Grant. *Battle Cries and Lullabies: Women in War from Prehistory to the Present*. Norman: University of Oklahoma Press, 1998.

Díaz Nosty, Bernardo. *La comuna asturiana: Revolución de Octubre de 1934*. Bilbao: Zero, 1974.

Dower, John W. *War without Mercy: Race and Power in the Pacific War*. New York: Pantheon Books, 1986.

Dudink, Stefan, Karen Hagemann, and John Tosh, eds. *Masculinities in Politics and War: Gendering Modern History*. Manchester: Manchester University Press, 2004.

Durgan, Andrew. *BOC 1930–1936: El Bloque Obrero y Campesino*. Barcelona: Editorial Laertes, 1996.

Ealham, Chris. *Class, Culture and Conflict in Barcelona, 1898–1937*. London: Routledge, 2005.

Ealham, Chris, and Michael Richards, eds. *The Splintering of Spain: Cultural History and the Spanish Civil War, 1936–1939*. Cambridge: Cambridge University Press, 2005.

Edles, Laura Desfor. *Symbol and Ritual in the New Spain: The Transition to Democracy after Franco*. Cambridge: Cambridge University Press, 1998.

Eksteins, Modris. *Rites of Spring: The Great War and the Birth of the Modern Age*. Boston: Houghton Miflin, 1989.

Elorza, Antonio. *La utopia anarquista bajo la Segunda República*. Madrid: Editorial Ayuso, 1973.

Elorza, Antonio, and Marta Bizcarrondo. *Queridos camaradas: La Internacional Comunista y España, 1919–1939*. Barcelona: Planeta, 1999.

Enders, Victoria Lorée, and Pamela Beth Radcliff, eds. *Constructing Spanish Womanhood: Female Identity in Modern Spain.* Albany: State University of New York Press, 1999.

Englund, Steven. "The Ghost of Nation Past." *Journal of Modern History* 64 (1992): 299–320.

Erice Sebares, Francisco. "Mujeres comunistas: La militancia femenina en al comunismo asturiano, de los orígenes al final del franquismo." In *Los comunistas en Asturias, 1920–1982,* edited by Valentín Brugos and Francisco Erice Sebares. Gijón: Ediciones Trea, 1996.

Falasca-Zamponi, Simonetta. *Fascist Spectacle: The Aesthetics of Power in Mussolini's Italy.* Berkeley: University of California Press, 1997.

Fernández, Alberto. "Octubre de 1934: Recuerdos de un insurrecto." *Tiempo de Historia* 2, no. 17 (April 1976): 11–21.

Fernández Llaneza, Carlos. *San Pedro de los Arcos.* Oviedo: Ayuntamiento de Oviedo, 1998.

Folguera Crespo, Pilar. "La II República. Entre lo privado y lo público (1931–1939)." In *Historia de las mujeres en España,* edited by Elisa Garrido. Madrid: Editorial Síntesis, 1997.

—— "Revolución y restauaración. La emergencia de los primeros ideales emancipadores (1868–1931)." *Historia de las mujeres en España,* edited by Elisa Garrido González, Madrid: Editorial Síntesis, 1997.

——, ed., *Otras visiones de españa.* Madrid: Editorial Pablo Iglesias, 1993.

Fraddosio, Maria. "The Fallen Hero: The Myth of Mussolini and the Fascist Women in the Italian Social Republic (1943–5)." *Journal of Contemporary History* 31, no. 1 (1996): 99–124.

Funck, Marcus. "Ready for War? Conceptions of Military Manliness in the Prusso-German Officer before the First World War." In *Home / Front: The Military, War and Gender in Twentieth-Century Germany,* edited by Karen Hagemann and Stefanie Schüler-Springorum. Oxford: Berg, 2002.

Fundación Pablo Iglesias. *Catálogo de los archivos de guerra civil de las Comisiones Ejecutivas del Partido Socialista Obrero Español y de la Unión General de Trabajadores.* Madrid: Editorial Pablo Iglesias, 1988.

García de Tuñón Aza, José María. *El Socialismo: Contra la ley.* Oviedo: Fundación Ramiro Ledesma Ramos, 2002.

García Delgado, José Luis. "Tensiones y problemas en la economía española de los primeros años trienta." In *Octubre 1934: Cincuenta años para la reflexión,* edited by Gabriel Jackson. Madrid: Siglo Veintiuno de España Editores, 1985.

García Delgado, José Luis, Manuel Tuñón de Lara, and José Álvarez Junco. *Los orígenes culturales de la II República.* Madrid: Siglo Veintiuno de España Editores, 1993.

Garrido, Elisa, ed. *Historia de las mujeres en España.* Madrid: Editorial Síntesis, 1977.

Gedi, Noa, and Elam Yigal. "Collective Memory: What Is It?" *History and Memory* 8, no. 1 (1996): 30–50.

Gentile, Emilio. *The Sacralization of Politics in Fascist Italy,* translated by Keith Botsford. Cambridge, Mass.: Harvard University Press, 1996.

Getman Eraso, Jordi. "Rethinking the Revolution: Utopia and Pragmatism in Catalan Anarchosyndicalism, 1930–1936." Ph.D. diss., University of Wisconsin, Madison, 2001.

Gillespie, Richard. *The Spanish Socialist Party: A History of Factionalism.* Oxford: Oxford University Press, 1989.

Gillis, John R., ed., *Commemorations: The Politics of National Identity.* Princeton, N.J.: Princeton University Press, 1994.

Gil Pecharromán, Julio. *Conservadores subversivos: La derecha authoritaria alfonsina (1913–1936).* Madrid: Eudema, 1994.

Glick, Thomas F. *Islamic and Christian Spain in the Early Middle Ages.* Princeton: Princeton University Press, 1979.

——. "Sexual Reform, Psychoanalysis, and the Politics of Divorce in Spain in the 1920s and 1930s." *Journal of the History of Sexuality* 12, no. 1 (January 2003): 68–97.

Gomez, Aurora G. *True Catholic Womanhood: Gender Ideology in Franco's Spain.* Dekalb: Northern Illinois University Press, 2000.

González, Miguel. *San Inocencio Canoura Arnau: Mártir en Asturias, 1934.* Madrid: Biblioteca de Autores Cristianos, 1999.

González Calleja, Eduardo. "Hacia una nueva 'guerra carlista' (1931–1939)." In *El Carlismo y la guerras carlistas: Hechos, hombres e ideas.* Madrid: La Esfera de los Libros, 2003.

——. "La violencia y la política." In *El Carlismo y la guerras carlistas: Hechos, hombres e ideas.* Madrid: La Esfera de los Libros, 2003.

——. "The Symbolism of Violence during the Second Republic." In *The Splintering of Spain: Cultural History and the Spanish Civil War, 1936–1939,* edited by Chris Ealham and Michael Richards. Cambridge: Cambridge University Press, 2005.

Graham, Helen. "The Eclipse of the Socialist Left: 1934–1937." In *Elites and Power in Twentieth-Century Spain,* edited by Frances Lannon and Paul Preston. Oxford: Clarendon Press, 1990.

——. *Socialism and War: The Spanish Socialist Party in Power and Crisis, 1936–1939.* Cambridge: Cambridge University Press, 1991.

——. *The Spanish Republic at War, 1936–1939.* Cambridge: Cambridge University Press, 2002.

——. "Women and Social Change." In *Spanish Cultural Studies: An Introduction,* edited by Helen Graham and Jo Labanyi, Oxford: Oxford University Press, 1995.

Graham, Helen, and Jo Labanyi, eds. *Spanish Cultural Studies: An Introduction.* Oxford: Oxford University Press, 1995.

Grayzel, Susan R. *Women's Identities at War: Gender, Motherhood, and Politics in Britain and France during the First World War.* Chapel Hill: University of North Carolina Press, 1999.

Grimau, Carmen. *El cartel republicano en la Guerra Civil.* Madrid: Ediciones Cátedra, 1979.

Gruber, Helmut, and Pamela Graves, eds. *Women and Socialism, Socialism and Women.* New York: Berghahn Books, 1998.

Gullace, Nicoletta F. "Sexual Violence and Family Honor: British Propaganda and International Law during the First World War." *American Historical Review* 102, no. 3 (June 1997): 714–47.

Gullickson, Gay L. *Unruly Women of Paris: Images of the Commune.* Ithaca, N.Y.: Cornell University Press, 1996.

Gutiérrez del Castillo, Arturo. "El movimiento revolucionario de 1934: Algunos aspectos a través de la prensa granadina." *Cuadernos de historia moderna y contemporanea* 3 (1982): 195–229.

Hagemann, Karen. "German Heroes: The Cult of Death for the Fatherland in Nineteenth-Century Germany." In *Masculinities in Politics and War: Gendering Modern History,* edited by Stefan Dudink, Karen Hagemann, and John Tosh. Manchester: Manchester University Press, 2004.

Hagemann, Karen, and Stefanie Schüler-Springorum, eds. *Home/Front: The Military, War and Gender in Twentieth-Century Germany.* Oxford: Berg, 2002.

Halbwachs, Maurice. *The Collective Memory.* New York: Harper and Row, 1980.

———. *On Collective Memory.* Chicago: University of Chicago Press, 1992.

Harris, Ruth. "The 'Child of the Barbarian': Rape, Race and Nationalism in France during the First World War." *Past and Present*, no. 141 (November 1993): 170–207.

Harrison, Joseph. *An Economic History of Modern Spain.* New York: Holmes and Meier, 1978.

Heywood, Paul. *Marxism and the Failure of Organised Socialism in Spain, 1879–1936.* Cambridge: Cambridge University Press, 1990.

Hoganson, Kristin L. *Fighting for American Manhood: How Gender Politics Provoked the Spanish-American and Philippine-American Wars.* New Haven, Conn.: Yale University Press, 1998.

Holguín, Sandie. *Creating Spaniards: Culture and National Identity in Republican Spain.* Madison: University of Wisconsin Press, 2002.

Horne, John. "Masculinity in Politics and War in the Age of Nation-States and World Wars, 1850–1950." In *Masculinities in Politics and War: Gendering Modern History,* edited by Stefan Dudink, Karen Hagemann, and John Tosh. Manchester: Manchester University Press, 2004.

Imágenes en guerra: memoria estampada en la España de los años 30. Valencia: Universitat de Valencia, 1998.

Irwin, William J. *The 1933 Cortes Elections: Origin of the Bienio Negro.* New York: Garland, 1991.

Irwin-Zarecka, Iwona. *Frames of Remembrance: The Dynamics of Collective Memory.* New Brunswick, N.J.: Transaction Publishers, 1994.

Jackson, Gabriel. *The Spanish Republic and Civil War, 1931–1939.* Princeton, N.J.: Princeton University Press, 1965.

James, Daniel. "Meatpackers, Peronists, and Collective Memory: A View from the South." *American Historical Review* 102, no. 5 (December 1997): 1404–12.

Jensen, Geoffrey. *Irrational Triumph: Cultural Despair, Military Nationalism, and the Ideological Origins of Franco's Spain.* Reno: University of Nevada Press, 2002.

Juliá, Santos. *Historia del socialismo español.* Vol. 3. Barcelona: Conjunto Editorial, 1989.

———. "La UGT de Madrid en los años treinta: Un sindicalismo de gestion." *Revista Española de Investigaciones Sociologicas* 20 (1982): 121–51.

———. "Los socialistas y el escenario de la futura revolución." In *Octubre 1934: Cincuenta años para la reflexión,* edited by Gabriel Jackson. Madrid: Siglo Veintiuno Editores, 1985.

———. *Madrid, 1931–1934: De la fiesta popular a la lucha de clases.* Madrid: Siglo Veintiuno Editores, 1984.

———. *Orígenes del frente popular en España (1934–1936):* Estudios de historia contemporánea siglo XXI. Madrid: Siglo Veintiuno Editores, 1979.

Julian González, Inmaculada. *El cartel republicano en la guerra civil española.* Madrid: Ministerio de Cultura, 1993.

Junta Electoral Central. *Elecciones generales: 22 junio 1986.* Madrid: Junta Electoral Central, 1990.

Kansteiner, Wulf. "Finding Meaning in Memory: A Methodological Critique of Collective Memory Studies." *History and Theory* 41 (May 2002): 179–97.

Kaplan, Gisela T. *Contemporary Western European Feminism.* New York: New York University Press, 1992.

Kaplan, Temma. *Red City, Blue Period: Social Movements in Picasso's Barcelona.* Berkeley: University of California Press, 1992.

Keene, Judith. " 'Into the Clear Air of the Plaza': Spanish Women Achieve the Vote in 1931." In *Constructing Spanish Womanhood: Female Identity in Modern Spain,* edited by Victoria Lorée Enders and Pamela Beth Radcliff. Albany: State University of New York Press, 1999.

Kent, Susan Kingsley. *Making Peace. The Reconstruction of Gender in Interwar Britain.* Princeton: Princeton University Press, 1993.

Kern, Robert W. *Red Years, Black Years.* Philadelphia: Institute for the Study of Human Issues, 1978.

Kertzer, David I. *Ritual, Politics, and Power.* New Haven, Conn.: Yale University Press, 1988.

Koshar, Rudy. *From Monuments to Traces: Artifacts of German Memory, 1870–1990.* Berkeley: University of California Press, 2000.

———. *Germany's Transient Pasts: Preservation and National Memory in the Twentieth Century.* Chapel Hill: University of North Carolina Press, 1998.

Kowalsky, Daniel L. *La Unión Soviética y la Guerra Civil Española: Una revisión crítica.* Barcelona: Crítica, 2004.

———. *Stalin and the Spanish Civil War.* 2004. Project Gutenberg-e, 2004, http://www .gutenberg-e.org/kod01/.

Kundrus, Birthe. "Gender Wars. The First World War and the Construction of Gender Relations in the Weimar Republic." In *Home/Front: The Military, War and Gender in Twentieth-Century Germany,* edited by Karen Hagemann and Stefanie Schüler-Springorund. Oxford: Berg, 2002.

Lannon, Frances. "The Church's Crusade against the Republic." In *Revolution and War in Spain, 1931–1939,* edited by Paul Preston. London: Methuen, 1984.

——. "Modern Spain: The Project of a National Catholicism." In *Religion and National Identity,* edited by Stuart Mews. Oxford: Basil Blackwell, 1982.

Leomar. *Balas reverentes: Antes el martir Lasaliano Hermano Jaime Hilario.* N.p: Fernando Franco, 1952.

Linz, Juan J. "From Great Hopes to Civil War: The Breakdown of Democracy in Spain." In *The Breakdown of Democratic Regimes,* edited by Juan J. Linz and Alfred Stepan. Baltimore: Johns Hopkins University Press, 1978.

Llorente Hernández, Angel. *Arte e ideología en el franquismo (1936–1951).* Madrid: Visor, 1995.

Lombardero Suárez, Manuel. *Asturias y los poetas.* Oviedo: Ediciones Nobel, 1996.

Lopez Lopez, Ramiro, and José María Reyes Lopez. *El nuevo beato de la dioceses: Hermano Marciano-José; Los mártires de Turón.* Sigüenza: Diócesis de Sigüenza-Guadalajara, 1990.

Lorenten, Lois Ann, and Jennifer Turpin, eds. *The Women and War Reader.* New York: New York University Press, 1999.

Lowe, Simon. "The Juventud de Acción Popular and the 'Failure' of 'Fascism' in Spain, 1932–1936." MA thesis, University of Sheffield, 2000.

Macarro Vera, José Manuel. *La utopia revolucionaria: Sevilla en la Segunda República.* Sevilla: Monte de Piedad y caja de ahorros de Sevilla, 1985.

Madariaga, María Rosa de. "Imagen del moro en la memoria colectiva del pueblo español y retorno del moro en la guerra civil de 1936." *Revista Internacional de Sociología* 46, no. 4 (1988): 575–99.

Malefakis, Edward. *Agrarian Reform and Peasant Revolution in Spain.* New Haven, Conn.: Yale University Press, 1970.

Mangini González, Shirley. *Memories of Resistance: Women's Voices from the Spanish Civil War.* New Haven, Conn.: Yale University Press, 1995.

Mar-Molinero, Clare, and Angel Smith, eds. *Nationalism and the Nation in the Iberian Peninsula: Competing and Conflicting Identities.* Oxford: Berg, 1996.

Martin, Benjamin. *The Agony of Modernization.* Ithaca, N.Y.: ILR Press, 1990.

Martin, Rupert, and Francis Morris. *No Pasaran! Photographs and Posters of the Spanish Civil War.* Bristol: Arnolfini Gallery, 1986.

Martín Nájera, Aurelio. *Fuentes para la historia del Partido Socialista Obrero Español y de la Juventudes Socialistas de España.* 2 vols. Madrid: Editorial Pablo Iglesias, 1991.

Mato Díaz, Ángel. *La lectura popular en Asturias (1869–1936).* Oviedo: Pentalfa Ediciones, 1992.

Maynes, Mary Jo. "Adolescent Sexuality and Social Identity in French and German Lower-Class Autobiography." *Journal of Family History* 14, no. 4 (1992): 397–418.

Mazariegos, Emilio L. *Juntos como un solo hombre: Mártires de Asturias 1934.* N.p.: Centro Vocacional LaSalle, 1989.

McDonough, Peter, Samuel H. Barnes, and Antonio López Pina. *The Cultural Dynamics of Democratization in Spain.* Ithaca, N.Y.: Cornell University Press, 1998.

Meaker, Gerald H. *The Revolutionary Left in Spain, 1914–1923*. Stanford: Stanford University Press, 1974.

Melman, Billie, ed. *Borderlines: Genders and Identities in War and Peace, 1870–1930*. New York: Routledge, 1998.

Menéndez García, Juan José. *Belarmino Tomás: Soberano de Asturias*. Gijón: Gran Enciclopedia Asturiana, 2000.

———. *Ramón González Peña "Generalisimo" de revolución*. Gijón: Gran Enciclopedia Asturiana, 2002.

Millan Jimenez, Antonio. *La poesía de Rafael Alberti (1930–1939)*. Cadiz: Diputación Provincial de Cadiz, 1984.

Miravitlles, Jaime et al. *Carteles de la República y de la guerra civil*. Barcelona: Centre d'Estudis d'Historia Contemporanea, 1978.

Moa, Pío. *El derrumbe de la Segunda República y la guerra civil*. Encuentro Editorial, 2001.

———. *Los mitos de la guerra civil*. Madrid: Esfera, 2004.

———. *Los orígenes de la guerra civil española*. Madrid: Ediciones Encuentro, 1999.

———. *Los personajes de la República vistos por ellos mismos*. Ediciones Encuentro, 2000.

Monge y Bernal, José. *Acción Popular: Estudios de biología política*. Madrid: Impr. Sáez Hermanos, 1936.

Montero, José R. *La CEDA: El catolicismo social y politico en la II República*. 2 vols. Madrid: Ediciones de la Revista de Trabajo, 1977.

Mosse, George L. *Fallen Soldiers: Reshaping the Memory of the World Wars*. New York: Oxford University Press, 1990.

———. *Masses and Man: Nationalist and Fascist Perceptions of Reality*. New York: Howard Fertig, 1980.

———. *Nationalism and Sexuality: Respectability and Abnormal Sexuality in Modern Europe*. New York: Howard Fertig, 1985.

———. *The Nationalization of the Masses: Political Symbolism and Mass Movements in Germany from the Napoleonic Wars through the Third Reich*. New York: Howard Fertig, 1975.

Munson, Elizabeth. "Walking on the Periphery: Gender and the Politics of Modernization." *Journal of Social History* 36, no. 1 (2002): 63–75.

Nash, Mary. *Defying Male Civilization: Women in the Spanish Civil War*. Denver: Arden Press, 1995.

———. " 'Ideals of Redemption': Socialism and Women on the Left in Spain." In *Women and Socialism, Socialism and Women*, edited by Helmut Gruber and Pamela Graves. New York: Berghahn Books, 1998.

———. "Identidades, representación cultural y discurso de género en la españa contemporánea." In *Cultura y culturas en la historia*, edited by Pedro Chalmeta. Salamanca: Ediciones Universidad de Salamanca, 1995.

———. " 'Milicianas' and Homefront Heroines: Images of Women in Revolutionary Spain." *History of European Ideas* 11 (1989): 235–44.

———. *Mujeres Libres: España, 1936–1939*. Barcelona: Tusquets, 1975.

———. *Mujer y movimiento obrero en España*. Barcelona: Fontamara, 1981.

———. "Un/Contested Identities: Motherhood, Sex Reform, and the Modernization of Gender Identity in Early Twentieth-Century Spain." In *Constructing Spanish Womanhood: Female Identity in Modern Spain,* edited by Victoria Lorée Enders and Pamela Beth Radcliff. Albany: State University of New York Press, 1999.

———. "Women and War: *Milicianas* and Armed Combat in Revolutionary Spain." *International History Review* 15, no. 2 (1993): 269–82.

Nash, Mary, and Susana Tavera, eds. *Las mujeres y las guerras.* Barcelona: Icaria Editorial, 2003.

Navarro Navarro, Francisco Javier. "La imagen en la propaganda política durante la Guerra civil española: prototipos y símbolos." *Imágenes en guerra: memoria estampada en la España de los años 30.* Valencia: Universitat de Valencia, 1998.

Nerone, John. "Professional History and Social Memory." *Communication* 11 (1989): 89–104.

Nerone, John, and Ellen Wartella. "Introduction: Studying Social Memory." *Communication* 11 (1989): 85–88.

New Jerusalem Bible. New York: Doubleday, 1985.

Nirenberg, David. *Communities of Violence: The Persecution of Minorities in the Middle Ages.* Princeton, N.J.: Princeton University Press, 1996.

Nora, Pierre. "Between Memory and History: *Les Lieux de Mémoire.*" *Representations* 26 (1989): 7–25.

Nora, Pierre. *Realms of Memory: Rethinking the French Past.* New York: Columbia University Press, 1996.

Núñez Perez, María Gloria. *Trabajadoras en la segunda república: Un estudio sobre la actividad económica extradoméstica (1931–1936).* Madrid: Ministerio de Trabajo y Seguridad Social, 1989.

Núñez Seixas, Xosé-Manoel. "Nations in Arms against the Invader: On Nationalist Discourse during the Spanish Civil War." In *The Splintering of Spain: Cultural History and the Spanish Civil War, 1936–1939,* edited by Chris Ealham and Michael Richards. Cambridge: Cambridge University Press, 2005.

Nye, Robert A. *Masculinity and Male Codes of Honor in Modern France.* Oxford: Oxford University Press, 1993.

———. *The Origins of Crowd Psychology: Gustave LeBon and the Crisis of Mass Democracy in the Third Republic.* London: Sage Publications, 1975.

O'Callaghan, Joseph. *Alfonso X and the Cantigas de Santa Maria: A Poetic Biography.* Boston: Brill, 1998.

Octubre 1936–1947–1937. Asturias. Oviedo: Editorial La Nueva España, 1947.

Ojeda, Germán. "La crisis económica asturiana de los años 30." In *Octubre 1934: Cincuenta años para la reflexión,* edited by Gabriel Jackson. Madrid: Siglo Veintiuno Editores, 1985.

Ordovas, José Manuel. *Historia de la Asociacíon Católica Nacional de Propagandistas: De la dictadura a la Segunda República 1923–1936.* Pamplona: EUNSA, 1993.

Palomino, Ángel. *1934: La guerra civil empezó en Asturias.* Barcelona: Editorial Planeta, 1998.

Paniagua, Xavier. *La sociedad libertaria.* Barcelona: Editorial Crítica, 1982.

Pastor Ugeña, Alfredo. *La Agrupacion Socialista Madrileña durante la Segunda Republica.* 2 vols. Madrid: Editorial de la Universidad Complutense de Madrid, 1985.

Payne, Stanley G. *El colapso de la República: Los orígenes de la guerra civil (1933–1936),* translated by Maria Pilar López Pérez. Madrid: La Esfera de los Libros, 2005.

———. Payne, Stanley G. *Falange. A History of Spanish Fascism.* Stanford: Stanford University Press, 1961.

———. *Fascism in Spain, 1923–1977.* Madison: University of Wisconsin Press, 1999.

———. *The Franco Regime, 1936–1975.* Madison: University of Wisconsin Press, 1987.

———. *Franco y José Antonio: El extraño caso del fascismo español.* Madrid: Editorial Planeta, 1997.

———. *A History of Fascism, 1914–1945.* Madison: University of Wisconsin Press, 1995.

———. "Political Violence during the Spanish Second Republic." *Journal of Contemporary History* 25 (1990): 269–88.

———. *Spain's First Democracy: The Second Republic, 1931–1936.* Madison: University of Wisconsin Press, 1993.

———. *The Spanish Civil War, the Soviet Union, and Communism.* New Haven, Conn.: Yale University Press, 2004.

Peirats, José. *La CNT en la revolución española.* 3 vols. Paris: Ruedo Ibérico, 1971.

Penniman, Howard Rae, and Eusebio Mujal-León. *Spain at the Polls, 1977, 1979, 1982: A Study of the National Elections.* Durham, N.C.: Duke University Press, 1985.

Pérez Díaz, Víctor. *The Return of Civil Society: The Emergence of Democratic Spain.* Cambridge, Mass.: Harvard University Press, 1993.

Pérez Ledesma, Manuel, José Álvarez Junco, and Rafael Cruz, eds. *Cultura y movilización en la España contemporánea.* Madrid: Alianza Editorial, 1997.

Peterson, V. Spike. "Gendered Nationalism: Reproducing 'Us' versus 'Them.' " In *The Women and War Reader,* edited by Lois Ann Lorenten and Jennifer Turpin. New York: New York University Press, 1999.

Preston, Paul. "Alfonsist Monarchism and the Coming of the Spanish Civil War." *Journal of Contemporary History* 7, no. 3/4 (1972): 89–114.

———. *The Coming of the Spanish Civil War.* London: Macmillan, 1978.

———. *Franco: A Biography.* New York: Basic Books, 1994.

———. "The Politics of Revenge: Francoism, the Civil War and Collective Memory." In *The Politics of Revenge,* edited by Paul Preston. London: Unwin Hyman, 1990.

———. "Spain's October Revolution and the Rightist Grasp for Power." *Journal of Contemporary History* 10, no. 4 (1975): 555–78.

———. *The Triumph of Democracy in Spain.* London; New York: Methuen, 1986.

Quién es quién en España. Madrid: Editorial Campillo, 1997.

Radcliff, Pamela Beth. *From Mobilization to Civil War: The Politics of Polarization in the Spanish City of Gijón, 1900–1937.* Cambridge: Cambridge University Press, 1996.

———. "La representación de la nación: El conflicto en torno a la identidad nacional y las prácticas simbólicas en la Segunda República." In *Cultura y movilización en la españa contemporánea,* edited by Manuel Pérez Ledesma. Madrid: Alianza Editorial, 1997.

——. "Women's Politics: Consumer Riots in Twentieth-Century Spain." In *Constructing Spanish Womanhood: Female Identity in Modern Spain,* edited by Victoria Lorée Enders and Pamela Beth Radcliff. Albany: State University of New York Press, 1999.

Radley, Alan. "Artefacts, Memory and a Sense of the Past." In *Collective Remembering,* edited by David Middleton and Derek Edwards. London: Sage Publications, 1990.

Rieber, Robert W. *The Psychology of War and Peace: The Image of the Enemy.* New York: Plenum Press, 1991.

Rieber, Robert W., and Robert J. Kelly. "Substance and Shadow: Images of the Enemy." In *The Psychology of War and Peace: The Image of the Enemy,* edited by Robert W. Rieber. New York: Plenum Press, 1991.

Roberts, Mary Louise. *Civilization without Sexes. Reconstructing Gender in Postwar France, 1917–1927.* Chicago: University of Chicago Press, 1994.

Robinson, Richard A. H. *The Origins of Franco's Spain: The Right, the Republic and Revolution, 1931–1936.* Newton Abbot, U.K.: David and Charles, 1970.

Roca i Girona, Jordi. *De la pureza a la maternidad: La construcción del género femenino en la postguerra española.* Madrid: Ministerio de Educación y Cultura, 1996.

Romero Salvadó, Francisco J. *Spain 1914–1918: Between War and Revolution.* London: Routledge, 1999.

Rosal, Amaro del. *1934: Movimiento revolucionario de octubre.* Madrid: Akal, 1983.

Rubin, David C., ed. *Remembering Our Past: Studies in Autobiographical Memory.* Cambridge: Cambridge University Press, 1996.

Ruiz, David. *Asturias contemporánea, 1808–1975: Síntesis histórica; Textos y documentos.* Madrid: Siglo Veintiuno de España Editores, 1981.

——. *El movimiento obrero en Asturias: De la industrialización a la Segunda República.* Oviedo: Amigos de Asturias, 1968.

——. *Insurrección defensiva y revolución obrera: El octubre español de 1934.* Barcelona: Editorial Labor, 1988.

Ruiz Ayucar, Angel. "Los 'intelectuales' y Asturias. Historia de una campaña internacional contra España y la Guardia Civil." *Revista de Estudios Historicos de la Guardia Civil* 4, no. 12 (1973): 9–42.

Salm, Luke. *The Martyrs of Turón and Tarragona: The De La Salle Brothers in Spain, 1934–1939.* Romeoville, Ill.: Christian Brothers Publications, 1990.

Sanabria, Enrique. "Anticlerical Politics: Republicanism, Nationalism, and the Public Sphere in Restoration Madrid, 1885–1912." Ph.D. diss., University of California, San Diego, 2002.

Sanchez, Sarah. *Fact and Fiction: Representations of the Asturian Revolution (1934–1938).* Leeds: Maney Publishing; Modern Humanities Research Association, 2003.

Sánchez García-Saúco, Juan Antonio. *La revolución de 1934 en Asturias.* Madrid: Editora Nacional, 1974.

Seifert, Ruth. "The Second Front: The Logic of Sexual Violence in Wars." *Women's Studies International Forum* 19, nos. 1–2 (1996): 35–43.

———. "War and Rape: A Preliminary Analysis." In *Mass Rape: The War against Women in Bosnia-Herzegovina,* edited by Alexandra Stiglmayer. Lincoln: University of Nebraska Press, 1994.

Sherman, Daniel. "Art, Commerce, and the Production of Memory in France after World War I." In *Commemorations: The Politics of National Identity,* edited by John R. Gillis. Princeton, N.J.: Princeton University Press, 1994.

Shubert, Adrian. *Death and Money in the Afternoon: A History of the Spanish Bullfight.* New York: Oxford University Press, 1999.

———. "A Reinterpretation of the Spanish Popular Front: The Case of Asturias." In *The French and Spanish Popular Fronts: Comparative Perspectives,* edited by Martin S. Alexander and Helen Graham. Cambridge: Cambridge University Press, 1989.

———. *The Road to Revolution in Spain: The Coal Miners of Asturias, 1860–1934.* Urbana: University of Illinois Press, 1987.

———. *A Social History of Modern Spain.* Winchester, Mass.: Unwin Hyman, 1990.

Sinclair, Alison. "The World League for Sexual Reform in Spain: Founding, Infighting, and the Role of Hildegart Rodríguez." *Journal of the History of Sexuality* 12, no. 1, (January 2003): 98–109.

Søland, Brigitte. *Becoming Modern: Young Women and the Reconstruction of Womanhood in the 1920s.* Princeton, N.J.: Princeton University Press, 2000.

Souto Kustrín, Sandra. "Taking the Street: Workers' Youth Organizations and the Political Conflict in the Spanish Second Republic." *European History Quarterly* 34, no. 2 (2004): 131–56.

———. "Y ¿Madrid? ¿Qué hace Madrid?" *Movimiento revolucionario y acción colectiva (1933–1936).* Madrid: Siglo Veintiuno de España Editores, 2004.

Spackman, Barbara. *Fascist Virilities: Rhetoric, Ideology, and Social Fantasy in Italy.* Minneapolis: University of Minnesota Press, 1996.

Stearns, Peter N. *Be a Man! Males in Modern Society.* New York: Homes and Meier Publishers, 1979.

Stiglmayer, Alexandra, ed. *Mass Rape: The War against Women in Bosnia-Herzegovina.* Lincoln: University of Nebraska Press, 1994.

Taibo, Carlos. *Izquierda Unida y sus mundos: Una visión crítica.* Madrid: Libros de la Catarata, 1996.

Taibo, Paco Ignacio II. *Asturias 1934.* 2 vols. Gijón: Ediciones Júcar, 1980.

Thébaud, Françoise. "The Great War and the Triumph of Sexual Division." In *A History of Women in the West: Toward a Cultural Identity in the Twentieth Century.* Vol. 5. Cambridge, Mass.: The Belknap Press of Harvard University Press, 1994.

Thurston, Robert W., and Bernd Bonwetsch, eds. *The People's War: Responses to World War II in the Soviet Union.* Urbana: University of Illinois Press, 2000.

Tomé, Sergio. *Oviedo: La formación de la ciudad burguesa, 1850–1950.* Oviedo: Colegio Oficial de Arquitectos de Asturias, 1988.

Tone, John Lawrence. "Spanish Women in the Resistance to Napoleon, 1808–1814." In *Constructing Spanish Womanhood: Female Identity in Modern Spain,* edited by Victoria Lorée Enders and Pamela Beth Radcliff. Albany: State University of New York Press, 1999.

Tortella, Gabriel. *The Development of Modern Spain: An Economic History of the Nineteenth and Twentieth Centuries.* Cambridge, Mass.: Harvard University Press, 2000.

Tosh, John. "Hegemonic Masculinity and the History of Gender." In *Masculinities in Politics and War: Gendering Modern History,* edited by Stefan Dudink, Karen Hagemann, and John Tosh. Manchester: Manchester University Press, 2004.

Townson, Nigel. *The Crisis of Democracy in Spain: Centrist Politics under the Second Republic, 1931–1936.* Brighton: Sussex Academic Press, 2000.

Tuñón de Lara, Manuel. *La II República.* 2 vols. Madrid: Siglo Vientiuno de España Editores, 1976.

Tusell, Javier. *La elecciones del frente popular en España.* 2 vols. Madrid: Editorial Cuadernos para el Dialogo, 1971.

Tyree, Robert. "Toward the Second Revolution: The Political Thought of Joaquín Maurín." Ph.D. diss., Northern Illinois University, 1996.

Ullman, Joan Connelly. *The Tragic Week: A study of Anti-Clericalism in Spain, 1875–1912.* Cambridge, Mass.: Harvard University Press, 1968.

Valdizán, Mariano. *Mártires de Turón Escritos.* Valladolid: Hermanos de las Escuelas Cristianas, 1999.

Vázquez Garcia, Juan Antonio. "El contexto económico de octubre del '34 en Asturias: La industria hullera." In *Octubre 1934: Cincuenta años para la reflexión,* edited by Gabriel Jackson. Madrid: Siglo Veintiuno Editores, 1985.

Verhey, Jeffrey. *The Spirit of 1914: Militarism, Myth and Mobilization in Germany.* Cambridge: Cambridge University Press, 2000.

Vidarte, Juan Simeón. *El bienio negro y la insurrección de Asturias: Testimonio.* Barcelona: Grijalbo, 1978.

Viñas, Ricard. *La formación de la Juventudes Socialistas Unificadas (1934–1936).* Madrid: Siglo Veintiuno de España Editores, 1978.

Vincent, Mary. *Catholicism in the Second Republic: Religion and Politics in Salamanca, 1930–1936.* New York: Oxford University Press, 1996.

——. "Gender and Morals in Spanish Catholic Youth Culture: A Case Study of the Marian Congregations 1930–1936." *Gender and History* 13, no. 2 (August 2001): 273–98.

——. "The Martyrs and Saints: Masculinity and the Construction of the Francoist Crusade." *History Workshop Journal* 47, no. 1 (1999): 68–98.

Warner, Marina. *Monuments and Maidens: The Allegory of the Female Form.* New York: Atheneum, 1985.

Watanabe, Chiaki. *Confesionalidad Católica y militanca política: La Asociación Católica Nacional de Propagandistas y la Juventud Católica Española (1923–1936).* Madrid: UNED Ediciones, 2003.

Wertsch, James V. *Voices of Collective Remembering.* Cambridge: Cambridge University Press, 2002.

Winston, Colin. *Workers and the Right in Spain, 1900–1936.* Princeton, N.J.: Princeton University Press, 1985.

Winter, Jay. *Sites of Memory, Sites of Mourning: The Great War in European Cultural History.* Cambridge: Cambridge University Press, 1995.

Winter, Jay, and Emmanuel Sivan, "Setting the Framework." In *War and Remembrance in the Twentieth Century,* edited by Jay Winter and Emmanuel Sivan. Cambridge: Cambridge University Press, 1999.

——, eds. *War and Remembrance in the Twentieth Century.* Cambridge: Cambridge University Press, 1999.

Wolf, Kenneth Baxter. *Christian Martyrs in Muslim Spain.* Cambridge: Cambridge University Press, 1988.

Wood, Nancy. *Vectors of Memory: Legacies of Trauma in Postwar Europe.* Oxford: Berg, 1999.

Woodward, Kenneth L. *Making Saints: How the Catholic Church Determines Who Becomes a Saint, Who Doesn't, and Why.* New York: Simon and Schuster, 1990.

Young, James Edward. *The Texture of Memory: Holocaust Memorials and Meaning.* New Haven, Conn.: Yale University Press, 1993.

INDEX

Brian D. Bunk is a visiting assistant professor in the department of history at the University of Massachusetts, Amherst.

Library of Congress Cataloging-in-Publication Data
Bunk, Brian D., 1968–
Ghosts of passion : martyrdom, gender, and the origins of the Spanish Civil War /
Brian D. Bunk.
p. cm.
Includes bibliographical references and index.
ISBN-13: 978–0-8223–3932–8 (cloth : alk. paper)
ISBN -13: 978–0-8223–3943–4 (pbk. : alk. paper)
1. Spain—History—Civil War, 1936–1939—Causes. 2. Asturias (Spain)—History—
Revolution, 1934. 3. Spain—History—Civil War, 1936–1939—Social aspects.
4. Spain—History—Civil War, 1936–1939—Participation, Female. I. Title.
DP257.B785 2007
946.081'1—dc22   2006027828